A Festschrift for Frederick B. Artz

A *Festschrift for Frederick B. Artz*

EDITED BY DAVID H. PINKNEY AND THEODORE ROPP

DUKE UNIVERSITY PRESS   DURHAM, NORTH CAROLINA   1964

© 1964, Duke University Press

Library of Congress Catalogue Card number 64-13717
Cambridge University Press, London, N.W.1, England

Printed in the United States of America
by the Seeman Printery, Inc., Durham, N. C.

Preface

Few undergraduate teachers of history in the United States have taught their subject so appealingly as to have attracted two score and more of their students into careers as professional historians. Even fewer have combined that accomplishment with the achievement of international reputations as productive scholars. Among these latter few, we know only one man in our time who has also achieved scholarly distinction in two different fields of history. Frederick B. Artz, for thirty-eight years a professor of history in Oberlin College, numbers among his former students more than fifty historians who hold chairs of history in American universities and colleges from Manhattan to Berkeley. His publications have established him as an authority on both the history of nineteenth-century France and the cultural history of the Middle Ages.

This rare accomplishment as teacher and scholar brings honor not alone to the man but to the college where he made his career and in a measure to all who share the distinction of being his students. The authors of this volume—all of them his students and all professional historians—and the College, eager to recognize and to acclaim his achievements, have chosen to publish a *Festschrift*, the traditional honor of scholars for an influential and respected colleague or master. *Festschriften* are usually reserved for university professors who have trained generations of graduate students. Probably not more than two or three undergraduate teachers of history in the United States can claim among their former students the professional historians necessary to produce such a volume of scholarly essays. A *Festschrift* is, therefore, an especially appropriate and distinctive monument to Professor Artz's uniquely fruitful career of distinguished teaching and scholarship.

We have made no attempt to center the essays on a particular theme. Professor Artz's interests in history have been catholic, and his students have made their careers in many fields of history—political, economic, social, and cultural—and in areas that range geographically around the world and chronologically from the Renaissance to the present. The essays reflect directly this diversity and more remotely the catholicity of Artz's own interests. Each stands by itself, a tribute of the author to a scholar whom he respects and esteems and to a teacher for whom he feels both gratitude and affection.

The editors acknowledge with warm thanks the generosity of the Board of Trustees of Oberlin College in making possible the publication of this volume. They are especially grateful, too, to President Carr and to Donald M. Love, Emeritus Secretary of the College, for their effective support of the project of the *Festschrift* from its inception, and to Thomas LeDuc, who as chairman of the Department of History at Oberlin aided in launching the project and who later helped the editors in many ways.

DAVID H. PINKNEY

October, 1962   THEODORE ROPP

Contents

Contents

A Festschrift for Frederick B. Artz

Frederick B. Artz: The Man and the Teacher, the Historical Scholar and Critic

THEODORE ROPP AND DAVID H. PINKNEY

In spite of their claims to realism, many historians are romantics. They are inevitably eclectics if they succeed in penetrating more than one era or area of the past and avoid the temptation to make it stand for all human experience. If history is both art and science, an historian's choice of subjects will reflect his own artistic and scientific bent and possibly the interests of his immediate audience. A sketch of his personality and career should thus try to answer four questions. What aspects of his personality attracted him to history and enabled him to communicate history to others? What were the characteristics of the institutions in which he was educated and which he served? Are these personal and institutional characteristics reflected in his publications? Do these last suggest particular problems faced by American scholars of his generation in his general field?

Frederick Binkerd Artz was born in Dayton, Ohio, on October 19, 1894. He was the only child of a cultivated and well-to-do middle-class family. Books he found in his home. The geography which he studied in grammar school gave him his first interest in Europe and its history. In high school he was fortunate in having excellent teachers of English literature and European history. With enough money from his family to travel widely and to live a comfortable life, relatively indifferent to mechanical marvels and to status, Frederick Artz, to use one of his favorite phrases, has lived at ease in a cultural Zion whose joys he has communicated by every means in his power. His ebullience, mimicry, and wit are reflections of the verve with which he tackled major historical subjects in a generation in which many of his colleagues mistook pedantry for historical science. This enthusiasm was the key to his ability to communicate his love of Europe, its history, and its culture to his students. It reflected a heritage in which learning and the arts were both respectable and respected, which insisted that scholarship and enthusiasm were not incompatible and that both were to be enjoyed and communicated.

The Oberlin which Frederick Artz entered in 1912 and to which he has devoted his life was a college that was still rather atypical in the Middle West. In the words of Artz's friend and modern Oberlin's historian, Donald M. Love, it was a college

of quiet culture and Olympian peace. There was a spirit of cooperation among faculty, administration, and students. The outside world existed but it was definitely outside, and it could wait. A polite interest was about all that students were required or expected to show in public affairs until they emerged from academic seclusion to find their way about in the world. The accepted theory of education was still that of grounding students in fundamental ways of thinking and in basic concepts which should later serve them in good stead in meeting particular situations. Immediate laboratory applications of all principles of social conduct were not regarded as necessary or desirable.[1]

Whether this was the kind of college that Henry Churchill King had visualized when he had become its president nearly ten years before, is not the question here. Fifty years later Frederick Artz still represented one part of Oberlin's late nineteenth-century compromise between the missionary college of the earlier half of that century and the new American scholarship. He had little real sympathy with Oberlin's earlier traditions of active social and religious reform. He found the traditional, aesthetic, and historical aspects of religion more satisfying and was as unsympathetic with Protestant enthusiasts as he was to be with the vague leftist pacificism of many Oberlin students during the thirties, or with the equally shallow conservative quietism of some of the second postwar generation. Liberal and humanist as he was, he saw no easy or quick solutions to humanity's problems. This attitude was as helpfully exasperating to the thoughtful young as his academic conservatism was baffling to several

1. *Henry Churchill King of Oberlin* (New Haven, 1956), p. 191.

generations of academic reformers. Neither attitude was con-
ducive to academic peace, but he communicated to those students who were fortunate enough to understand him something
of his humane scepticism of human perfectibility and his enthusiasm for genuine progress.

Frederick Artz is thus an old-fashioned Liberal. His emotional commitments are primarily aesthetic in an age when American
historians have toyed with model-making and methodology,
philosophers have become lost in semantics, and literary critics
have counted commas. He is as repelled by the gracelessness of
their jargon as by its lack of content. If he gleefully exploded
the balloons of the academic organization men and the academic
anarchists, he regarded both as threats to the view of the academic good life which he acquired in Oberlin before the First
World War. This picture should not, however, suggest a dys-
peptic Oberlin Mr. Chips. Frederick Artz's academic funda-
mentalism, valuable as it has been to Oberlin, was balanced by
his positive commitment to scholarship.

This commitment was perhaps best represented by the great
classical scholar and Oberlin teacher, Charles Beebe Martin, and
parts of Donald Love's description of Professor Martin apply to
Frederick Artz: a "keen and sensitive appreciation of the beautiful in art and literature and a tradition of scholarship which led
generations of Oberlin students to do thorough undergraduate
work and to seek thereafter advanced university degrees," and,
he might have added, in the best possible graduate institutions.
Frederick Artz does not have Professor Martin's "brusque manner"; he surely has the latter's "trenchant and sometimes devastating wit." Most of Professor Martin's colleagues, Mr. Love
noted, were not research scholars. "The vast majority are remembered by those who studied under them primarily as great
teachers."[2]

This was surely the case with Frederick Artz's own "great"
teacher, Charles H. A. Wager, who sprinkled his courses with
considerable contempt for formally organized scholars. Dr.
Wager was ostensibly little interested in undergraduate teaching as preparation for graduate work. Frederick Artz, on the

2. *Ibid.*, p. 149.

other hand, was particularly effective in that role because of his own participation in and contact with both American and European scholarship and scholars. These two great undergraduate teachers really answered the supposedly current question of the interference of research with undergraduate teaching. Dr. Wager, by example at least, seems to have thought that it did. Frederick Artz, like Charles Beebe Martin, has never subscribed to this view. Though his personal situation may have made it easy for him to combine research and teaching, this combination is one source of an influence that has aided more than fifty of his students to Ph.D.'s in history. In his efforts to encourage students to go on to graduate work, he was ably seconded by his colleague in American History, Robert S. Fletcher. Artz's teaching, on the other hand, clearly shows Professor Wager's influence. Both men were deeply interested in ideas and the arts. Both preferred authors who displayed taste and style, careful organization, and feeling for large canvases and major problems. Both were evocative and magnetic teachers with a phenomenal gift for bringing the past to life.

Not surprisingly, Frederick Artz was most interested at Harvard in Charles H. Haskins' courses in French and medieval history and in Irving Babbitt's courses in comparative literature. These men, he thinks, first interested him in the comparative history of ideas. These teachers, too, were interested in large subjects. They too were able to communicate the "feel" of whole systems of thought and society. If Artz had taught graduate courses at any institution except the top few, one wonders how gladly he would have suffered the foolish and the unprepared or turned them to necessary thesis hackwork. Oberlin gave him more than six thousand undergraduates to lecture and inspire, and scores of able candidates for honors. Few American college teachers of his generation could really have hoped for more.

As the second part of this essay shows in detail, Artz represents an American scholarship in European history that is passing from the scene. Unless they were willing to become expatriates, those scholars who were the most effective undergraduate teachers of European history represented an older European scholarly tradition, one of broad and humane understanding and enthusiasm for the European past, one that compared and synthesized, while too many of Europe's own scholars were becoming tools of a sterile historical nationalism. Artz's style is closer to the French *précis* than to the English essay, but closer still to the works of those Americans who represented the generation that trained him, that of Haskins, Carl Becker, or Preserved Smith.

Like them, Frederick Artz is personally engaged with the best of Europe's past, and this engagement explains his ability to communicate its feeling. Here too, the record is only a pale reflection of his personality. He made the first of twenty-one trips to Europe in the summer of 1914, graduated from Oberlin as a member of Phi Beta Kappa and with honors in history in 1916, and taught at Antioch College for a year. In the summer of 1917 he volunteered for the United States Army and served nearly two years in France. He spent four months as a student at the University of Toulouse, entered the Harvard Graduate School in 1919, and was awarded his Ph.D. in 1924. He has taught in Oberlin ever since. He opposed isolationism and appeasement well before Pearl Harbor. His famous witticisms, like most witticisms that are worth anything, were directed at ideas rather than at people. They expressed his deep sense of the eternal fitness of things and his deeply felt love of the best in European civilization.

He belongs, of course, to the generation of E. M. Forster, Ernest Hemingway, F. Scott Fitzgerald, E. E. Cummings, and William Faulkner. All but the first are dead, all differed in their reactions to that civilization's travail. During his most influential years, when both men were moving against the tide, Artz's attitudes are most comparable perhaps to those of Forster. In "My Own Centenary" the latter wrote in 1927:

Sir Vincent has, we believe, frequently come into contact with the younger generation, and has checked with the kindliness of which he is a past-master their self-styled individualism—an individualism which is the precise antithesis of true genius. They confuse violence with strength, cynicism with open-mindedness, frivolity with joyousness—mistakes never made by Forster who was never gay until he had earned the right to be so, and only criticized the religious and social institutions of his time because they were notoriously corrupt. We know what the twentieth century was.[3]

We should be proud to recognize that this was the creed of many American teachers of European history. It is Frederick Artz's creed as a scholar, teacher, and citizen. It was part of the creed of his Oberlin. It gave life to his scholarship. It made him one of the most influential college teachers of his whole generation.

*   *   *

To the question, "Who is Frederick B. Artz?" a doctoral candidate in history in 1939 would have replied, "The historian of the Bourbon Restoration." His counterpart in 1959 would have answered, "The author of *The Mind of the Middle Ages.*" These contrasting replies reflect an unusual duality in Artz's career as a historian. Before the World War of 1939-45 he wrote one book and a number of articles on the history of France, most of them on the Bourbon Restoration, 1814-1830, and established himself as the leading American scholar of the Restoration. After the war he turned to cultural history and before his retirement wrote two books—one on the cultural history of the Middle Ages, the other on the history of literature, art, and music in early modern Europe. He continued through reviews, editorial advice, and comments at scholarly meetings to play a rôle, as critic, in American historical writing on France of the nineteenth century.

The confrontation on paper of these two faces of a historian's life makes at first sight a surprising contrast, but there was no real break in Artz's career. His postwar activities continued interests clearly evident in his work before the war. Indeed, his first venture into the history of the Bourbon Restoration was a diversion from an earlier youthful commitment to intellectual and cultural history. As a graduate student at Harvard he thrice won the Bowdoin Prize with essays in intellectual history.[4] He intended to write his doctoral dissertation in that field, and he proposed several topics to Professor Haskins, who was then chair-

3. Reprinted in *Abinger Harvest* (New York, 1936), pp. 61-62.
4. "The Origins of the Contemporary Mind" (Bowdoin Prize, 1920); "Machiavelli and Machiavellianism" (1922); "Marsiglio of Padua and His Place in the History of Political Philosophy" (1924).

man of the Department of History. Haskins replied tartly that if that were what he was interested in he had better go to Columbia! Shunning this desperate course, Artz asked the advice of Robert H. Lord, then a professor of Harvard, who suggested a subject in the political history of the Bourbon Restoration—the Polignac minister of 1829-30. Prince Polignac headed King Charles X's last government, and his inept handling of the affairs of his office led to the Revolution of 1830 and the end of the Restoration. Artz's research took him through the contemporary printed sources—histories, memoirs, journals—and to the Archives nationales in France, where he worked in police and prefectoral records. From his findings he wrote two typescript volumes entitled "The Polignac Ministry," and they were accepted as his dissertation at Harvard in 1924. It was essentially a narrative, political history of the formation, activities, and downfall of the ministry. Although never published it has remained a useful reference, especially for its bibliography, and it is still consulted in the Widener Library, where a copy is on deposit.

In the year following completion of the dissertation Artz made his first appearance before his profession, staking his initial public claim to the Bourbon Restoration as a field of research. At the annual convention of the American Historical Association in Ann Arbor in December, 1925, he presented a paper on the electoral system in France during the Restoration. He described the functioning of the system—the methods of campaigning, the governments' efforts to influence elections, and the meetings of the electoral colleges. For his materials he drew largely on published monographs, although he did include some illustrative matter directly from the archives. The paper was a valuable summary of existing knowledge of the subject, and in 1929 the *Journal of Modern History*, the newly established publication of the Modern European History Section of the American Historical Association, published it in its second number.[5] Until the appearance two years later of Artz's own book, in which he in-

5. "The Electoral System in France during the Bourbon Restoration, 1815-1830," *Journal of Modern History*, I (1929), 205-18. This journal cited hereinafter as *J.M.H.*

corporated the essence of this article, it was the only authoritative publication on the subject.

Historians in France learned of this foreign scholar's invasion of a neglected period of their history when in 1929 the *Revue d'Histoire moderne*, the journal of the Société d'Histoire moderne, published Artz's article "La Crise des incendies en 1830 et les compagnies d'assurance."[6] It dealt with an epidemic of fires that destroyed many farm buildings in the French provinces, particularly in Normandy, during the spring and summer of 1830 preceding the Revolution in late July of that year. The origins of these fires baffled the authorities at the time, and they have puzzled historians ever since. They occurred at the time of a bitterly contested election campaign, and the Ultra Royalists accused the Liberals of setting them to discredit the government; the opposition accused the Polignac ministry and the clergy of using arson to frighten electors into voting for official candidates. Artz, citing reports he had found in police records in the Archives nationales, concluded that probably agents for insurance companies set the fires. Fire insurance policies covered seven-year periods, and they had first been sold in the provinces in 1816. A similar epidemic of fires occurred in that year and another in 1822-23, seven years later. Many policies were again up for renewal in 1830, and zealous agents were out with matches to demonstrate the need for their services. Here was a neat answer to a vexing problem, appealing in its reasonableness and simplicity. The evidence, however—seven documents from one carton in the Archives nationales—was largely hearsay or circumstantial, and Artz's answer was a useful suggestion, not a definitive solution of the mystery.

A second article in the *Revue d'Histoire moderne*, this one on political parties in France during the Restoration, appeared in 1931.[7] It was a summation, largely from published monographs, supplemented by memoirs and archival sources, of existing knowledge of the doctrines and leadership of political groupings under Louis XVIII and Charles X. The author's conclusion that

6. IV (1929), 96-105. In the *Revue* the article was erroneously entitled "La Crise des assurances en 1830 et les compagnies d'assurances."
7. "Les Debutes des partis modernes en France (1815-1830)," *Revue d'Histoire moderne*, VI (1931), 275-89.

the success of the Liberals' organization and propaganda after 1827 made the Revolution of 1830 inevitable appears now to be too sweeping, for it sets aside the undoubted influence of the economic depression and the enigmatic role of the working class in Paris in producing the explosion of July, 1830.

In 1931 the Harvard University Press published Artz's *France under the Bourbon Restoration, 1814-1830.* The first serious book in English on the subject, it rescued from neglect a period that Artz's own studies had convinced him was the most fecund in all French history since Waterloo. "The Bourbon Restoration in France," he had written, "saw the beginnings of a modern parliamentary regime, the rise of liberal Catholicism, of socialism, of positivism, and of the romantic school in literature and the fine arts."[8] Wishing to present these varied aspects of life and thought, and economic development as well, he eschewed a conventional chronological narrative and instead treated his subject in five topical chapters: "The Beginnings of a Modern Parliamentary Government in France," "The Clerical Question," "The Rise of a New Economic Order," "The State of Society," and "The Romantic Revolt." The first chapter he based in part on police and prefects' reports and on contemporary newspapers. The remaining four were syntheses of the work of other historians published in the century since 1830. Although it was the first book of a young scholar, eminent members of the profession thought it worthy of their attention. Professors Allison of Yale, Guérard of Stanford, and C. K. Webster of the University of London reviewed it in the principal English-language journals. In Germany the monumental *Historische Zeitschrift* published a short notice on it.[9] The comments were generally favorable, although as often happens in the case of works cutting across several of the conventional fields of history, the reviewers found fault with the sections dealing with their specialties, applauded those in which they themselves were least at home. French critics discovered nothing new in the book but, nonetheless, praised it,

8. *American Historical Review,* XXXV (1929-30), 913. This journal cited hereinafter as *A.H.R.*

9. *A.H.R.,* XXXVII (1931), 113-15; *J.M.H.,* III (1931), 499-501; *English Historical Review,* XLVII (1932), 715-16; *Historische Zeitschrift,* CXLVI (1932), 181-82.

in the words of one of them, as "a work of serious and intelligent popularization" for Americans.[10] In the thirty years since its publication the book has stood up remarkably well. It is still the standard work in English on the Bourbon Restoration; it has introduced many generations of American students to the period; and its extensive and critical bibliographies have been a boon to scholars and students alike. After long being out of print it has recently been reprinted.[11]

The publication and favorable reception of this book established Artz as the American authority on the Bourbon Restoration in France. Since then few important books on the period have appeared that editors of one or another of the historical journals have not given to him to review. It was he who introduced to American readers the magisterial works of De Bertier de Sauvigny, now the leading French authority on the Restoration.[12] When in the 1950's the American Historical Association undertook to publish a new *Guide to Historical Literature,* the editors called upon Artz to prepare the sections on the Bourbon Restoration and the July Monarchy.[13] His services as critic have been steadily in demand in other ways. Editors seek his advice on manuscripts dealing with his period of French history, and from 1932 to 1935 he served on the Board of Editors of the *Journal of Modern History.*[14] For thirty years he has been a familiar figure at meetings of French historians in the United States. His comments and criticism, sometimes formally as a member of session, at other times spontaneously from the floor, have always been trenchant, always heard with respect, and over the years they have been influential on American historical scholarship of France.

Neither the limits of the Bourbon Restoration nor the frontiers of France, however, confined Artz's professional interests,

10. *Rev. d'Hist. mod.,* VII (1932), 205; *Revue historique,* CLXXIV (1934), 241.

11. The reprint has been published by Russell and Russell, New York, 1963.

12. *A.H.R.,* LV (1950), 595-97; LXI (1956), 392-93.

13. George F. Howe, *et al.* (eds.), *The American Historical Association's Guide to Historical Literature* (N.Y., 1961), pp. 476, 494.

14. From 1941 to 1958 Artz served on the Board of Editors of the *Journal of Central European Affairs,* a learned review established in 1941 under the sponsorship of Oberlin and Carleton colleges, the universities of Colorado and Indiana, and the Slavic Department of Harvard University.

even in the early years of his career. At a session of the American Historical Association in December, 1929, he read a paper on "Michelet and French Nationalism," and about the same time he contributed to the *Encyclopaedia of the Social Sciences* an article on Ercole Consalvi, cardinal and Papal secretary of state during the pontificate of Pius VII (1800-1823).[15] A few years later he spoke to his colleagues in the American Historical Association on the gaps in historical knowledge of Europe from 1815 to 1850.[16] He urged especially the need for general interpretative works covering these years or even longer—a comprehensive history of German society in the first half of the nineteenth century comparable to Halévy's books on English history in the same period, for example; an international history of European literature from 1750 to 1850, an international history of Philhellenism. When he turned his attention to monographic studies he emphasized subjects "along the edges of the old disciplines," such as the history of education or of the financing of early industry, but he still showed his liking for broad, international subjects by recommending studies of the movement of ideas across national frontiers. One such suggestion, the study of the cultural influence of the United States on Europe, a reversal of the then almost exclusive concern with cultural transmission in the opposite direction—westward across the Atlantic, has since attracted the attention of a number of historians.[17]

The combination of a reputation in the field of the Bourbon Restoration and interest in the whole of European history made Artz an obvious choice as a contributor to the multi-volume history of modern Europe projected by Harper and Brothers in the early 1930's. The editor, William L. Langer of Harvard, chose twenty American historians of Europe to distil into twenty volumes of readable synthesis, appealing to the layman, the essence

15. IV, 210.
16. Published as "European Civilization 1815-1850: Some Unfinished Business," *J.M.H.*, IX (1937), 304-13.
17. Cf. Halvdan Koht, *The American Spirit in Europe, a Survey: Transatlantic Influences* (Philadelphia, 1949); Merle Curti, *Prelude to Point Four: American Technical Missions Overseas, 1838-1938* (Madison, 1954); Durand Echeverria, *Mirage in the West: A History of the French Image of American Society to 1815* (Princeton, 1957); Russell M. Jones, "The French Image of America: 1830-1848" (unpublished doctoral dissertation, University of Missouri, 1957).

of the great mass of historical scholarship on European history since the Middle Ages. To write the volume on the post-revolutionary years, 1814 to 1832, Langer selected Artz, and his book, entitled *Reaction and Revolution, 1814-1832,* was published in the autumn of 1934, sharing with Crane Brinton's *A Decade of Revolution* the distinction of being the first of the twenty volumes to appear. The book was most successful in its treatment of general ideas and cultural trends—liberalism, idealism, romanticism, and what Artz called in a happily descriptive phrase, "the search for a principle of authority." Here he achieved the kind of international synthesis he urged upon his colleagues. The best parts of the volume made it a valuable introduction to an age of European history little known outside scholarly circles, and it has been widely used as a college textbook. Its extensive bibliographies and its wide range of factual material gave the volume utility as a work of reference. By 1961, when the thirteenth revised printing came on the market, more than 15,000 copies had been sold.[18]

After his completion of this general book some of Artz's professional colleagues urged him to return to monographic research, and following their recommendation and his own advice to choose objects on the periphery of the old disciplines he undertook a study of the history of technical education in France. This project occupied most of his scholarly attention through the remainder of the 1930's. Its first fruits appeared as an article, "Les Débuts de l'Education technique en France, 1500-1700," in the *Revue d'Histoire moderne* in 1937.[19] The following year the same review published a second part of the study, bringing the story to 1789.[20] Two final installments, "L'Enseignement technique en France pendant l'époque révolutionnaire, 1789-1815," appeared after the war in 1946 as the leading articles in two successive numbers of the most distinguished of French historical journals, the *Revue historique.*[21] The study was important not for France alone but for the history of education and the advancement of technology in all the European world, because

18. Letter from William L. Langer, Dec. 4, 1961.
19. XII (1937), 467-519.
20. XIII (1938), 361-407.
21. CXCVI (1946), 257-86, 385-407.

France was the poineer in the development of technical education. Until the eighteenth century such training was left to apprenticeship and experience in industry and in the army and the navy; officers and industrialists alike looked on theoretical education in science and mathematics with a mixture of distrust and hostility. In the eighteenth century the picture changed. In 1747 the French state established two engineering schools—the Ecole des Ponts et Chaussées and the Ecole des Mines—and in the succeeding hundred years created a group of engineering schools unequaled elsewhere in the world—the Ecole du Génie militaire, the Ecole du Génie navale, the Conservatoire national des Arts et Métiers, the Ecole centrale des Arts et Manufactures, and crowning the edifice of French technical education, the great Ecole polytechnique, which quickly became the most prestigious school in France and set the pattern of technical education throughout Europe and the United States. Drawing chiefly on contemporary publications and the monographs of other scholars and occasionally utilizing documents in the Archives nationales Artz reconstructed this rich history from the emergence in the sixteenth and seventeenth centuries of an awareness of the need for special technical education through the foundation of the greatest schools during the years of the Revolution and the Empire, and he skilfully related these ideas and accomplishments to contemporary intellectual developments and to the changing needs of industry and of the armed forces. Artz originally proposed to continue the study to 1850, and since his retirement he has again taken up this final part of the project. The four long articles as they stand are the best work on the subject, and they constitute Artz's principal original contribution to French historical scholarship.

Even before he completed the last of these articles his interests had been distracted from the eighteenth and nineteenth centuries by the dismal realities of the twentieth. Alarmed by the precipitous decline in Europe of the liberalism he admired, the mounting victories of totalitarianism, and the descent into war of the continent he loved, he turned his energies to contemporary issues. At the last convention of the American Historical Association before the outbreak of the war in Europe he had presented a paper comparing the two Bonapartist dictatorships and showing their similarities and contrasts with the fascist dictatorships, and in it there was no mistaking his anxiety for the future.[22] After the fall of France in 1940 he wrote for Farrar and Rinehart's series *America in a World at War* a pamphlet entitled *1917 and 1941*. Here in burning words he poured out his indignation against Americans for their indifference to the threat of a German victory. This was no scholarly, analytical article but a desperate call to action. "The lights of our civilization are going out," he warned. "If they are relighted, the Americans and the English will relight them."

The frame of mind reflected in this pamphlet was not one to stimulate historical scholarship, and during the war years Artz set aside his old scholarly interests. After the war ended he appeared on the program of the first full-scale postwar convention of the American Historical Association in 1946 as a critic of a paper on French constitutionalism, but this was more an indication of his prewar reputation in the profession than a presage of a return to an active and creative role in French historical scholarship. Now his interests in cultural history prevailed over narrower research interests, and he undertook to write a work of synthesis and popularization. He chose, however, not the field he knew best, where his very specialization might be a handicap, but the cultural history of the Middle Ages, frankly acknowledging that no medievalist would dare such an ambitious undertaking. Behind his choice lay formal training in medieval history under Haskins at Harvard, a quarter of a century of teaching the subject at Oberlin, and an even longer period of reading and reflecting on it. The outcome was in the words of one reviewer a book of "rare wisdom and ripe scholarship." It was published in 1953 by Alfred Knopf as *The Mind of the Middle Ages, 200-1500 A. D.; an Historical Survey.*[23] Medievalists might complain that it did not embody all the latest scholarship, that the author's selection of facts and personalities was arbitrary, and that this or that interpretation was dubious. One critic protested that

22. Published as "Bonapartism and Dictatorship," *South Atlantic Quarterly,* XXXIX (1940), 37-49.
　23. A second edition was published in 1954, a third in 1958.

Artz was far too sympathetic to all things medieval; another declared that he could never really understand his subject because he was so unsympathetic to all things medieval. But the book commanded respect. *Speculum,* journal of the Medieval Academy of America, devoted five full pages to a critical review of it, and the reviewer concluded that it was "a good book, a credit to its author, and, if judged relatively rather than absolutely, a first-rate book—a valuable contribution to the historiography of the Middle Ages."[24] Another critic compared it to "that distinguished . . . classic," Preserved Smith's *A History of Modern Culture,* a particularly apt comparison because Artz was a warm admirer of that work and of its author and had certainly been influenced by Smith's conceptions of cultural history.[25] The volume's broad coverage of the field from Imperial Rome to the Reformation, from Britain to Islam, its successful integration of music, art, philosophy, and science into the medieval scene, its explanatory notes that included many quotations from sources, and its critical bibliographies gave it a broad appeal. It has been used widely as a textbook in colleges and universities, and a growing body of American college graduates sees the intellectual and artistic life of the Middle Ages through the eyes of Frederick Artz.

The book gave Artz a new reputation in the historical profession. When he next presented a paper before the American Historical Association, in 1956, his subject was in medieval and early modern history. Here, too, he came not as the professional presenting work of original research but as the informed outsider offering an answer to the sweeping question "When and How Did the Modern World Begin?" He had kept a foot in the camp of the French historians, appearing as a critic at a session on the Second French Empire at the American Historical Association's convention in 1953. In 1957 at the annual conference of the Society for French Historical Studies he was the chairman of a meeting on his original subject, the Bourbon Restoration. But this old friend did not win him back. He was by the

24. XXVIII (1953), 858-62. The reviewer was Thomas C. Van Cleve of Bowdoin College.
25. *N.Y. Times Book Review,* May 3, 1953, p. 16 (review by J. H. Randall, Jr., of Columbia University).

latter date at work on another synoptic book in cultural history continuing the history of literature and the arts that he had carried through the Middle Ages in his preceding book. Entitled *From the Renaissance to Romanticism; Trends in Style in Art, Literature, and Music, A.D. 1300-1830*, it appeared in the fall of 1962 under the imprint of the University of Chicago Press.

By 1962 Artz's second career, that of the cultural historian and synthesizer, had clearly prevailed over that of the research scholar. Other research scholars might regret that he left them, regret the loss of the continued application of his talents to problems that interest them. Had he taught in a university with a large research library and had graduate students to direct in his own specialty, perhaps he would have persisted in his first role. The demands of undergraduate teaching certainly had the opposite influence, reinforcing his already strong interests in the broad view of history. The war and the mounting threats to the values of Western civilization in his lifetime perhaps undermined his faith in the value of the meticulous study of little subjects; for him the times demanded historians who could communicate an appreciation of the ideas and the humane values that over the centuries have gone into the composition of the Western tradition. But even without this pressing imperative, synoptic history written for the layman, not for the professional scholar, is the ultimate achievement of historians. It is the finished fabric in which the monographs of specialists are the threads. The ability to weave this complex fabric and to make it appealing is probably the rarest of talents in the historical profession of Artz's time. Here lay his greatest gifts, and here he made the contribution for which he will be longest remembered as a historian.

Patronage, Piety, and Printing in Sixteenth-Century Europe*

ROBERT M. KINGDON

Scholars have devoted much study to early printers as technicians, as humanists, and as agents of propaganda. They have devoted comparatively little to early printers as businessmen.[1] Yet they were, of necessity, men of business and occasionally ones of considerable astuteness and vision. Surviving records of their business activities are not as complete as one might wish. Some can be found, however, and they merit more intensive and more technical study than they have yet received. Two sets of these records have attracted my own attention: one scattered among the manuscript collections of the State Archives of Geneva, Switzerland, the other in the Plantin-Moretus Museum of Antwerp, Belgium. The collections in Geneva include notaries' copies of contracts and the minutes of judicial sessions of city councils relating to the affairs of a number of local printers. Of these Genevan printers, two interested me particularly: Henri Estienne, the great publisher of humanist texts, and his brother François. The museum in Antwerp preserves the actual account

* This essay is a revised version of one I read to the Humanities Society of the State University of Iowa in 1958. I thought it appropriate to this volume, because of Mr. Artz's interest in early books and their printers, an interest which helped stimulate my own first work on this subject. Part of the research upon which this essay is based was made possible by a grant from the Penrose Fund of the American Philosophical Society.

1. Among the more important exceptions to this rule are the suggestive synthetic study of Lucien Febvre and Henri-Jean Martin, *L'apparition du livre* (Paris, 1958), and the technical articles of Raymond and Florence de Roover on the business operations of Christopher Plantin: Raymond de Roover, "The Business Organization of the Plantin Press in the Setting of Sixteenth Century Antwerp," *Gedenkboek der Plantin-Dagen, 1555-1955* (Antwerp, 1956), pp. 230-46 (volume hereinafter cited as *Plantin Gedenkboek*); Florence Edler [de Roover], "Cost Accounting in the Sixteenth Century: The Books of Account of Christopher Plantin, Antwerp, Printer and Publisher," *Accounting Review*, XII (1937), 226-37.

books and the business correspondence of Christopher Plantin, who operated what was probably the largest publishing business of the time.[2] Comparison of the business operations of several small-scale printers of Calvinist Geneva with those of a single large-scale printer of Catholic Antwerp suggests to me several interesting generalizations. They concern certain relations among patronage, piety, and the printing industry.

Many, perhaps most, of the really well-known printers of the early modern period depended on patronage. The most generous patrons available were kings and princes. The Estienne firm secured its significant contemporary reputation with materials the purchase of which was financed by subsidies from the kings of France. The link between the two was first made strong during the career of Robert Estienne the elder, father of the Henri Estienne upon whose activities we shall focus.[3] Robert had won subsidies for his publishing house in Paris from King Francis I, who was particularly interested in encouraging the new humanistically oriented classical scholarship inspired by the Renaissance in Italy. He used these grants to commission the manufacture of some of the finest types the world has ever seen, not only fine Latin types, but also Greek and Hebrew ones. One of his most important uses of these materials, however, got him into serious trouble. An edition of the Bible which he published with his own annotations aroused the fury of the members of the Sorbonne faculty, the intellectual guardians of the Catholic orthodoxy of that day. Their persecution goaded Robert Estienne into giving free rein to certain of his own growing religious inclinations. He turned Protestant and fled to Calvin's Geneva, successfully smuggling much of his invaluable equipment along with

2. The standard study of the Estiennes is Ant. Aug. Renouard, *Annales de l'imprimerie des Estienne* (2nd ed., 2 vols.; Paris, 1843; recently reprinted without date by Burt Franklin, New York). The standard study of Plantin is Max Rooses, *Christophe Plantin: imprimeur anversois* (Antwerp, 1883). Both have been supplemented but not replaced by more recent studies cited below. Another important source of information on Plantin is the *Correspondance de Christophe Plantin*, ed. Max Rooses and J. Denucé (9 vols.; Antwerp and other cities, 1883-1918), and M. van Durme, *Supplément à la correspondance de Christophe Plantin* (Antwerp, 1955). Hereinafter cited as Renouard, *Estiennes*; Rooses, *Plantin*; Plantin, *Corr.*

3. Elizabeth Armstrong, *Robert Estienne, Royal Printer: An Historical Study of the Elder Stephanus* (Cambridge, 1954), provides the most complete scholarly study of his career.

him. This decision robbed Estienne of his patron, but he was well enough established by now to carry on his business without much difficulty until his death in 1559.

His son Henri, however, did have to face the patronage problem. Henri Estienne had been superbly educated and was even more of a scholar than his father. His contributions to the editing and analysis of Greek texts still demand scholarly attention. The fact that he published so many works of erudition, however, and published them in provincial Geneva, made his financial problems even more difficult than those of his father. The city possessed no one with wealth and interest enough to become the patron required by the needs of Henri Estienne's business. He could not, furthermore, leave Geneva. His father's printing equipment had been willed to him on condition that he never move it from that city. If he ever did decide to violate this condition, the equipment would revert to the city government for use in ways that would support municipal charities. The pious deacons and councilors of Geneva were constantly on the watch to see to it that Estienne did not try to move anything out of town. More than once he was called before governmental councils and forced to submit to exhaustive questioning on rumors that he had planned to leave the city.[4]

Fortunately for scholarship, Henri Estienne did find patrons willing to subsidize his publishing business, even though it remained in Geneva. Two of them were especially important: Ulrich Fugger and King Henry III of France.

Ulrich Fugger of Augsburg, the only member of that fabulously wealthy family of international financiers to develop Protestant leanings, had decided to collect a library that would contain the best examples of every author, every subject, and every language. To house this library, he arranged to purchase one of the finest houses in the city of Geneva, for the very large sum of 2000 écus. To fill this library and to secure for it personal parchment editions of works he particularly treasured, Fugger contracted with Henri Estienne to become "his printer." This

---

4. For a more detailed and documented account of these quarrels, see Robert M. Kingdon, "The Business Activities of Printers Henri and François Estienne," *Aspects de la propagande religieuse* (Geneva, 1957), pp. 258-75; hereinafter cited as Kingdon, "Estiennes."

agreement was reached in 1558, even before the death of Estienne's father. It provided that Estienne was to receive an annual stipend of 300 livres outright, supplies of parchment, and a loan of 1500 livres at a rate of interest not specified. In return Fugger was to receive one copy in parchment of every book printed by Estienne. To see to it that Estienne kept his part of the bargain, Fugger sent to Geneva a personal agent—Henry Scringer, a noted Scottish humanist and lawyer.[5]

Fugger's patronage provided the financial basis for much of Estienne's most important work. Unfortunately it lasted only a decade. Relatives of Ulrich Fugger, motivated perhaps by alarm at his heavy expenses, perhaps by jealousy, perhaps by religious orthodoxy, soon secured a court order restraining him from spending money for cultural purposes. By 1568 the Fugger subsidies had stopped. Estienne spent much of the rest of his life trying to regain them. He seems finally to have reached some sort of agreement with Fugger's heirs, but only toward the end of his life, too late to do him any good.

Estienne, meanwhile, had turned to a grandson of the patron who had made his father's reputation—to Henry III. The king was a decadent and frivolous man who lacked the religious fanaticism that dominated so many of his contemporaries. This made it possible for a Protestant like Estienne to visit the royal court. In doing so he succeeded in impressing or at least amusing the king, who, in 1579, agreed to grant him an annual pension of 300 livres, to be paid through the royal ambassador to the Swiss Leagues. The king also promised Estienne a special grant of 100 écus, but this the printer never did collect because he unwisely neglected to bribe a corrupt royal treasurer.

Christopher Plantin managed to tap an even richer vein than did Henri Estienne. His principal patron was Philip II, King of Spain and also ruler of a vast empire including all of what is today the Netherlands and Belgium, much of present-day Italy,

---

5. For more on the Fugger patronage of Henri Estienne, see Kingdon, "Estiennes," and sources therein cited; also Paul Lehmann, *Eine Geschichte der alten Fuggerbibliotheken* (2 vols.; Tubingen, 1956-1960), *passim.*; E.-H. Kaden, "Ulrich Fugger et son projet de créer à Genève une 'librairie' publique," *Geneva*, N.S. VII (1959), 127-36 (valuable for texts appended to it); Henri Delarue, "A propos du différend Ulrich Fugger-Henri Estienne en 1561," *Mélanges offerts à M. Paul-E. Martin* (Geneva, 1961), pp. 497-502.

parts of France, and a good deal of Latin America. Plantin in-
sinuated his way into the king's graces with the help of two
friends, both of whom came to hold key positions at the royal
court. One was Antoine Perrenot de Granvelle, Bishop of Arras,
Cardinal of the Roman Catholic Church, who became Philip's
regent for the Low Countries, then his ambassador in Italy, finally his first minister.[6] The other was Gabriel de Zayas, one of the
royal secretaries—not the most important of them, he was too
lazy for that—but the one who managed to stay in favor the
longest. Both had known Plantin when he was still a minor
bookbinder and then a one-press printer in Antwerp. He had
filled special commissions for each, and must have made a favorable impression on both.[7]

The project with which Plantin and his friends won the attention of the Spanish court was a proposal to publish a new
polyglot Bible.[8] The Complutensian Polyglot of Alcala, a multi-
lingual text of the Bible in Latin and the original languages of
Greek and Hebrew, prepared by a group of scholars under the or-
ganizational direction of Cardinal Cisneros de Ximenez, had long
since gone out of print. Scholarly interest in the text of the Bible
had, however, grown with the controversies rising out of the
Reformation. Plantin, therefore, proposed to produce a revised
and improved version of this pioneer work. For such a project
he needed subsidies. To be executed properly it required the
assistance of a group of scholars with competence in Latin,
Greek, and Hebrew. It required fonts of type in each of those
languages. It required access to the best available Biblical manuscripts, many of them in the custody of the Vatican. To complicate matters further, Plantin proposed the addition of a "Chal-
dean" or Aramaic text wherever one was available. All these
factors necessitated an enormous initial expense. The return
could not be expected to be great, since the Polyglot would be

6. On Granvelle's patronage of Plantin, see the studies of M. van Durme,
e.g., "Granvelle et Plantin," *Estudios dedicados a Menendez Pidal,* VII (Madrid,
1957), 225-72.
7. On Zayas' early relations with Plantin, see the document published in
Rooses' *Plantin,* pp. 392-93, and *passim.* Other aspects of their relationship are
illuminated by the many letters between them published in Plantin, *Corr.*
8. For a good recent discussion of this project, see Colin Clair, *Christopher
Plantin* (London, 1960), chap. iv, pp. 57-86. Hereinafter cited as Clair,
Plantin.

of use only to scholars with competence in the several Biblical languages.

In 1566 Plantin ran off a few sample proofs of his proposed Polyglot and took them to the internationally famous Frankfort Book Fair to sound out the market. Several German noblemen reportedly expressed considerable interest in subsidizing the project. Meanwhile, however, Plantin had written to friend Zayas in Spain. Zayas persuaded his royal master to follow the glorious example of his predecessors in subsidizing Biblical scholarship, in the process overcoming the suspicion of some of the more conservative Spanish religious—that editions of this sort undermined orthodoxy. Philip II agreed to grant subsidies large enough to cover all the expenses of the project. As in all the enterprises that attracted his attention, he insisted on close supervision. To effect this, he sent to Antwerp a learned Spanish doctor, B. Arias Montanus, to work with Plantin in directing the project. Plantin welcomed Montanus into his home, wined and dined him, became his bosom friend, and won another useful contact with the Spanish crown.

The Polyglot Bible was not a commercial success. Plantin published only 1200 copies for general sale, and he never did sell them all. Some remained in the stocks of his books inventoried after his death. But the book nevertheless made his reputation. It was a scholarly and artistic triumph. It confirmed Philip II in his initial high opinion of Plantin's abilities, and led to the establishment of a continuing and profitable connection between the two. The king awarded Plantin several large printing commissions. He also appointed Plantin to the newly created post of "Proto-typographer," a royal agent charged with supervising the printing industry throughout the Low Countries. Plantin or assistants he selected were to investigate the competence and religious orthodoxy of every printer working in that area. Each printer was required to submit affidavits from ecclesiastics who could testify to his piety and orthodoxy, and from magistrates who could testify to the soundness of his moral reputation. Plantin himself was responsible for testing each man's technical competence and knowledge of languages. This measure obviously served the double purpose of enforcing standards of competence and religious conformity. It also placed Plantin in a position of power that could not be challenged by any of his business rivals.[9]

With this new office Plantin also won the right to publish proclamations, both of the king and of local governmental and ecclesiastical authorities. For example, when Philip II decided to circulate a version of the new Index of Prohibited Books suggested by the Council of Trent, Plantin was given the job of printing and distributing copies throughout the Low Countries.

These prosperous relations between Plantin and his sovereign were rudely interrupted by the turn of political events in the area, in particular by the horrifying sack of Antwerp in 1576, commonly called the Spanish Fury. Plantin later bitterly accused the king of failing to honor his agreements.[10] While it is clear that the volume of printing Plantin did for the king fell off after 1576, there is reason to suspect that this accusation was not entirely sincere. It was released to the public at a time when Plantin was keeping some of his presses running by accepting commissions from heretic Dutch Calvinists, thus scandalizing all good Catholics. He had even done work for the Estates-General of the Northern Provinces, the institution then in nominal charge of the full-fledged revolt against the authority of Philip II.

Even Plantin's accusations and Spanish suspicions about his devotion to orthodoxy could not dissolve the connection between the Spanish crown and the Plantin firm. His heirs established ever more cordial relations with the successors to Philip II, and orders continued to pour into Antwerp. The Plantin press maintained its respectable prosperity for centuries following, down practically until the time the steam press and the linotype machine rendered its equipment hopelessly archaic.

These capsule accounts of the search by Estienne and Plantin for patrons should suggest the extent to which a large-scale, successful, sixteenth-century printer had to become a politician. Expanded versions of these accounts would make it even more obvious that complicated and devious intrigues were necessary

9. Plantin as king's proto-typographer see Clair, *Plantin,* chap. vi, pp. 105-12.

10. In a public letter issued from Leiden in 1583, published in Rooses, *Plantin,* pp. 410-17.

forerunners to the substantial wealth and international reputations these men acquired. Research into the careers of other
printers might well confirm this pattern. In this connection, study
of the Aldine press of Venice, which with the Estienne press and
the Plantin press is often reputed to be one of the three greatest
of the century, would probably prove particularly interesting.
For a time at least, this press gained much of its working capital
from the papacy. Paul Manutius, the second of the Aldines and
the one contemporary to the men we have studied, moved his
operations for a while to Rome, where he could work more closely with the great reforming popes who were his patrons.[11]

The second main generalization I want to advance is even
broader. It can be applied, I believe, to almost all the printers
of the sixteenth century, not just to the well-known and powerful. It deals with the relation between printing and religion.
This relation seems to me to be a close one, and one of great
importance to both. I would even go so far as to suggest that
the rise of a printing industry in the West with all its enormous
consequences in creating mass literacy, mass education, mass
government, and mass participation in a highly organized economy, is a consequence of certain peculiarities in the Christian
religion that have dominated the Western ethos. Christianity has
long been distinguished by the peculiar importance it places on
written Scripture as an ultimate source of truth—hence a persistent demand for many copies of the Bible and of devotional
books based wholly or partly on the Bible, such as the breviary
and the psalter. This demand may well have stimulated Guten-
berg's crucial invention of movable type. The book that is generally held to have earned him the reputation of founder of the
printing industry was, after all, a Bible. This demand, furthermore, would logically have been tremendously increased by intellectual developments during the late fifteenth and the early
sixteenth centuries. First many scholars of the Renaissance, then
the religious leaders of the Reformation, renewed and strength-
ened the Christian emphasis on the importance of Scripture.

11. Ant. Aug. Renouard, *Annales de l'imprimerie des Alde* (3rd ed.; Paris,
1834; reprinted Bologna, 1953), especially pp. 442-50 for Manutius' arrangements with the papacy.

These religious leaders, in addition, stimulated a continuing demand for versions of the Scripture in the vernacular languages. All these developments may well account for the impressive growth of the printing and publishing industry in the course of the sixteenth century.[12]

The straws in the wind pointing me toward these conclusions are fragmentary statistics of the number of copies in sixteenth-century editions. By modern commercial standards these editions were quite small. An average edition for Plantin consisted of 1250 to 1500 copies. Books that were popular or widely used he might publish in editions of 2500 copies, as he did, for example, with his Virgil. Books that were costly or of limited interest he published in smaller editions of a few hundred copies. And Plantin was one of the giants of the industry. This state of affairs is hardly surprising, given the relatively primitive state of printing technology, the relatively small size of the literate public, and the high cost of some of the raw materials that went into books. Paper in particular was very expensive. The stocks of paper for a book would sometimes cost twice as much as the money wages for all the men engaged in composing and printing it.[13]

I have found, however, three great exceptions to these general rules on edition size, one in Geneva, two in Antwerp. All were of books strikingly alike. They were the Huguenot psalter, which was published by a syndicate of printers in Geneva and various other cities, and the Roman missal and Roman breviary, whose publication was superintended from Rome but engrossed for the Spanish Hapsburg domains by Plantin. Let me dwell on two— the Huguenot psalter and the Roman breviary. (Arrangements for the publication and distribution of the Roman missal were almost identical to those for the breviary.)

A vernacular psalter was an essential for practically every literate member of the Protestant congregations being formed all over Europe in the course of the sixteenth century. The singing

12. Cf. the somewhat different but not necessarily incompatible theories on printing and intellectual developments advanced by Walter J. Ong, S.J., in his *Ramus, Method and the Decay of Dialogue* (Cambridge, Mass., 1958), pp. 307-14, and in several of his recent articles.

13. For sample figures of edition sizes and printing costs, see de Roover in *Plantin Gedenkboek*, pp. 235-36.

of the Psalms by laymen and clergy together, in their native tongue, was a part of the service of divine worship which the Reformers believed to be recommended by the Bible itself. Among French-speaking Protestants, the psalter which became most popular was based on translations prepared by the poet Clément Marot and the powerful Calvinist minister Theodore Beza, set to music by Louis Bourgeois and others.[14] Versions, translations, and excerpts of it still provide an important guide to worship for Protestants of the Calvinist tradition all over the world.

The largest early editions of this psalter were prepared in 1561-62, the years of partial toleration of Protestantism in France that made possible the peak of the Calvinist campaign to reform Christianity in that country. Arrangements for their printing were supervised by author Beza, who during this period spent most of his time away from his regular charge in Geneva, guiding the formation both of the Reformed Church of France and of the Huguenot party. For technical help, Beza turned to Antoine Vincent, a prosperous Calvinist printer and publisher, whose business centered in Lyons, but who spent much of his time superintending the operations of a branch in Geneva. Vincent and his son undertook to arrange the publication of the Huguenot psalter by a multitude of printers in many of the cities serving the French market. Eight per cent of the costs of these editions was to be turned over to charitable work, either directly or through the Vincents. This 8 per cent was regarded as an author's right, and may thus have been one of the first percentage royalties in history, even though based on cost of production rather than on sales. The essence of these arrangements was confirmed by a royal "privilege" or copyright, granted for ten years by the King of France, late in 1561. Several months later Vincent licensed more than a dozen printers of Paris to proceed with the production of these psalters—this in the city which was not only the political capital of France but also the historic intellectual center of religious orthodoxy in western Christendom. Soon

14. For a comprehensive study of this subject, see O. Douen, *Clément Marot et le psautier huguenot* (2 vols.; Paris, 1878-1879). The whole subject is now being reworked by Pierre Pidoux of Territet, Switzerland.

afterward, Vincent concluded a licensing agreement with an Orleans printer. It is obvious that he also concluded similar agreements with printers in Lyons and Geneva. Apparently he even recruited Plantin for his syndicate. In 1564 Plantin, still a relatively unknown Antwerp printer without any royal connections, obtained a four-year local "privilege" from the regent of the Low Countries for the printing of this psalter. Other printers in other cities also entered the syndicate.[15]

Information on actual production of these Huguenot psalters is difficult to find. There seem to be no Protestant printers' records as complete as those of Plantin. Scattered records in Geneva, however, make it clear that the printing of the psalter in that city was handled by a local syndicate. When its members squabbled among themselves, a newly established municipal regulatory commission, charged with many of the same responsibilities for protecting orthodoxy and technical competence that Plantin was to exercise as royal "Proto-typographer," stepped in to bring order to local arrangements. The commission allocated quantities of psalters among competing printers, fixed common prices, and regulated the quality of printing and paper used in the books. Printers not meeting minimum standards of quality were forced to cut back operations, and in some cases were driven entirely out of business.

The records of this dispute reveal that during the peak years of 1561 and 1562, the Genevan members of this syndicate produced 27,400 copies of the Huguenot psalter. Of this total, 10,800 copies were produced in a second set of editions allocated by the printing commission.[16] Since this total of 27,400 copies was only a fraction of the entire number published, obviously the total of all these editions must have been really immense for the period. It seems entirely possible that members of Vincent's syndicate ran off more than 100,000 psalters altogether.

Information on distribution of these Huguenot psalters is also

15. On all these arrangements, see E. Droz, "Antoine Vincent: la propagande protestante par le psautier," *Aspects de la propagande religieuse,* pp. 276-93.
16. For more information on these figures, see Robert M. Kingdon, *Geneva and the Coming of the Wars of Religion in France, 1555-1563* (Geneva, 1956), p. 100. On Genevan printing during this period in general, see Paul Chaix, *Recherches sur l'imprimerie à Genève de 1550 à 1564* (Geneva, 1954); hereinafter cited as Chaix, *Recherches.*

difficult to find. Many of the Genevan printers, notably Henri Estienne, regularly attended the international book fairs in Frankfort. But they seem to have looked to Frankfort primarily as an outlet for their classical and scholarly books. Wholesale booksellers clearly did distribute tremendous quantities of books. The most important of them seems to have been Laurent de Normandie, a French emigrant who established his business in Geneva. He must have arranged for distribution of a good part of the psalters published in that city. The inventory of his property prepared following his sudden death in 1569 has recently been uncovered and published.[17] It reveals that De Normandie carried several thousand copies of this psalter in a stock of almost 35,000 volumes. These and other records make it clear that itinerant book peddlers called "colporteurs" handled much of the actual retail distribution of the Huguenot psalters.

The size of the market for psalters had many interesting economic consequences for the printing industry. One of the more striking can be found in a number of contracts drafted for François Estienne, a poor younger brother of Henri Estienne, who was also a master printer in Geneva.[18] François never was able to tap the rich patronage that financed his brother's operations. In fact, he does not seem to have had much money or capital of any kind. Henri tried to transfer some of his equipment to François, but the Geneva Council, at the urging of Fugger's agents, blocked this transfer, for fear it was a trick to evade the paternal will, which required that all the Estienne property remain in Geneva. François, therefore, had to depend on his own resources. He managed to finance his operations by using stocks of testaments and psalters which he had already printed or was planning to print, as collateral to obtain loans and stocks of paper. This expedient kept him going for about ten years. Then his business failed and he left Geneva. Of all the books he published he normally used only the testaments and psalters as collateral. Apparently only they commanded a market wide and steady enough to persuade other businessmen to extend him

17. By Heidi-Lucie Schlaepfer, in pp. 184-230 of her "Laurent de Normandie," *Aspects de la propagande religieuse*, pp. 176-230.
18. See Kingdon, "Estiennes," *passim.*

necessary credit. If it can be demonstrated that this method of carrying on business was widespread, it would surely be obvious that most of the printing industry depended on religious staples. The average small printer, who could not make the contacts that won wealthy patrons, must often have been obliged to print or obtain stocks of a popular religious book in order to keep the rest of the business going.

The approximate Catholic equivalents to the Protestant psalter are the breviary and the missal. The breviary is perhaps the closer equivalent since its heart is the Psalms of the Old Testament. Its use is perhaps more limited, since it is normally used only by priests, only rarely by laymen. On the other hand, its use is almost certainly more intensive, since every priest in those days was normally expected, and is nowadays obliged, to use a breviary for the saying of his offices every single day. It is a rare Protestant who sings many hymns every single day.

Breviaries had, of course, been printed before the sixteenth century. But the Catholic Counter Reformation provided a tremendous stimulus to the breviary trade.[19] This stemmed not only from an undoubted increase in priestly piety, but also from an important change in the breviary text. One of the many reforming demands that faced the Roman Catholic Church in that period of confusion and strife was for a single authoritative standard of devotional practice, and wide enforcement of that standard. After several false starts, in two of which Platin participated, this task was finally accomplished by the liturgical decrees of the Council of Trent. In this, as in so many other fields, the Tridentine Fathers repudiated reforms that seemed modernizing, particularizing, or of a Protestant tendency, and repaired to a more antique and universal standard. The nature of that standard had been suggested by the plan for liturgical reforms proposed by members of the conservative Theatine order. In the Council's concluding decrees of 1563, the job of drafting the actual text of the reformed breviary was entrusted to the Vatican. The specialists hired by the Vatican finished work by 1568, and the official

19. Two general histories of the Roman breviary which contain useful chapters on the Tridentine reforms: Pierre Batiffol, *Histoire du Bréviaire romain* (Paris, 1893); Dom Suitbert Bäumer, *Histoire du Bréviaire*, trans. fr. the German with useful additions by Dom Réginald Biron (2 vols.; Paris, 1905).

text was then released to the printers. At the same time a papal bull banned use of any other breviary, excepting only those that won explicit papal approval or that could claim a prescriptive right of use over a period of two hundred years.

This touched off a mad scramble for the right to publish the new breviary. The printers who won out were Paul Manutius, of the famous Aldine press, and Christopher Plantin.[20] Manutius, as papal printer, got the copy of the official text and a papal "privilege" theoretically granting him the sole right to publish the book. Plantin, thanks to some shrewd bargaining and pressure brought to bear by his old friend and patron, Cardinal Granvelle, won a license to print the new breviary in the Low Countries. It was agreed that a tenth of Plantin's production would be sent to Manutius to pay him for this concession. This was soon commuted to cash payments equivalent to a tenth of the value of Plantin's production. He printed more than seven thousand copies of the Roman breviary under the terms of this agreement.

After a few years, however, Plantin began looking for ways to evade further payments to Manutius. It was not only the expense that irked him. It was also the bother. In those days transferring large sums of cash over great distances involved arrangements that could become complicated or slow. He finally found a safe method of evasion in a new arrangement with the King of Spain. Philip II had already decided to promulgate in his realms a breviary with a text slightly different from that prepared for the Vatican. With the help of Zayas, Plantin persuaded Philip to place orders with him for mammoth quantities of these breviaries and other devotional books, enough to supply the needs of all the clergy in Spain. Since the text of these breviaries was not to be quite the same as the text promulgated in Rome, Plantin felt himself released from his agreement with Manutius and ceased making his payments.

The text of the new Spanish breviary was the personal work of the king. He felt it was slightly more orthodox and slightly more grammatical than the pope's text. Since Roman Catholi-

20. For a documented account of what follows, see Robert M. Kingdon, "The Plantin Breviaries: A Case Study in the Sixteenth-Century Business Operations of a Publishing House," *Bibliothèque d'Humanisme et Renaissance* (1960), pp. 133-50.

cism then depended heavily on the secular support of the Spanish crown, there was little the pope could do but approve these changes. He granted the clergy of Spain special permission to use the royal breviary. That these changes were accurately incorporated into the volumes Plantin published was guaranteed by the king's close personal supervision of their publication. One of the most psychologically revealing sets of manuscripts preserved in Antwerp is a set of printers' proofs for this breviary. They had been sent to Spain by Plantin. They were returned with marginal corrections in the hand of some royal scribe but with additional corrections and comments in the spidery hand of Philip II himself.[21]

The order for Spanish breviaries, and the other Spanish orders for devotional books which quickly followed it, constituted a major business coup for Plantin. This was not only because they released him from his obligations to Manutius. The size alone of these orders was enough to guarantee the prosperity of any printer. In the five years during which the agreement remained in effect Plantin delivered 15,505 breviaries to agents of the Spanish crown. He apparently delivered even more missals and in addition thousands of psalters, antiphonaries, diurnals, and books of hours. He also printed or purchased for sale to the king quantities of other books for the royal library. Most of these books were supplied to the king at retail prices. Plantin offered his royal customer few of the wholesalers' discounts he normally offered to those who bought from him in quantity. This must have made his profits truly impressive. It is no wonder that during this period he was able to expand his printing plant from one that was merely among the biggest in Europe to one that had at least four times as many presses as the plants of such rivals as Henri Estienne and Antoine Vincent.[22] It was also during this period that Plantin acquired the tremendous stock of types, type matrices, and punches that was to serve his descendents for the next three hundred years. One expert typographer estimates the

21. Museum Plantin-Moretus, Archives, No. 122, "Missale et Breviarium," p. 146, *inter alia.*

22. On the controversial question of how many presses Plantin actually operated, see de Roover in *Plantin Gedenkboek*, pp. 240-41, and Clair, *Plantin*, p. 283. Sixteen is the minimum estimate. The number of presses allocated to each Genevan printer is revealed by a text published in Chaix, *Recherches*, p. 32.

Plantin stock to contain three times as many sixteenth-century type matrices as the other three surviving collections of real size combined.[23]

This high prosperity, we have already noticed, was ended by the Spanish Fury of 1576. Relations between the Plantin-Moretus press and the Spanish crown, however, continued for centuries thereafter. The most important element in this trade, moreover, continued to be the supply of breviaries and other devotional books to the Spanish market. That market soon grew to include not only Spain proper but also her overseas colonies. Traces of the impact of Plantin's devotional books can even be found in Latin American art of the colonial period.[24]

Altogether Plantin sold at least twenty-two thousand breviaries during the first eight years of his production of them. When we realize that he was only the most important of dozens of printers who were publishing this volume (the Manutius "privilege" had been ignored or violated all over Europe), it becomes clear that the Roman breviary, like the Huguenot psalter, was one of the best sellers of the century.

The channels through which Plantin distributed his breviaries are clearly revealed by his records. In general, all of his books were distributed through four main ones: (1) retail sale through his own shop in Antwerp, (2) wholesale distribution through sales to booksellers, publishers, and other buyers at the semi-annual international book fair in Frankfort, (3) wholesale distribution through booksellers doing business in the Low Countries, northern France, parts of southern England, and the upper Rhineland, (4) quantity sale to patrons who arranged their own methods of further distribution.

Most of the breviaries were distributed by the third and fourth of these methods. By the time his business had grown to sizable proportions, Plantin was selling only a small percentage of his books in his retail shop. The records of those sales reveal, however, that an important percentage of them were of breviaries and other devotional books, particularly in the years immediately

---

23. Harry Carter, in "Plantin's Types and Their Makers," *Plantin Gedenkboek*, pp. 253-54.

24. For an interesting example, see Pál Kelemen, *Baroque and Rococo in Latin America* (New York, 1951), p. 213, plates 139 and 191.

following the release of the Tridentine texts. At the Frankfort book fairs Plantin also sold a few breviaries, but only a few. As we have already noted, the Frankfort market was apparently mostly for scholarly classical volumes of international interest.

Booksellers seem to have distributed most of the breviaries Plantin printed under the Manutius contract. Many of them were also printers and publishers on their own account, and most of them also sold books to Plantin. Barter appears to have been common in the sixteenth-century book trade. None of these other traders could operate on the same scale as Plantin, however, so practically every account was settled by cash payments to him. On almost all of these accounts Plantin allowed a substantial discount, averaging about 15 per cent, although it varied considerably and seems to have been negotiated separately with the settling of each individual account.

Patrons distributed the rest of Plantin's breviaries. By far the most important of these, of course, was Philip II. He set up his own elaborate distribution network within Spain under the direction of a religious order that maintained headquarters in the royal palace. Plantin also had other patrons. Many of them were bishops or abbots, who probably distributed the devotional books sent to them directly to clergymen under their jurisdiction.

These two generalizations on the sixteenth-century publishing industry suggest a third. For both of them tend to de-emphasize the role in society of the humanist and to emphasize the precariousness of his calling. Such a conclusion may disappoint those who are dedicated today to the pursuit of the humanities. It was commonly believed in the sixteenth century that really thorough training in the languages of classical antiquity was the hallmark of an educated man, and this belief was held more widely and was subject to much less challenge than it is today. It was also accepted that the printing industry could contribute to this training by its production of classical texts. The printers we have considered did make contributions to this cause. The Greek texts of Henri Estienne and the Polyglot Bible of Plantin provide proof of that. And yet careful study of the business operations of these same men makes it clear that these prestige editions did not pay their own way. The market for books of scholarship, then as now, was narrowly restricted and widely scattered. These publications were subsidized, either by the generous patronage of men of power or by profits gained by catering to the popular thirst for religious consolation. Plantin sold at least twenty, possibly thirty times as many breviaries as he sold Polyglot Bibles. Henri Estienne depended on profits from the sale of Bibles and on outright gifts from patrons to underwrite the production of the Greek texts for which he is famous. Piety and patronage made scholarship possible.

Nationalism and Science—Sir Joseph Banks and the Wars with France

A. HUNTER DUPREE

The eighteenth century casts an image that calls modern man back to the Age of Reason as to his own better self. No part of the noble dream of the eighteenth century has a more haunting attraction in the anxieties of the nuclear era than the true internationalism of science that soared above the noise of battle. "The sciences are never at war," wrote Edward Jenner in 1803.[1] Scientists now believe as an article of faith that the truth that is their calling transcends nationality, and that the intrusion of national interest is a monstrous distortion of the real nature of science. Hence they fondly and enviously hark back to the supposedly idyllic state of the *philosophes* with only a trace of a smile at the naïve innocence of those delightfully civilized times.

Among the famous and admired examples of eighteenth-century internationalism in science is Benjamin Franklin's appeal that American warships and privateers during the Revolution not obstruct the voyage "of that most celebrated Navigator and Discoverer Captain Cook."[2] Another impressive example is the visit of Sir Humphry Davy to Paris in 1813, when the Duke of Wellington was fighting through the Pyrenees.[3]

The best example of such an attitude was the "Great Panjandrum of British Science,"[4] Sir Joseph Banks, President of the

1. Sir Gavin de Beer, *The Sciences Were Never At War* (London, 1960), p. 197, quotes a letter of Edward Jenner to the Institut National of France, 1803: "The Sciences are never at war. Peace must always preside in those bosoms whose object is the augmentation of human happiness."
2. *Ibid.*, p. 26.
3. *Ibid.*, pp. 204-208.
4. J. C. Beaglehole, Introduction to *The Voyage of the Endeavour, 1768-1771* (*The Journals of Captain James Cook on His Voyages of Discovery*) (Cambridge, 1955), p. cxxxvi.

Royal Society of London from 1778 to 1820. "It has, indeed," he
wrote to Jean-Baptiste-Joseph Delambre in 1804, "been always
my wish to promote the scientific intercourse among nations,
notwithstanding any political divisions which might subsist between them. . . ."[5]

Sir Gavin de Beer has now performed the signal service of
gathering documents bearing on the theme of science and nationalism from 1690 to 1815 in a single volume entitled *The Sciences
Were Never at War*. Of his 208 pages of documents for the
entire period of more than a century, 165 pages revolve closely
around Sir Joseph Banks. In selecting his documents to illustrate
a single theme De Beer has expressed his sense of the importance
of the subject and has saved other scholars much grubbing in
the global tangle of Banks's papers. Yet the very importance of
the internationalism of science in the twentieth century bids other
scholars not to rest with his collection. For De Beer has largely
contented himself with letting the documents speak for themselves. And what do they say?

One can grant at the outset some of the happier features of
the eighteenth-century situation—a group in both France and
England, for example, who considered themselves set off by the
possession of enlightened ideas and a long tradition of affection-
ate intercourse with each other. One can also add a belief as a
part of the Enlightenment that reason triumphant would be superior to national rivalries; witness the attitude of the visitors from
outer space in Voltaire's story of *Micromégas*.

An even more striking contrast between the Age of Reason
and our own is the difference in attitude toward the usefulness
of science. The usefulness of science as an expression of reason
was one of that generation's fondest affirmations. Yet no one saw
in the science of that day, however useful, the key to military
power by weapons research. The applicability of science to
practical problems had not reached the point where science was
in many instances a direct resource for war. That generation,

5. De Beer, *The Sciences Were Never At War*, p. 136, quotes this letter from
the copies in the British Museum. The original, a lone fugitive, came to rest
among the letters of the American botanist Asa Gray, at the Gray Herbarium
of Harvard University, where it several years ago attracted the attention of the
present author and started the line of reflections that have culminated in this
paper.

which went through endless and acrimonious discussions of the concept of "contraband of war," had no good reason to consider science in that category. Collections of dried plants did not then and do not now provide the sinews of war. Even a *Nautical Almanac* had more relevance for an exploring voyage than for fleet actions in the close waters of the English Channel.

These statements of differences between the eighteenth and twentieth centuries are fairly comfortable rough generalizations. Yet the insistent and emotional espousal of the theme that science was once international and completely above the strife of nations implies a golden age to which the twentieth century should look back with envy. The internationalism of science is indeed so strongly held as an article of faith that to question the existence of the golden age in the eighteenth century takes on the overtone of treason to science. Yet this whole subject is too close to survival in the modern world to be left to an uncritical faith, however generous. For beneath the evocation of the golden age of internationalism in science lurks a major dilemma about the nature of science itself and its relation to society in the modern world.

In the first place, most of the ringing declarations of internationalism in science as collected by Sir Gavin de Beer stem not from the seventeenth and eighteenth centuries but rather from the period of the wars against revolutionary France, 1793 to 1815. And in the collection, as in these years, Sir Joseph Banks is the crucial central figure. Just here lies the dilemma. For in these years and in these wars, and in Britain and France—the great protagonists—lies the origin of an exclusive nationalism that has become the overriding theme of modern history. How is it that the crystallization of nationalism and the heyday of internationalism in science took place at precisely the same time and in the same historical milieu?

The easy and seductive answer to this question is to say that science is by nature international—that there is no such thing as a British biology or a French chemistry. The facts are everywhere the same; any evocation of national influence on science is a species of anti-intellectualism. But to take such a stand, overlooking for the moment its incompleteness, is to put forward a momentous, almost fantastic proposition: Science, alone of the social activities of man, operates independently of its social environment. In this case science alone of the social activities of man is then independent of the strongest force in modern history, nationalism. Should this proposition really hold up, it would provide a guide for the solution of the major problems facing the twentieth-century world. And there is no lack of advocates of an international science divorced from the nation state system.[6] But before attacking the big problems with all the certainty of righteousness, it would be well to examine carefully in the correspondence of Sir Joseph Banks during the wars with France that golden age celebrated by Sir Gavin de Beer.

One of the striking things about the negotiation between the British and French during the Wars of the Revolution is the presence on both sides of veterans—not merely of science—but of the great explorations of the age of Captain James Cook. Sir Joseph Banks, of course, had founded his whole scientific career on his adventures as the gentleman botanist of Cook's first voyage. And, less happily, the case which dominated British thoughts in the early 1800's was the detention by the governor of Isle de France (Mauritius) of Captain Matthew Flinders on his return from the exploration of Australia. Even the belated gesture of the First Class of the French National Institute in electing Alexander Dalrymple a corresponding member in 1811[7] echoed the very beginning of the great age of exploration. Out of the great war for empire (1754-1763) Dalrymple had emerged as the primary figure in the search for a *Terra Australis* by the British until Cook came along to destroy the dream of a Southern continent.[8]

On the French side also many of the actors were veterans of the quest for *Terra Australis* and the consequent exploration of the South Seas. The first big case of scientific exchange that Banks arranged was the return to France of the collections of La Billardière, a botanist who had accompanied D'Entrecasteaux

6. Robert Jungk, *Brighter Than a Thousand Suns* (N. Y., 1958), is an egregious example of a book which lays great stress on an international science as a kind of alternative loyalty to the nation state.

7. De Beer, *The Sciences Were Never At War*, p. 191. The First Class of the Institut National comprised the physical and mathematical sciences and corresponded closely to the *Académie royale des Sciences* of the *ancien régime*.

8. Beaglehole, Introduction to *The Voyage of the Endeavour*, pp. ci-civ.

in search of La Pérouse.[9] Louis-Antoine Bougainville had made his voyage around the world immediately before Cook's first voyage, and significantly his name appears among those Frenchmen who in 1800 petitioned Banks as president of the Royal Society of London to provide a safe-conduct for Nicholas Baudin, who was planning an expedition in the same Australian waters as Flinders, the British captain who indeed encountered the French expedition and assisted them.

Thus in order to understand the motives of the main actors in the drama of international science in the early 1800's, it is necessary to look back at the system of exploration that grew up in the 1760's. France and Britain were struggling hard for the continent of North America and for the subcontinent of India, as Bougainville, a mathematician who served as an officer under General Montcalm at Quebec, knew only too well. After the Treaty of Paris in 1763 Bougainville had established a colony on what are now the Falkland Islands, but the French had decided that a renewal of the struggle that had been so disastrous for them was injudicious at the moment. As a result of British protest Bougainville had withdrawn his colony and ceded French claims to Spain, but he substituted an exploring expedition beyond the Straits of Magellan, his classic voyage around the world.[10]

Bougainville was the disciple of a provincial French intellectual and jurist, Charles de Brosses, whose collected information on explorations in the South Seas might point to yet another continent over which France and Great Britain could struggle, *Terra Australis*. De Brosses was also a theoretician of exploration who recognized the necessity of two ingredients in any penetration into the southern Pacific, where the challenge of the environment and distance was so severe that little more was known than had been discovered by Magellan two and a half centuries earlier. De Brosses insisted that nationalistic motives and the financial support of governments were necessary for successful expeditions. Also, good child of the Enlightenment that he was, he recognized that an expedition to bring back anything of value

9. De Beer, *The Sciences Were Never At War,* pp. 45-68.
10. Louis-Antoine Bougainville, *Voyage autour du monde* (Paris, [1771]).

must have a scientific corps and be dominated at least in the early phases by a quest for knowledge.[11] All of the great expeditions from Bougainville and Cook through La Pérouse and D'Entrecasteaux to Flinders and Baudin followed the pattern dreamed of by De Brosses—national aspiration plus science.

If De Brosses' *Terra Australis* had materialized as another North America, a great war for empire would doubtless have been fought over it. But instead the coral reefs and great expanses of water in the South Pacific made European penetration into the whole area from Tierra del Fuego to the Dutch East Indies a choice between survival and disaster, as La Pérouse found to his cost. The result was a kind of truce for the exploring expeditions to the South Seas. Even a state of war in Europe did not shake the sometimes grudging co-operation of European ships to the eastward of Java. The need for succor at remote outposts and the dearth of communication with the civilized world conspired to establish the principle, as a matter of reciprocity, that an exploring ship, even if a naval vessel, was in a special category. It is against this background and the conscious attempt of both the British and the French to maintain this truce during the Napoleonic Wars that both the safe-conduct for Baudin and the sad fate of Flinders must be judged. When the members of the Institut National, including Bougainville, asked for a passport for Baudin to get him past the British cruisers in European waters, they appealed to humanity and science but precisely within the framework of the truce that had so many South Seas precedents.

The *Institut national* considers that it is precisely at the moment when war still burdens the world that the friends of humanity should work for it, by advancing the limits of science and of useful arts by means of enterprises similar to those which have immortalised the great navigators of our two nations and the illustrious men of science who have scoured the sea and land to study nature, Sir, where they could do so with the greatest success.[12]

Banks's answer, while acceding to the principle of his French counterparts, had definite ideas as to the limits of the truce, and

11. See A. C. Taylor, *Le Président de Brosses et L'Australie* (Paris, [1937]).
12. A.-L. de Jussieu and others to Sir Joseph Banks, May 16, 1800, De Beer, *The Sciences Were Never At War*, p. 238.

those limits did not include impairing the blockade functions of the British fleet against contraband of war. "If . . . any difficulties occur," he wrote to the French commissioner in London, "in the arrangements of the Passports I will most willingly use my utmost endeavours & promote arrangements on that head satisfactory to the National Institute provided they do not interfere with the necessary precautions which every nation must adopt for the security of their Colonies and the consequent prosperity of the Realm."[13]

While the British honored their passport to Baudin, who received good treatment from both Flinders and local authorities when in real need in Australian waters, the detention of Flinders at Mauritius seemed a barbarous violation of the South Seas truce. Yet if one examines the circumstances of Flinders' arrest, it is easy to see that the same principles of exemption of a ship of discovery from ordinary rules were here also at work. Flinders had a passport from the French, but he was not in the ship, the *Investigator,* for which the passport was issued, but rather in the little *Cumberland.* He bore dispatches from the governor of New South Wales which referred to the possibility of military action against the Spaniards in Peru and Chile. Thus the French governor had the excuse to assert that a voyage of discovery had passed into the sphere of national interest. As Flinders, held prisoner of war, wrote home to Banks:

Having no idea that the dispatches had any reference to war, since it was a time of peace when I left Port Jackson, I did not see the necessity of throwing them overboard at a hazard. To be the bearer of any dispatches in time of peace cannot be incorrect for a ship on discovery more than for any other. I do not however presume to blame Governor King. After a misfortune has taken place we all see very well the proper steps that ought to have been taken to avoid it.[14]

A second fact that shaped Banks's policy during the years 1793 to 1815 and that had quite as much effect as his clear understanding of the limited nature of the South Seas truce was the virulence of the opposition within Britain to any form of truckling with the enemies of the nation, especially Bonaparte. Wil-

13. Sir Joseph Banks to Louis-Guillaume Otto, June 13, [1800], *ibid.,* p. 93.
14. Quoted in H. C. Cameron, *Sir Joseph Banks* (London, 1952), p. 97.

liam Cobbett, who had learned all the arts of the hard school of partisan journalism in the new nation of the United States, had been pro-British and anti-French in the party wars of America. In 1800 he brought his talents home to London and took up the cry against a government that on October 1, 1801, signed the Preliminaries of London with Napoleon.[15]

Sir Gavin de Beer makes much of the fact that Banks was elected a Foreign Associate of the First Class of the Institut National while war was still in progress. Yet December 26, 1801, was after the preliminaries had been signed even if before the final Treaty of Amiens of March 25, 1802. The magnitude of the breach during the previous war and the lessening of tension on the occasion of the Preliminaries is indicated by the long list of those elected along with Banks—Henry Cavendish, John Herschel, Nevil Maskelyne, and Joseph Priestley (who had emigrated to the United States some years before).[16] In his letter to the Institut National, written on January 21, 1802, Banks injected a note of political commentary in his gratification at the election.

To be the first elected to be an associate of the first Literary Society in the world surpassed my most ambitious hopes and I cannot be too grateful toward a Society which has conferred upon me this honour and toward a nation of which it is the literary representative—a nation which during the most frightful convulsion of the late most terrible revolution never ceased to possess my esteem; being always persuaded, even during the most disastrous periods, that it contained many good citizens who would infallibly get the upper hand and who would re-establish in the heart of their countrymen the empire of virtue, of justice, and of honour.[17]

Such sentiments "so repugnant to the genuine feelings of an Englishman" were enough for the likes of Cobbett. His *Weekly Political Register* went after Banks in an attack signed "Misogallus," which in April, 1802, appeared as a separate pamphlet pub-

15. See Lewis Melville, *The Life and Letters of William Cobbett in England & America* (London, 1913), I, 117-42. For a general account of the Peace of Amiens, Geoffrey Bruun, *Europe and the French Imperium 1799-1814* (N. Y., 1938), pp. 50-54.

16. Cameron, *Banks,* p. 249.

17. De Beer, *The Sciences Were Never At War,* p. 104; also quoted in Cameron, *Banks,* p. 250.

lished by the firm of Cobbett and Morgan.[18] The author accused
Banks's paragraph of being

replete with sentiments which are a compound of servility, disloyalty,
and falsehood; sentiments which ought never to be conceived by an
English heart, never written by an English hand, and least of all by
yours. . . , elevated to a station in which the country might be ex-
cused for looking up to you as the jealous guardian, not the betrayer,
of its literary credit.[19]

No more nationalistic a conception of the role of the titular
head of the scientists of a country has been framed in the twentieth century. "Misogallus" would not admit that the scientific
by-products of Napoleon's Egyptian campaign were worthy of
approbation.

Your *"respectable brothers"* of the French Institute may perhaps be
intoxicated by the incense which you have lavished before their altar
of Atheism and Democracy; for, although they were companions of
the *respectable Buonaparté* [sic] in his expeditions, and plundered
libraries and cabinets with as much alacrity, and as little scruple, as
he displayed in treasuries and in churches, I do not believe that the
ungrateful nations whom they robbed ever composed such a brilliant
eulogium on their talents and their virtues.[20]

Harking back to Banks's part in the return of the collection of
La Billiardière to France under the revolutionary government,
"Misogallus" charged that "you cannot forget that you disposed
of it by sending it all to France, with no authority but your own,
with no pretence except that *the philosophers of the two nations
were not at war*. Thus, Sir, you imposed an obligation on the
French, which they have repaid, it seems, to your exquisite gratification."[21]

   "Misogallus's" intent was to bring Banks into an unpatriotic
disgrace, and he probably had the effect of limiting Banks's freedom of action. Even De Beer, who seems loath to admit the
existence of the "Misogallus" attack, confesses that there was
"indignation in England," and "opposition to Banks's re-election

18. Misogallus, *A Letter to the Right Honourable Sir Joseph Banks, K. B.*
(London, 1802). A copy is in the New York Public Library.
   19. *Ibid.*, p. 7.
   20. *Ibid.*, pp.7-8.
   21. *Ibid.*, p. 12.

as President of the Royal Society."[22] Yet "Misogallus," despite
the fog of his invective, put his finger on two aspects of Banks's
policy that go a long way toward explaining his operations with
the French. In the first place, the thing that most outraged
"Misogallus" was the fact that Banks considered his election to
the Institut National "the highest and most enviable literary distinction which I could possibly attain" when he was in fact already President of the Royal Society of London. That Banks
considered the French scientists as a group more distinguished
than any he could muster in Britain is probably true. Secondly,
Banks thought in terms of reciprocity, of deliberately doing good
turns for French scientists so that they might repay him by equally good deeds, not so much to himself as to other Fellows of the
Royal Society.

Since the Revolutionary era was one of great brilliance for
French science, the scientific organizations of the Napoleonic
Empire were so closely allied to the nation-state itself that it is
possible to speak of "French science" without resorting to pusil-
lanimous phraseology like "science in France." Banks saw on the
letters which came to him from across the Channel the names of
Laplace, Lalande, Cuvier, Berthollet, and De Jussieu. Anyone who
attempted to keep up with the scientific literature of the first
fifteen years of the nineteenth century needed the results of
French investigation more than those of any other. Certainly
Banks saw the national interest of Britain, not a betrayal of it, in
sending the *Nautical Almanac* for 1807 to France while Napoleon
was collecting troops at Boulogne.[23] His payment was the return
flow of French publications that his French counterpart, Jean-
Baptiste Delambre, perpetual secretary of the First Class of the
Institut National did not fail to provide.[24]

Sir Joseph's major effort at reciprocity, however, had to do
with men. In the 1790's his great triumph, which gave him an
investment of good will to be collected later, was to play a
vigorous if somewhat secondary role in the release of the French

22. De Beer, *The Sciences Were Never At War*, p. 104; Edward Smith, *The Life of Sir Joseph Banks* (London, 1911), pp. 210-12, gives an account of the affair.

23. Sir Joseph Banks to Jean Baptiste Delambre, second letter of Jan. 30, 1804, De Beer, *The Sciences Were Never At War*, p. 138.

24. *Ibid.*, pp. 173-74.

geologist Déodat de Dolomieu. Yet even in the 1790's Banks recognized severe limitations on any claim that a scientist should be released simply because he was a scientist. Dolomieu had participated in Napoleon's Egyptian campaign, and on his way home fell into the hands, not of the British, but of the government of Naples. And the problem was not that Dolomieu was captured but rather that he was held as a criminal rather than as a prisoner of war. Banks wrote to Sir William Hamilton, British Ambassador to Naples, that Dolomieu "is in some danger of being tried as a Criminal, tho' his situation appears to a common observer clearly to be that of a Prisoner of War."[25] It was a touchy business influencing a decadent ally, even through Lady Emma Hamilton and her friend the "Gallant Admiral."[26] Hence when Dolomieu thanked him profusely, Banks set him right rather stiffly as to the role the Royal Society of London played in the release.

Tho', Sir, your unfortunate situation caused a visible regret in all men of Science here, who were acquainted with the active part you have always taken in promoting the increase of human knowledge, and tho' all of them in their private capacities, I have no doubt, did all in their power to promote an interference of our Government in your favour, yet, Sir, it is necessary I should inform you that the Royal Society, as a body, took no measure whatever, or indeed ever publickly took cognizance of your situation; we in England, Sir, are as firmly attached to Royal Government as you can be to Republican; and, whatever our private wishes might be, we did not think it proper or decent to speculate upon the conduct of a king . . .; or, as a public body, to take matters of a political nature in any shape under our consideration.[27]

Hence whatever Banks was willing to do in the amelioration of the lot of recognized scientists caught in the toil of war, he explicitly committed the Royal Society against a policy of internationalism by reciprocity.

The rupture of the Peace of Amiens gave Banks his most ample opportunity to use his standing with the Institut National in securing the release of Britons held in France. Because of the principle of reciprocity Banks found himself in the business of

25. Sir Joseph Banks to Sir William Hamilton, Nov. 8, 1799, *ibid.*, p. 83.
26. Sir Joseph Banks to Lady Hamilton, Nov. 8, 1799, *ibid.*, pp. 84-85.
27. Sir Joseph Banks to Déodat de Dolomieu, July 16, 1801, *ibid.*, p. 103.

assisting Frenchmen held in Britain in hopes of securing the release of members of the Royal Society. Over this whole situation
loomed the figure of Flinders, held at Mauritius as a prisoner of
war in violation of the South Seas truce and despite the good
treatment by the British of Baudin. While Banks never failed to
exploit membership in the Royal Society as a means of getting
the intercession of the Institut National, he did on a number of
occasions also intercede for non-scientists. This was hardly a free
flow of personnel between warring nations, but rather an uneasy
exchange of civilians in a system informally paralleling the officially arranged exchanges of prisoners of war. As Georges Cuvier
wrote to one of the beneficiaries, James Forbes, F.R.S., in 1804,
the Institut

has taken up your case with the Minister of War, and . . . it has supported your requests with all the arguments provided by your age,
your scientific works, and especially the reciprocity called for by the
services rendered by Sir Joseph Banks and the Royal Society to
Frenchmen who found themselves in need of their protection.[28]

Indeed the British government put a stop to the practice,
much to Banks's displeasure it is true, when his good offices extended to a prisoner of war captured in combat. Pierre-Bernard
Milius was captain of a French frigate which struck to H.M.S.
Phoenix. But he was also a veteran of the French expeditions to
the South Seas and could open his appeal to Banks with a sentence designed to warm a naturalist's heart.

It is to the worthy shipmate of Captain Cook that I offer a small collection of rare birds, saved from the hazards of war. I beg you, Sir,
to accept it as a feeble token of the respect in which you are held
by all those who have sailed the wide seas and are in a position to
appreciate the services which your talents and enlightenment have
rendered to humanity.[29]

Banks interceded for Milius to the extent of pleading his ill-
health and of trying to work up French pressure for Flinders, but
the Admiralty had plans for a straight exchange of Milius for an
unscientific Captain of the Royal Navy who was a prisoner of
war in France. After an acrimonious exchange of correspondence

28. Georges Cuvier to James Forbes, May 9, 1804, *ibid.*, p. 252.
29. Pierre-Bernard Milius to Sir Joseph Banks, Sept. 3, 1804, *ibid.*, p. 141.

with the First Lord of the Admiralty, Banks withdrew from the negotiation of these exchanges in 1806, when reciprocity in detained scientists may be said to have failed.

The question of how a limited passage of persons and information could be allowed by belligerents without opening themselves to spies is one worthy of some comment. That scientists could be military spies was fully recognized during the wars with France, and Banks was interested neither in infiltrating the French nor in opening the gates of Britain to French spies under the banner of the internationalism of science. Napoleon was capable on occasion of suspecting a British man of science of espionage, which in 1804 elicited from Banks this statement of principle:

> . . . if I cannot maintain a correspondence with learned Englishmen in France, without being accused of employing them for political objects; and if Gentlemen of known reputation and honour cannot visit your country for the purpose of giving and receiving scientific information, without being exposed, on every turn of public affairs, to the vile imputation of acting as spies . . . it will be impossible for me either to preserve a constant intercourse of good offices between the men of science in the two nations, or to ensure for learned Frenchmen, who may come to England, those marked attentions and civilities, which it is my wish that they should receive in time of war as well as peace.[30]

Much depended in this foreboding statement on the assertion that scientists were "Gentlemen of known reputation and honour." The accord which Banks wished for here, based on reciprocity, did not, as we have seen, extend beyond 1806.

That technical knowledge could be used for espionage was the basis for an earlier charge Banks made against the French during the troubled peace of Amiens. The "appointment of Engineers under the character of commercial agents, has destroyed all confidence in the recommendation of a Frenchman."[31] Literary persons might maintain communication in time of war only if they did not spy or pass "intelligence of the strength or weakness of Military posts." Thus if Banks's own principles were transferred to an era where scientific information itself constituted the stuff of military strength or weakness, they would call

30. Sir Joseph Banks to Delambre, Jan. 30, 1804, *ibid.*, p. 136.
31. Sir Joseph Banks to Antoine-François Fourcroy, May 4, 1803, *ibid.*, p. 111.

for a cessation of the very interchange which De Beer celebrates Banks as advocating.

Sir Joseph Banks stands out in the time of the wars with France not as the advocate of an absolute internationalism in science in time of war but rather as a tough and resourceful negotiator of British scientific interests in the first great national struggle of modern history. If this view is correct, the paradox is removed from the ringing internationalism of some of the words which Sir Gavin de Beer's documents undoubtedly contain. The internationalism of Banks was a product of his national policy, with limits on several sides. Science did not escape the rise of nationalism but adapted to it. The South Seas truce, the principle of reciprocity, the gain for British science in seeing the publications of France, the barking of the ignorant and vindictive Gallophobes like Cobbett, the necessity of staying completely clear of espionage, all shaped Banks's policy toward a France whose revolution he despised and whose chief Consul he was certain could never conquer "our own soil." Co-operation with the Institut National in and out of the state of war between France and England was a means to an end in national policy, however affectionately the terms were couched.

Why then have so many, including Sir Gavin de Beer, looked upon this first turmoil of nationalism as a period when the sciences were never at war? The key is found in De Beer's very first sentence in his introduction: "The modern world is become so accustomed to the notion of total war and its implications of maximal effort by whole populations, that it is difficult to realise that during the lifetime of our own grandfathers a very different system prevailed."[32] The difficulty in understanding Banks lies precisely in this assumption of differences between the early nineteenth century and the present. Without arguing the extent to which the First and Second World Wars were "total wars" in any absolute sense, one can look at the period since 1945 and speculate that limited war, not total war, may be the true characteristic of national struggle in the twentieth century. And in a limited war precisely the kind of dilemmas that faced Banks open up today. The cessation of communication is not complete,

32. *Ibid.*, p. ix.

and the possession of research potential on both sides makes interchange of information desirable despite the difficulties. The principle of reciprocity again rears its head. The possibility of discussions that do not bear too directly on military strength and weakness becomes an opening to be treasured and improved.

Sir Joseph would be very nearly an ideal negotiator for a program of scientific exchange between the West and the Soviet Union. He would believe fully in the desirability of an accommodation, but he would brook no nonsense. And far in the background, as one hears the crash of surf on coral at Tahiti or sees Captain Cook and his young botanist treating with the Maoris on New Zealand, an even more daring challenge for a transposed Sir Joseph becomes imaginable. Among the negotiations which the scientific communities of the Western World—tied despite themselves to their national support—must successfully pursue are treaties of knowledge with the underdeveloped nations of the world.

The Myth of the French Revolution of 1830*

DAVID H. PINKNEY

"The history we read," recently declared an English historian, "is, strictly speaking, not factual at all, but a series of accepted judgments."[1] Few of the judgments that historians have made about the past have had wider acceptance than the conception of the years 1830-1832 as the beginning of a new era in Western Europe. The Revolution in France and the Reform Act in England were the climactic events that consummated the change and set off the two great liberal powers of the west from the autocratic and aristocratic states of the center and east. Here editors of historical series find new authors, textbook writers begin second volumes or new chapters, professors give examinations, and students hopefully relax in anticipation of studying the more familiar middle class era that, they are assured, lies ahead.

In the history of France the key piece in this pattern is the view of the Revolution of 1830 as the Bourgeois Revolution, a revolution in which the rising bourgeoisie wrested control of the state from the landed aristocracy.[2] The Great Revolution of 1789 also has been seen as a bourgeois revolution because of the benefits that revolutionary legislation brought to the bourgeoisie, but on that revolution there are many rival and conflicting judgments. The stereotype of *the* Bourgeois Revolution has been fixed almost uncontested on the events of 1830. Indeed, this judgment has become a veritable article of faith, and it is virtually impossible

* I am indebted to the John Simon Guggenheim Memorial Foundation and to the University of Missouri Research Council for grants that made possible the research on which this essay is based.

1. Geoffrey Barraclough, *History in a Changing World* (Oxford, 1955), p. 14.
2. See, for examples, Louis Blanc, *Histoire de dix ans, 1830-1840* (6e éd.; Paris, 1846), I, 350, II, 31-32; Alexis de Tocqueville, *The Recollections* (New York, 1949), pp. 2-3; Georges Weill, *L'Eveil des nationalités et le mouvement libéral (1815-1848)* (Paris, 1930), pp. 97, 103; J. Lucas-Dubreton, *La Royauté bourgeoise, 1830* [Paris, c.1930], chap. i, "La Révolution bourgeoise."

to challenge successfully because of the ambiguity of its terms. "Bourgeois" and "bourgeoisie" lack precise meaning. They may indicate a man's status in society, as they ordinarily did in eighteenth-century France, where everyone except noblemen, peasants, and manual laborers might come within varying definitions of "bourgeois." They may designate, as they did for Marx, a man's function in the economy, indicating that he obtains his income through ownership of means of production. Either broad definition included in France of 1830 men whose situations and interests were widely and significantly different—wealthy bankers and small shopkeepers, industrialists and artisans, professional men, and the large official class of civil servants.[3] Clearly not all of these won control of the state in 1830 nor even had the same political convictions and aims. The phrase "control of the state" is equally ambiguous. What constitutes "control"? How can it be measured historically? These questions have no generally accepted answers. Without some answers, however, and without a definition of "bourgeois" any discussion of a bourgeois revolution is doomed to futility.

Among the students of social classes and of the French Revolution of 1830 "bourgeois" has been more precisely defined than it ordinarily is in general context. It is used to mean only the *grande bourgeoisie*—the wealthy businessmen. The Revolution of 1830 is then seen as an event in which the rising class of bankers and manufacturers and wholesale merchants displaced the landed aristocracy in the control of the French state.[4] This more

3. Cf. Alfred Cobban, "The Vocabulary of Social History," *Political Science Quarterly*, LXXI (1956), 1-17; Halvedan Koht, "The Class Struggle in Modern History," *Journal of Modern History*, I (1929), 353-60; M. Vovelle and D. Roche, "Bourgeois, rentiers, propriétaires; éléments pour la définition d'une catégorie sociale à la fin du XVIIIᵉ siècle," *Actes du quatre-vingt-quatrième Congrès national des Sociétés savants 1959; Section d'Histoire moderne et contemporaine* (Paris, 1960), pp. 419-21; René Rémond, *La Droite en France de 1815 à nos jours* (Paris, 1954), pp. 77-78.

4. For a sophisticated statement and defense of this thesis, see Jean Lhomme, *La Grande Bourgeoisie au pouvoir (1830-1880)* (Paris, 1960). E. de Beau de Loménie, *Les Responsabilités des dynasties bourgeoises*, Tome I, *De Bonaparte à MacMahon* (Paris, [c.1943]), is concerned not with a class but with certain bourgeois families; the Revolution of 1830 brought a significant increase to their economic and political power, but in Beau de Loménie's view they achieved their power on the occasion of Napoleon's *coup d'état* of 18 Brumaire in 1799 and never lost it, not even during the Restoration. He does not, moreover, distinguish between the *grande bourgeoisie*, on the one hand, and the official class and professional men, on the other. Rémond, *La Droite en France*, pp. 74-79,

carefully delineated conception of the Bourgeois Revolution en-
joys a firm place in the historiography of France and in the literature of revolutions.

The validity of this historical judgment can, nonetheless, be
challenged. The nature of the challenge depends on the chal-
lenger's assumptions about the meaning of that still difficult term
"control of the state." The American historian, Sherman Kent, as-
suming that control rested with the electorate, challenged the
conception of the regime of Louis-Philippe as a bourgeois monarchy by showing that the electorate was overwhelmingly composed of the landed gentry, not of the *grande bourgeoisie*.[5] On
equally defensible methodological grounds one may assume that
control lies in the hands of members of parliament and high administrative officials. Starting from that assumption this essay disputes the validity of the conception of the Revolution of 1830 as a
bourgeois revolution by demonstrating that the Revolution did
not give the *grande bourgeoisie* any significantly increased hold
on the public offices. After the violence of July was passed and
the new king firmly installed upon the throne, the number of
bankers, manufacturers, and *négociants* in parliament and the
key offices of state was small, scarcely more than before the
Revolution.

The Revolution of 1830 did bring new men into public office.
The change of men was probably the most revolutionary aspect
of the Revolution. The replacement of officeholders began at the
top with king and ministers and quickly spread down through
both houses of parliament, the administration, the courts, and
the army to obscure sub-prefects, mayors, and junior officers.
The Chamber of Peers and the Chamber of Deputies purged
their own ranks. In the Ministry of the Interior, Guizot in a
month swept out all but three of the old prefects. Before the
year's end Dupont de l'Eure in the Ministry of Justice replaced
more than four hundred members of the magistracy. All the
commanding generals of the nineteen military districts under

---

sees an "Orleanist right" triumphant in 1830, but he differentiates it from
Lhomme's *grande bourgeoisie*; it was, he maintains, "only very partially a business bourgeoisie"; its principal source of wealth was still the land.

5. Sherman Kent, *Electoral Procedure under Louis-Philippe* (New Haven,
1937).

Charles X lost their commands. Probably at no other time did France experience so thorough a purge of the higher offices of state so rapidly. In December, 1830, the men who governed France were not the same men who had governed the country six months earlier. Conventionally one would here conclude that the old were the landed aristocracy, the new, the *grande bourgeoisie*. In fact, the social composition of the new group of office-holders was little different from that of the old.

Louis-Philippe, the first of the new men, has gone down in history as the Bourgeois King, but socially he was as far removed from the bourgeoisie as Charles X. A prince of the royal blood and one of the great landed proprietors of France, he can be classified only with the aristocracy. In 1825 he was among the former émigrés who applied for indemnification for property confiscated during the Revolution, and he and his sister received some twelve million francs, by far the largest sum awarded to any family.[6] His much publicized decision to send his elder sons to public school in Paris was less than democratic in practice. In royal style each son had his private tutor, and at the school they took their lunches apart from the other students and were served special dishes. On the playground they associated only with boys selected by their father.[7] In the 1820's the Duke entertained in the Palais-Royal in a manner more regal than did the King himself in the Tuileries. The ball he gave for his brother- and sister-in-law, the King and Queen of Sicily, on the occasion of their visit to Paris in the spring of 1830 astounded those who saw it by its extravagant display of wealth. "We are dancing on a volcano," declared an anxious guest, and looking out at the riotous crowd of spectators gathered in the palace gardens, he might well have been concerned with the consequences of his host's display of extravagance at a time of economic depression.[8] Later, when Louis-Philippe was safely on the throne

6. A. Gain, *La Restauration et des biens des émigrés* (Paris, 1929), II, 192, 223-31.

7. M. D. R. Leys, *Between Two Empires* (London, 1955), p. 180; T. E. B. Howarth, *Citizen-King: The Life of Louis-Philippe, King of the French* (London, 1961), p. 136; Agnes de Stoeckl, *King of the French: A Portrait of Louis-Phillippe, 1773-1850* (London, 1951), pp. 101-102.

8. *Le Moniteur universel* (Paris), June 2, 1830, p. 598; Rodolphe Apponyi, *Vingt-cinq ans à Paris (1826-1850)* (Paris, 1913-26), I, 1-4, 243-44, 260-62;

his behavior corresponded more closely to bourgeois standards, but his liberal bourgeois supporters learned to their dismay that he did not share their ideas on parliamentary government. No Bourbon was more unwilling than he to become a mere reigning figurehead.

Change in the membership of the Chamber of Deputies began when the revolutionary days were scarcely past. All during August, 1830, and into September letters of resignation flowed to the desk of the Chamber's president from deputies who concluded that they could not or should not serve under the new King.[9] Late in the month the chamber speeded the process by requiring all public officeholders, including deputies and peers, to take an oath of fidelity to the new King and of obedience to the revised Charter. The law gave deputies two weeks, peers one month, in which to take the oath, and failure to do so was considered equivalent to resignation.[10] Twenty-one deputies refused to take the oath and were treated as having resigned; some fifty resigned outright; and others were excluded by the annulment of their elections.[11] In all, some eighty deputies, approximately 20 per cent of the membership, left the Chamber before the year's end and were replaced by new men.[12]

To fit the stereotype of the Revolution dislodging the landed aristocracy and enthroning the businessmen, most of the retiring deputies should have been proprietors; their successors, merchants, bankers, and manufacturers. An actual count shows among the retiring deputies five businessmen and twenty-one proprietors; among the newcomers, eleven businessmen and twelve proprietors. The shift is in the expected direction but very small and far from sufficient in the total composition of the Chamber to move control of parliament from one social category to another. A comparison of the composition by social classes of the Chamber of Deputies in 1829 and of the Chamber at the beginning of 1831, after the purge and replacement had been com-

Archives nationales, F⁷3884, Préfecture de Police de Paris, "Bulletin de Paris," June 1, 1830; Howarth, *Citizen-King,* p. 140.

9. *Moniteur,* Aug. 11–Sept. 5, 1830.
10. *Bulletin des lois,* 9ᵉ Série, Tome I, 1ᵉ Partie, pp. 66-67 (1830).
11. *Ibid.,* 9ᵉ Série, T. I, 2ᵉ Partie, pp. 138-42, 169, 170, 171, 255, 495, 547, 671; *Moniteur,* Aug. 6, 1830, pp. 852-55, Aug. 18, 1830, pp. 915-16.
12. *Almanack royal pour l'an MDCCCXXIX* (Paris, 1829), pp. 117-30.

pleted, shows that the Revolution for all its reshuffling of deputies had made surprisingly little change in the Chamber.[13]

Composition of the Chamber of Deputies		
	1829	*1831*
Business men (*grande bourgeoisie*)	14%	17%
Professional men	5	12
Public officeholders	40	38
Proprietors	31	23
Unidentified	10	10

Proprietors dropped from slightly less than one-third of the membership to about one-fourth, but in 1831 they still enjoyed a margin of some thirty seats over the businessmen.[14]

The Chamber of 1831 can be made to appear predominantly bourgeois in composition by combining the wealthy businessmen, the professional men, and the civil servants into a single category. So, too, can the Chamber of 1829. But in neither case does this sustain the thesis of the *grande bourgeoisie au pouvoir* because neither the official class nor the professional men in France of the eighteenth and early nineteenth centuries can properly be identified with the wealthy business class. The public officeholders of 1830, like the royal officials of the eighteenth century, are a group that does not fit into the Marxian categories, based on English experience, of aristocracy, bourgeoisie, and proletariat. Their values, interests, aims were not the same as

13. The names of retiring and new deputies were obtained from the *Bulletin des lois* and *Le Moniteur universel*. The membership rolls of the Chamber of Deputies in 1829 and in 1831 were taken from the *Almanach royal, MDCCCXXIX*, pp. 117-30, and the *Almanach royal et national pour l'an MDCCCXXXI* (Paris, 1831), pp. 86-94. The social and economic identification of the deputies is based on information from Adolphe Robert, *et al.*, *Dictionnaire des parlementaires français* (Paris, 1891), Vols. I-V, *passim.*; Gustave Vapereau, *Dictionnaire universel des contemporaines* (Paris, 1858), *passim.*; and *Almanach royal MDCCCXXIX*, pp. 117-30.

14. Even after the electoral law of 1831 had nearly doubled the number of eligible voters (from 94,000 to 166,000) by reducing the tax qualification, the landed proprietors continued to dominate the electorate numerically. One authority has estimated that 82 to 90 per cent of the voters in 1831 obtained their livings from ownership of land and only 8 to 14 per cent from manufacturing or commercial enterprises. The body of citizens eligible to serve in the Chamber of Deputies, for whom there was a higher tax requirement, had essentially the same composition.—Kent, *Electoral Procedure*, pp. 9, 26, 54, 58.

those of the *grande bourgeoisie*.[15] The professional class, chiefly lawyers, which made up an eighth of the Chamber in 1831, were more akin to the official class than to the businessmen, for their careers, too, were in considerable degree dependent upon favors from the state. Few of the lawyer deputies had not been on the public payroll at one time or another.[16] Professorships in the state schools were plums dangled before physicians and scholars. Public funds or public prosecution could make or break the careers of journalists and writers. Once in office and in favor themselves these men found their interests bound up with those of the great block of officeholders that dominated the Chamber and that became the parliamentary foundation of Louis-Philippe's and Guizot's achievement in the 1840's of a rule more personal than any Charles X ever achieved.

The change in ministers after the Revolution accurately reflected the alteration of the class composition of the Chamber. Here, too, was no clear-cut shift from landed proprietors to businessmen. Polignac's ministry of nine members had included no businessmen and two proprietors, but it was heavily weighted with men who had made their careers in the civil and military services. Among their successors—the twenty men appointed to cabinet posts between July, 1830, and the middle of March, 1831—the predominance of officeholders remained essentially unchanged. None among them is identifiable as a proprietor.[17] Marshal Soult, who became Minister of War in November, 1830, was a general turned businessman. He had made his name and his fortune in the Imperial armies, but during the Restoration he turned his energies and his money to industry, and in 1830 he was actively involved in mining, smelting, and transportation enterprises in the Midi. Two others were prominent bankers, and

15. Cf. Alfred Cobban, *The Myth of the French Revolution* (London, [1955]), pp. 14-19; Marcel Reinhard, "Sur l'histoire de la Révolution française," *Annales: économies-sociétés-civilisations*, 14ᵉ Année (1959), pp. 550-62.

16. Robert, *Dictionnaire des parlementaires*, Vols. I-V, *passim*.

17. *Almanach royal, MDCCCXXXI*, pp. 65-66; Robert, *Dictionnaire des parlementaires*, Vols. I-V, *passim.*; *Biographie universelle et portative des contemporaines* (Paris, 1836), Vols. I-IV and Supplement, *passim.*; Vapereau, *Dictionnaire, passim.*; C. Mullié, *Biographie des célébrités militaires des armées de terre et de mer de 1789 à 1850* (Paris, 1851), I, 96-99, II, 528-30; Marcel Rousselet, *La Magistrature sous la Monarchie de Juillet* (Paris, 1937), p. 452; Lamothe-Langon, *Biographie des préfets depuis l'organisation des préfectures (3 mars 1800) jusqu'à ce jour* (Paris, 1826), pp. 324-25.

their role in the Revolution and their entry into the ministry, disproportionately magnified, is perhaps a principal source of the myth of the Bourgeois Revolution of 1830. Jacques Laffitte was head of a leading banking house of Paris and a former regent of the Bank of France, and Casimir Périer owned a family business that had widespread interests in industry, shipping, and real estate as well as finance. Laffitte and Périer were ministers without portfolio in Louis-Philippe's first government, and in November, 1830, Laffitte was named to the Ministry of Finance.[18]

In most of the key posts—Interior, Justice, Finance, Foreign Affairs—were men of different origin and attachments—officeholders and professional men like their predecessors. Baron Louis, the first Minister of Finance, had managed to serve almost all regimes during his lifetime. He began his public career in a purchased office of the Parlement de Paris ten years before the Revolution of 1789, filled a number of diplomatic missions for Louis XVI in the early 1790's, and under the Empire rose through the ranks of the civil service to high place in the Ministry of Finance. On three occasions before 1820 he served Louis XVIII as Minister of Finance, and in August, 1830, enjoying a reputation as an expert in public finance, he was again called to head the same ministry.[19] Guizot, the Minister of the Interior, the son of a lawyer and himself trained as a lawyer, had made his career and reputation as a professor and writer of history, although in the early years of the Restoration he was briefly secretary-general of two ministries and an officer of the Council of State.[20] The new Minister of Justice, Dupont de l'Eure, was a career judge; he had entered the magistracy during the Revolution and under the Empire rose to the presidency of the Imperial Court of Rouen, where he remained until dismissed in 1817.[21] Molé, the Minister of Foreign Affairs, was a son of a president of the Parlement de Paris. He entered the imperial civil service as an *auditeur* of the Council of State in 1806, became a prefect two years later and Minister of Finance in 1813, and he continued in public service

18. Robert, *Dictionnaire des parlementaires*, III, 518, IV, 584-85; Bertrand Gille, *Recherches sur la formation de la grande entreprise capitaliste (1815-1848)* (Paris, 1959), pp. 98-101.
19. Robert, *Dictionnaire des parlementaires*, IV, 182-84.
20. *Ibid.*, III, 291-92.
21. *Ibid.*, II, 498-99; Rousselet, *Magistrature*, p. 23.

under the moderate royalist governments of the early years of the Restoration.[22] Among the remaining thirteen men called to ministerial posts in the months immediately following the Revolution, ten had made their careers and reputations in the civil or military services.[23]

France was not, of course, governed by king, ministers, and parliament alone. The councillors of state, the prefects, the *procureurs-généraux* of the royal courts, the top-ranking military commanders were as influential in determining the present situation of the country and its future course. Through their ranks the Revolution of 1830 swept like a great broom, and following it came swarming into office a multitude of new men. The purge was intended in part to remove the unreliable and to install dependable officials. "Authority," proclaimed the new King in the first week of his reign, "should be in the hands of men firmly attached to the national cause."[24] Out went the still devoted supporters of the old regime, out went those no longer devoted but suspected of having served the Bourbons too zealously in the past, and out, too, went still others who had showed insufficient enthusiasm during the "Three Glorious Days" of revolution in July. But at least an equally powerful motive behind the purge was the need to find jobs for thousands of Frenchmen who saw in the Revolution an opportunity to achieve that common French ambition of getting on the public payroll. "A taste for holding office and a desire to live on the public money," wrote Tocqueville in his *Recollections*, "is the great and chronic ailment of the whole nation. . . ."[25] The "Revolution of the Job-Seekers" brought thousands into the streets, not to man the barricades but to besiege the ministries and the Commission des Recompenses nationales (established in August, 1830, to reward "the heroes of July"[26]) demanding rewards for real or fancied services during the Revolution or for opposition to the Bourbons during the Restoration.

22. Robert, *Dictionnaire des parlementaires*, IV, 385.
23. *Ibid.*, Vols. I-V, *passim*. Among the entire body of ministers in the eighteen years of the July Monarchy essentially the same pattern of class affiliation is apparent. Of the sixty men who held portifolios under Louis-Philippe thirty-six were civil servants, and only seven were businessmen.—Charles Pouthas, "Les Ministères de Louis-Philippe," *Revue d'histoire moderne et contemporaine*, I, (1954), 108.
24. *Bulletin des lois*, 9e Sér., T. I, 2e Partie, pp. 27-28 (1830).
25. Tocqueville, *Recollections*, pp. 31-32.
26. *Bulletin des lois*, 9e Sér., T.I, 2e Partie, pp. 93-94 (1830).

The old and ailing Benjamin Constant complained that in a single week in August six to seven thousand persons called at his house to bespeak his support of their quests for government jobs.[27] Lafayette was said to have endorsed 70,000 job applications.[28] Michelet wrote an urgent letter to his friend Quinet pressing him to hurry to Paris to claim a place before all were taken.[29] *Le Globe,* an opposition newspaper in Paris during the preceding reign, had to suspend publication a few weeks after the Revolution because most of its staff and contributors resigned to take jobs with the new government.[30]

The Council of State, that Napoleonic creation that survived all the revolutions of the nineteenth and twentieth centuries, was not immune to revolutionary house-cleaning. Of the thirty-four members in 1829 twenty-four were out by the end of 1830. To the ten councillors retained the new regime added fifteen of its own appointees.[31] All who can be identified were, like most of their predecessors, lawyers or civil servants.[32] The purge of individuals did not deliver this potent instrument into the hands of the businessmen. It remained a stronghold of the professional civil servants.

Since the time of Cardinal Richelieu most French governments have operated at the local level through the intendants and their Napoleonic successors, the prefects, and since the First Empire each new regime has filled the prefectoral posts with its own supporters.[33] In 1830 Guizot took charge of the reconstitution of the service, a task for which he had been prepared by his term as Secretary-General of the Ministry of the Interior during the purge that followed the fall of Napoleon in 1814.[34] Appointed Commissioner of the Ministry of the Interior on August 1, 1830,

27. Constant to C. J. B. Hochet, Aug. 19, 1830, Bibliothèque nationale, MSS Dept., N.A.Fr. 11909.
28. C. J. Gignoux, *La Vie du Baron Louis* (2e éd.; Paris, [c.1928]), p. 230.
29. Richard H. Powers, *Edgar Quinet: A Study in French Patriotism* (Dallas, 1957), p. 60.
30. Charles de Remusat, *Mémoires de ma vie* (Paris, [c.1959]), II, 366-67.
31. *Almanach royal MDCCCXXIX,* pp. 88-89; *Almanach royal MDCCCXXXI,* p. 68.
32. Robert, *Dictionnaire des parlementaires,* Vols. I-V, *passim.*
33. Brian Chapman, *The Prefects and Provincial France* (London, 1955), p. 32.
34. Charles Pouthas, *Guizot pendant la Restauration* (Paris, 1923), p. 8.

he at once began to fill the pages of the *Bulletin des lois* with ordinances dismissing old prefects and naming their successors. Before the month was out all save three of Charles X's prefects had been ousted; with them went 142 of his sub-prefects.[35] For replacements the new regime drew on former prefects of the Empire, dismissed prefects and sub-prefects of the Restoration, other civil servants, journalists, deputies, and army officers. The number of nobles among the prefects dropped from sixty-four to thirty, and the number designated especially as members of "old" or "illustrious" families dropped from nine to one. But there was no influx of businessmen or sons of business families. Perhaps seven of the new prefects could be classified as coming from the *grande bourgeoisie* and among the retiring prefects only three, but the majority of the corps after the Revolution was composed of men whose careers and social positions were made in employment of the state.[36]

The purge of local officials reached down to the mayors of cities. The Revolution brought new mayors to forty-seven of the fifty largest cities of France.[37] Biographical information on these local figures is difficult to find, but data on about a fifth of them suggest that in municipal government the business class may have experienced a modest increase in influence as a consequence of the Revolution. Among the mayors who were replaced nobles and proprietors predominated. Among the new, businessmen outnumbered both the proprietors and the professional men. Here is a step, perhaps, in the slow rise of the *grande bourgeoisie* to political power, but at most a very small one. The evidence is so limited and the offices clothed with so little power that the larger picture of continuity in the balance of class influence is not altered.[38]

35. *Annuaire historique universel pour 1830* (Paris, 1832), Appendix, p. 145; *Bulletin des lois*, 9e Sér., T. I, 1e Partie, pp. 25, 32, 33-34; 2e Partie, pp. 5-6, 15-18, 26-27, 29-30, 46-48, 58-60, 67-68.

36. *Annuaire historique 1830*, Appendix, pp. 145-46; Lamothe-Langon, *Biographie des préfets, passim*; Vapereau, *Dictionnaire, passim*; Robert, *Dictionnaire des parlementaires*, Vols. I-V, *passim*; *Nouvelle biographie générale depuis les temps le plus reculés jusqu'à nos jours* (Paris, 1855-70), XVIII, 381-83, XX, 726-27.

37. *Almanach royal MDCCCXXIX*, pp. 543-46; *Almanach royal MDCCCXXXI*, pp. 555-58.

38. Robert, *Dictionnaire des parlementaires*, Vols. I-V, *passim*; Vapereau, *Dictionnaire, passim*; *Biographie universelle*, I-IV and Supplement, *passim*; A.

In Paris the barricades were scarcely down when the press began an attack on the law courts. The judges, the prosecutors, and their assistants were only flatterers of the Bourbon government, and most of them deserved dismissal. "Almost the entire bench," stormed *Le Constitutionnel* of August 7, 1830, "must be renewed." Bernard, the new procurer-general of the Royal Court of Paris, gave the attack official sanction in declaring early in August that henceforth the laws would be applied by magistrates "without reproach."[39] The task of eliminating those unfit to serve the new regime fell to the Minister of Justice, Dupont de l'Eure, who had been ousted from the presidency of the Royal Court of Rouen in 1817, and to Merilhou, Secretary-General of the Ministry, who had lost his place in the Royal Court of Paris in the purges following the One Hundred Days. In four months this dedicated pair, often working eighteen or nineteen hours a day, replaced 426 members of magistracy.[40] The judges of the highest court, the Court of Cassation, were untouched, but a new procurer-general of the court was appointed. Thirteen of the twenty-seven royal courts throughout the country received new presiding judges. The key figures in the administration of justice were the procurers-general of the royal courts, the approximate counterparts of the federal district attorneys in the United States, although more powerful in highly centralized France. They were responsible for the enforcement of laws, for bringing violators to justice, and for keeping the Minister of Justice informed of threats to order in their districts. Of the twenty-seven in office in July, 1830, only three continued to hold their places at the end of August.[41] The new procurers not only exercised the usual important powers of their offices but had a role in shaping the new regime in the courts; Dupont de l'Eure appointed most of them within a few days of his taking office, and he depended on them for advice on the purge of judges and other court officials.[42]

Kleinclausz, *Histoire de Lyon* (Lyon, 1952), III, 77; Franklin Ford, *Strasbourg in Transition, 1648-1789* (Cambridge, 1958), p. 250.

39. Rousselet, *Magistrature*, p. 32.

40. *Ibid.*, pp. 33, 452; *Bulletin des lois*, 9e Sér., T. I, 1e Partie, pp. 7, 10, 20; Robert, *Dictionnaire des parlementaires*, IV, 344-45.

41. *Almanach royal MDCCCXXX*, pp. 368-405; *Almanach royal MDCCCXXXI*, pp. 281-319.

42. Rousselet, *Magistrature*, pp. 34-36.

One may search their biographical records in vain, however, for evidence that the new procurers represented the business community any more than did their predecessors. The duties of their offices required that they have legal training, and all of them on whom information is available were lawyers, magistrates, or former magistrates. If they may be said to represent any class, it was the professional class and the kindred official class, the same groups that had occupied pre-eminent place in the parliaments and administration since the first years of the Great Revolution.[43]

Pursuit of evidence of change in the class structure of the officeholding elite becomes increasingly unrewarding as one moves further into the ranks of professional officials. Although the Revolution of 1830 here, too, brought extensive changes in persons holding office, both the dismissed and the newly appointed were necessarily professional men or civil servants. The case of the procurers-general illustrates the point. The same necessity prevailed in the army. To assure its control over the armed forces the new government dissolved the Royal Guard, dismissed the Swiss Guard and repatriated its officers and men, hurried off a new general to Algeria to win the loyalty of Charles X's newly victorious Army of Africa, abolished the post of governor in the nineteen military districts, and replaced every one of the commanding generals in these districts and most of the corps and division commanders.[44] All of the new commanders, new and old alike, were professional soldiers. A clue to class distinctions among them is their titles of nobility, but it proves unrewarding. All of thirty-three top-ranking officers dismissed from commands held noble titles—eight of them granted by Napoleon; thirty-three among thirty-nine newly appointed top commanders were also nobles. The latter included a few more parvenus—fifteen of them had been ennobled by Napoleon—but not enough to distort the similarity of the two essentially professional groups.[45]

43. *Ibid.*, pp. 38, 77, 85-86, 89, 453-54, 456, 492; *Biographie universelle,* Vols. I-IV and Supplement, *passim*; Vapereau, *Dictionnaire, passim*; Robert, *Dictionnaire des parlementaires,* Vols. I-V, *passim.*
44. *Annuaire historique 1830,* pp. 261-62; *Moniteur,* Aug. 15, 1830, p. 903; *Almanach royal MDCCCXXXI,* pp. 587-603.
45. *Biographie universelle,* Vols. I-IV and Supplement, *passim*; Mullié, *Biog-*

After the smoke had blown away, the barricades disappeared, and the scramble for jobs subsided, one might see hundreds of new faces in the places of political, administrative, judicial, and military authority, but socially they looked so much like their predecessors that no significant change is discernible. In terms of classes the elite of the office holders was essentially unchanged by the Revolution.

Men are not differentiated by class alone, nor does class affiliation necessarily determine the behavior of legislators and government officials. Political ideas and political loyalties are at least equally important in influencing men in their exercise of official power, and one should ask, therefore, if the "Revolution of the Job-Seekers" brought to office men whose political loyalties were significantly different from those of their predecessors.

Biographical records do not ordinarily offer clear-cut definitions of their subjects' politics, nor, indeed, could they be expected to in a time of such political fluidity as the years between 1780 and 1850, wherein fall the political careers of the men who are the subject of this study. Occasionally a victim of the purge of 1830 is designated in records as an "ultra" or "very pious," a newcomer as a "carbonari" or ambiguously as a "liberal." A number of the retiring officials had been émigrés during the Revolution, which at first would seem to identify them politically, but most of them had returned and accepted appointments under Napoleon.

Among the scores of biographies of the new deputies and officials in 1830 one item of political interest does persistently recur; that is the holding of public office under the Empire. Among the twenty men who were appointed to ministerial posts in the first seven months of the new regime eighteen had been officials of the Empire, twelve in high place, and twelve had been loyal to Napoleon even in the critical One Hundred Days of 1815. One was the son of an imperial minister. Of the six who survived to see the revival of the Empire in 1852, five again became servants of the Emperor.[46] The Chamber of Deputies

---

46. Robert, *Dictionnaire des parlementaires*, Vols. I-V, *passim*; *Biographie*

at the beginning of 1831 included among its 428 members 82 former officials of the Empire, 60 veterans of Napoleonic armies, and 66 deputies who held Napoleonic titles of nobility. Eleven lived on to assume the dignity of senator of the Second Empire.[47]

When Louis-Napoleon appeared before the Chamber of Peers in September, 1840, on trial for his life following his attempted *coup* at Boulogne, he declared, ". . . finding myself within these Senate walls, filled with memories of my childhood, among you whom I knew, gentlemen, I cannot believe that I can justify myself here or that you can be my judges." He reminded his listeners that they had served the Empire, that like him they would avenge the defeat of Waterloo. "No," he concluded, "there is no quarrel between you and me. . . ."[48] He spoke as though he were addressing a Bonapartist assembly and with some justification; the list of peers who sat in the high court that autumn reads like a "Who's Who" of the Empire.[49] He might have spoken in similar terms to the Chamber of Peers in 1831. Its membership, fallen from three hundred in 1829 to 191 two years later, included 112 peers who had held public office under Napoleon, and 88 of its members bore titles granted by the Emperor.[50]

In the civil and military services the ratio of men with imperial connections was similarly high. Among the ninety-eight men named to prefectures after the Revolution thirty-six were former imperial officials, and twenty-three of these had either refused to serve under the Bourbons or been rejected by them.[51] Twelve among thirty new procurers-general had been in public office during the Empire.[52] All of the army officers named to the top military posts in 1830 had held commands in the armies of Napoleon, and all but two had rallied to his cause when he re-

universelle, Vols. I-V and Supplement, *passim*; Vapereau, *Dictionnaire, passim*; Mullié, *Biographie*, I, 96-99; Lamothe-Langon, *Biographie des préfets*, pp. 324-25.

47. Robert, *Dictionnaire des parlementaires*, Vols. I-V, *passim*.

48. *Moniteur*, Sept. 29, 1840, p. 2033.

49. *Ibid.*, Oct. 7, 1840, p. 2082.

50. *Almanach royal MDCCCXXIX*, pp. 107-14; *Almanach royal MDCCCXXXI*, pp. 78-84; Robert, *Dictionnaires des parlementaires*, I-V, *passim*.

51. Lamothe-Langon, *Biographie des préfets, passim*; Vapereau, *Dictionnaire, passim*; *Biographie universelle*, Vols. I-IV and Supplement, *passim*; Robert, *Dictionnaire des parlementaires*, I-V, *passim*.

52. Rousselet, *Magistrature*, pp. 38, 77, 85-86, 89, 453-54, 456, 460, 492; *Biographie universelle*, Vols. I-IV and Supplement, *passim*; Vapereau, *Dictionnaire, passim*; Robert, *Dictionnaire des parlementaires*, Vols. I-V, *passim*.

turned to Elba in 1815.[53] The new Minister of War was Count Gérard, a man of humble origin who rose to the rank of lieutenant-general in the imperial armies and became a count of the Empire. In 1815 Napoleon was about to make him a marshal of France when the fall of the Empire ended his military career for the next fifteen years. On August 11, 1830, he was named Minister of War and the following week received his long-delayed marshal's baton, not from the Emperor but from Louis-Philippe. He commanded the French army in Belgium in 1831, and three years later he was president of the council of ministers. In 1852 Louis-Napoleon made him a senator of the revived Empire.[54] His successor as Minister of War in November, 1830, was another imperial count and Napoleonic general, Marshal Soult.[55] One might object that no army officers could be found who were not Napoleonic veterans, but there were a few—and more who had chosen to side with the Bourbons during the One Hundred Days; eleven of the latter group held high commands under Charles X and were removed in 1830.[56]

The mere fact of having held public office under the Empire or even of having an imperial title of nobility was no proof of Bonapartism. Yet these men must have had a potent, even though covert, attachment to the Empire. For many it was the Empire that had launched them in successful public or military careers. Before the Revolution of 1789 few among them could have aspired to the eminence that the Empire offered. They were indebted to Napoleon for his keeping careers open to talents and to his conquering armies for the opportunities they offered to military officers and to civil officials who administered the conquered lands. In 1814 and 1815 scores of them saw their careers ended or cut-off unfulfilled by the return of the Bourbons. The Empire in retrospect must have looked like a golden age of unlimited horizons. The new Prefect of the Department of the Seine-Inférieure in 1830, for example, began his public career in 1806 as an *auditeur* of the Council of State; two years later at

53. Mullié, *Biographie*, Vols. I-II, *passim*.
54. *Ibid.*, I, 563-66; Robert, *Dictionnaire des parlementaires*, pp. 157-58; *Bulletin des lois*, 9e Sér., T. I, 2e Partie, p. 9 (1830); *Biographie des membres du Sénat* (Paris, 1852), p. 121.
55. Mullié, *Biographie*, II, 537.
56. *Ibid.*, Vols. I-II, *passim*.

the age of twenty-five he became Prefect of the Ariège; in 1810 he moved to a prefecture in Italy and remained there until the French were driven out in 1814. Appointed imperial Prefect of the Nord during the One Hundred Days, he was dismissed by the returning king, his career apparently ended at the early age of thirty-two. He held no public office again until 1830, when the Revolution restored him to his administrative calling.[57]

The new procurer-general of the Royal Court of Paris in August, 1830, had his career as a magistrate cut off by the Second Restoration, and from 1815 to 1830 he engaged in the private practice of law. The Revolution of 1830 enabled him to resume his career, and he finally fulfilled it as a member of the Court of Cassation under Louis-Napoleon.[58] At Toulouse the new procurer-general was the imperial procurer originally appointed in 1813 and recalled by Dupont de l'Eure in August, 1830, after a fifteen-year interruption in his career.[59]

Many of the officers appointed to high military commands in 1830 had spent the fifteen years after Waterloo in exile, and all had spent part of the period at least in retirement.[60] Certainly the decade and a half of the Restoration were frustrating years for ambitious military men accustomed to the boundless opportunities of the Empire. For them the Revolution of 1830 renewed careers, revived hopes, awakened old ambitions. Not without good reason did Louis-Napoleon make special efforts to cultivate army officers when in the 1830's he first sought to build a following in France.[61]

Indeed, the Revolution of 1830 may have come close to being a Bonapartist revolution. Until the fourth day of the Revolution a revival of the Empire was a more likely prospect than the establishment of an Orleanist monarchy. In the nineteen months preceding the Revolution the Criminal Division of the Ministry of Justice, assiduously in pursuit of anti-government activities, re-

57. Lamothe-Langon, *Biographie des préfets*, p. 198; Charles Durand, *Les Auditeurs au Conseil d'Etat de 1803 à 1814* (Aix-en-Provence, 1958), pp. 9-10, 20-22; Robert, *Dictionnaire des parlementaires*, II, 503.

58. Vapereau, *Dictionnaire*, p. 177.

59. Robert, *Dictionnaire des parlementaires*, II, 178.

60. Mullié, *Biographie*, Vols. I-II, *passim*.

61. F. A. Simpson, *The Rise of Louis Napoleon* (3rd. ed.; London, 1950), pp. 90-91.

ported twenty-eight pro-Napoleonic incidents and none at all for either the Duke of Orleans or the republic.[62] Sailors of the French fleet in Greece learning of the fall of Charles X but not knowing who had succeeded him shouted "Vive Napoléon" or "Vive la République"; apparently no one thought of Orleans.[63] In Paris during the revolutionary days of July crowds in the streets mixed cries of "Vive l'Empéreur" with "A bas les Bourbons" and "Vive la Charte,"[64] and Napoleonic veterans fought in the front ranks of the insurrectionary forces.[65] When the widow of Marshal Suchet and her sister, both bearers of imperial titles but both also close friends of the Duchess of Berry, daughter-in-law of Charles X, fled their town house in the Faubourg Saint-Honoré on July 29, they left instructions with servants that if the Royal Guard broke into the house, the large portrait of Napoleon hanging on the wall should be covered; if the people broke in, it should be uncovered.[66]

The faithful Gourgaud, Napoleon's aide-de-camp during the One Hundred Days and his companion on Saint-Helena, went on July 29 to Laffitte's house, the headquarters of the liberal deputies, and protested against the candidacy of the Duke of Orleans, and a number of army officers supported him.[67] Had he been prepared with a substitute, he might have had some success, for Orleans was far from being a popular candidate in Paris. Crowds had defaced or destroyed signs bearing the Orleans arms, and a mob had tried to sack the Orleans estate office on the Rue Saint-

62. Arch. nat., Inventaire de la Série BB[18] (Ministère de Justice, Correspondance de la Division criminelle), Tome I.

63. Comte d'Alton-Shée, *Mes mémoires (1826-1848)* (Paris, 1869), I, 53.

64. Arch. nat., CC 550, Chambre et Cour des Pairs, Affaire du 25 Juillet 1830, Carton, Officier de Paix, to Chef de la Police municipale, July 26, 1830; Rapport de Boussiron, Officier de Paix, July 26, 1830; CC 551, Chambre et Cour des Pairs, Affaire du 25 Juillet 1830, Bosche to Président, Chambre des Pairs, Oct. 22, 1830; Arch. nat., F[ld] III 81 Vendée, Commission des Récompenses nationales, J. B. Baudry to Baudry père, Aug. 11, 1830.

65. Archives du Département de la Seine, V[bis] 1 & 2, Comm. des Récomp. nat., 4e Arrond., Dossiers individuels; V[bis] 153, Comm. des Récomp. nat., 11e Arrond., Dossiers individuels; Arch. nat. F[ld] III 45, Comm. des Récomp. nat., Dossier Bonnecasse; Arch. nat., F[9] 1155, Affaires militaires, Combattants de Juillet, Affaires particulières, Dossier Brivois.

66. D' A. Cournet, *Souvenirs, 1760-1850* (Paris, 1913), pp. 133-34.

67. Blanc, *Histoire de dix ans*, I, 325-26; *Procès-verbal de la réunion préparatoire des electeurs du deuxième arrondissement . . . offert à messieurs les électeurs par M. Jacques Lefebvre* [Paris, n.d.], pp. 6-7.

Honoré.[68] Orleans' eldest son, the Duke of Chartres, was seized
by revolutionaries in Montrouge and narrowly escaped with his
life.[69] Louis-Philippe's first proclamation as Lieutenant-General
of the Kingdom was torn from the walls, and men charged with
posting it were beaten up in the streets of Paris.[70] Even on his
reputedly triumphant visit to the Hôtel-de-Ville on July 31, he
was greeted with shouts of "Plus de Bourbons" from men who
saw him as just another Bourbon.[71]

But the supporters of the Empire were unprepared. Napoleon
II was far away and scarcely known in France. No old general
whose name would stir the populace mounted his horse or drew
his sword for the Empire. Probably avid for renewed careers
and new honors the generals preferred the promise of the better
organized Orleanist solution to a gamble on the dubious cause
of a distant and almost unknown new Napoleon. Of all the
Napoleonic generals Gourgaud alone appeared at Laffitte's to
plead for the Empire, and only one declared for the Republic.
All the others joined the Orleanists.[72]

Who, then, did rule France after the Revolution of 1830?
Different men, certainly, filled public offices. Bonapartists or ex-
Bonapartists, or, at least, men indebted to the Bonapartes took
over scores of high posts. It cannot be said, however, that they
formed a Bonapartist party or that in important matters of policy
they followed a distinctively Bonapartist line or behaved in
any way that set them apart from their fellows who had no close
imperial connections. They and the other new officeholders of
1830 and 1831, elected and appointed, represented essentially the
same social classes as their predecessors. "There has been no
revolution," declared Casimir Périer in 1830. "There has been
only a change in the person of the king."[73] Had he added, "and

68. Arch. nat., F[ld] III 45, Dossier Bonneau; F[ld] III 46, Dossier Boyaud.
69. Paul Thureau-Dangin, *Histoire de la Monarchie de Juillet* (2e éd.; Paris,
1888), I, 10.
70. Armand Marrast, "Document pour l'histoire de France," MS, Bibliothèque
historique de la Ville de Paris, Série 23, Carton 1830.
71. Blanc, *Histoire de dix ans*, I. 343, 348; Thureau-Dangin, *Histoire*, I, 19;
Armand Marrast, *Programme de l'Hôtel de Ville ou récit de ce qui est passé
depuis le 31 juillet jusqu' au 6 août 1830* (Paris, 1831), p. 5.
72. Blanc, *Histoire de dix ans*, I, 325-26.
73. Quoted in S. Charléty, *La Monarchie de Juillet (1830-1848)* (E. Lavisse
[ed.], *Histoire de France contemporaine*, Vol. V), p. 5.

a change in the persons of public officials," he would have expressed the essence of the Revolution as it affected the balance of social classes in public office in France. After the Revolution the landed proprietors, the official class, and the professional men continued to predominate in the key offices of state as they had under the Empire and the Bourbon Restoration. Here the Revolution had introduced no new regime of the *grande bourgeoisie*.[74]

74. Since the completion of this essay two important publications relevant to it have appeared—Adeline Daumard, *La Bourgeoisie parisienne de 1815 à 1848* (Paris, 1963), and Charles H. Pouthas, "La Réorganisation du Ministère de l'Intérieur et la reconstitution de l'administration préfectorale par Guizot en 1830," *Revue d'histoire moderne et contemporaine*, IX (1962), 241-63.

The Wu-shih-shan Incident of 1878

ELLSWORTH C. CARLSON

One strand of China's nineteenth-century response to the "Western impact" was a persistent anti-foreignism. Hostility to the Western "barbarians" and to Chinese association with them was clearly evident in the refusal of the Cantonese, in the years after the Opium War, to allow the foreigners to exercise the right, granted by the Treaty of Nanking, to reside in the city of Canton. With the growth of Chinese-Western contact—especially with the expansion of the missionary movement—anti-foreignism became increasingly widespread until it finally erupted, at the turn of the century, in the Boxer Rebellion, in which large numbers of foreign missionaries and Chinese converts were massacred. Although the Boxer Rebellion has been the subject of an extensive literature, many less spectacular and less tragic anti-foreign incidents which occurred in the preceding decades remain relatively unstudied.

The subject of this study is what was known as the Wu-shih-shan (Black Stone Hill) incident, which occurred in Foochow in August, 1878. The roots of this incident, in which a Chinese mob destroyed a mission school on Wu-shih-shan, go back to the opening of the port of Foochow for trade and foreign residence shortly after the Opium War and especially to the beginnings of Protestant missionary activities in and around the city.

Although most anti-foreign activity in Foochow, including the Wu-shih-shan incident, was directed mainly at missionary activity, hostility to the presence of foreigners was apparent even before the missionary appeared on the scene. After the Opium War the Chinese were exceedingly reluctant to open Foochow, which unlike Amoy, Ningpo, and Shanghai, was a major administrative and cultural center, being the seat of the governor-general of

Fukien and Chekiang, and the location of periodic civil service examinations for the *chu-jen* degree. On the insistence of the foreigner, however, Foochow was officially opened to trade and foreign residence in June, 1844, although, except for the illegal sale of opium over the side of ships outside of the harbor, the trade did not reach a significant volume for more than a decade.[1]

The opening of Foochow was not accomplished without vigorous protest from the inhabitants of the city, especially from officials and educated members of the upper class or gentry, who will usually be referred to here as the literati. Repeated proclamations had to be issued calling for respect toward foreign strangers. Especially strong was the resistance to foreign residence within the walled city; accordingly, most foreigners lived in the suburbs. Only by stubborn insistence did the first British consul succeed in locating his consulate within the city walls. The Chinese officials finally agreed to the consulate's use of what had been a temple on Wu-shih-shan, but resentment on the subject continued.[2]

Wu-shih-shan, which figured importantly in the incident of 1878, is located in the southwest quarter of the walled city of Foochow and rises several hundred feet above the main level of the city. At the time of the opening of Foochow it was the site of numerous ancestral and Taoist temples and of "pleasure grounds" to which the inhabitants of Foochow would saunter at their leisure. It was also a place of study and the location of a club of the Foochow literati.[3] The first Protestant missionary to take up work in Foochow, Stephen Johnson of the American Board, spoke of Wu-shih-shan as a "commanding eminence in the midst of a great natural amphitheater" and said that

1. John King Fairbank, *Trade and Diplomacy on the China Coast: The Opening of the Treaty Ports* (Cambridge, Mass., 1953), I, 102, 155, 162-63, 286, 289, 292, 293.

2. *Ibid.*, I, 157, 162-63, 203-204. George Smith, *A Narrative of an Exploratory Visit to Each of the Consular Cities of China and to the Islands of Hongkong and Chusan in Behalf of the Church Missionary Society in the Years 1844, 1845, 1846* (London, 1847), pp. 335-37. Robert S. Maclay, *Life Among the Chinese* (New York, 1861), pp. 85-86, 127-29. See comments of Hsü Chi-yü, governor of Fukien, in memorial of August 13, 1850 in *Ch'ou-pan i-wu shih-mo: Hsien-feng ch'ao* (A complete account of the management of barbarian affairs: Hsien-feng period, Peiping: Palace Museum, 1930) II, 2b. This latter documentary collection will be cited hereinafter, for the Hsien-feng reign period, as IWSM-HF.

3. Smith, *Narrative*, pp. 331-33; Sun Ming-en, memorial of Aug. 25, 1850, IWSM-HF, II, 15b-16.

among all the places I have yet visited, there is no one commanding so many advantages in respect to climate, romantic situation, prospect of the city, its adjacent beautiful and fruitful plains, its peaceful, meandering river, and the encircling mountains, as the Black Rock Hill, now the residence of Her Britannic Majesty's Consul. . . .[4]

The opening of the treaty ports, as provided in the Treaty of Nanking, and the issuance of Imperial edicts in 1844 and 1845 providing for toleration of Christianity paved the way for the beginnings of Protestant missionary work in Foochow and the other treaty ports. Interest in the possibility of missionary work in Foochow was stimulated by the report of the Reverend George Smith, who visited there at the end of 1845 in behalf of the Church Missionary Society. Several things about Foochow attracted the attention of missionary societies: its hundreds of thousands of people in need of salvation, its influence as an administrative and cultural center over a wide area, its physical beauty, and its healthful climate.[5]

The first society actually to open work in Foochow was the American Board of Commissioners for Foreign Missions. Stephen Johnson, a missionary of that society who had worked among Chinese in Bangkok, Siam, arrived in Foochow by a ship engaged in the opium trade on January 2, 1847.[6] Before the year was over the first American Methodist (Northern) missionaries had arrived.[7]

The Church Missionary Society of the Church of England, whose work was to be the target of the Wu-shih-shan incident in 1878, was the third mission to establish a permanent work in

4. Letter of Stephen Johnson, quoted in *Missionary Herald*, XLIV (1848), 148.

5. Kenneth Scott Latourette, *A History of Christian Missions in China* (New York, 1929), pp. 228-32; 242-70; Smith, *Narrative*, pp. 327-75; views concerning Foochow of American Board missionaries Doty (stationed at Amoy), Johnson, Cummings, and Baldwin appear in *Missionary Herald*, XLII (1846), 161-63; XLIV (1848), 148, 155; XLV (1849), 222-23; XLVI (1850), 345-46.

6. Extracts from Johnson's early letters from Foochow, telling of his arrival and beginnings of his work were published in *Missionary Herald*, XLIII (1847), 224-26, 356-57. Complete texts of these letters and other letters and reports from Johnson and American Board missionaries who arrived later are available in American Board of Commissioners for Foreign Missions, archives of missionary letters, deposited in Houghton Library, Harvard University, 16.3.3(2), 16.3.5(1), 16.3.5(2), to be cited below as ABC.

7. Richard Terrill Baker, *Ten Thousand Years: The Story of Methodism's First Century in China* (New York, 1947), pp. 39-40.

Foochow. The first C.M.S. missionaries, R. D. Jackson and W. Welton, the latter having medical training, arrived in May, 1850.[8]

The missionaries of the two American societies reconciled themselves for the time being to the unwillingness of the Chinese to allow them to reside in the walled city and established their residences and places of work in the suburbs, but Jackson and Welton did not. They decided to insist on their right, which in the opinion of the British government had been granted in the Treaty of Nanking, to reside within the walled city. In June, with the help of the officer then in charge of the British consulate, Jackson and Welton succeeded in renting rooms in Shen-kuang-szu, one of the temples on Wu-shih-shan. The priests were agreeable, and the documents were stamped in the office of the District Magistrate.[9]

It was only a few days, however, before the prospect of missionary residence on Wu-shih-shan evoked heated and violent Chinese protest.[10] Leadership in the protest was taken by the Foochow literati and by several Chinese officials who were critical not only of missionary residence on Wu-shih-shan but also of those local officials—especially the district magistrate, the governor of Fukien, and the governor-general of Fukien and Chekiang —whose mismanagement of "barbarian affairs" had permitted the

8. "Journal of Occurrences," *Chinese Repository*, XIX (1850), 460; *Missionary Herald*, XLVII (1851), 40.

9. "Journal of Occurrences," *ibid.*, XIX (1850), 459-60; Eugene Stock, *The Story of the Fuh-kien Mission of the Church Missionary Society*, (3rd. ed.; London, 1890), pp. 15-16; memorial of Sun Ming-en, dated Aug. 25, 1850, IWSM-HF, II, 15b-16b; joint memorial of Liu Yün-k'o and Hsü Chi-yü, dated Sept. 1, 1850, IWSM-HF, II, 17b; letter of July 23, 1850 from William L. Richards of the American Board, *Missionary Herald*, XLVII (1851), 40.

10. Since David Tod Roy, graduate student at Harvard University, has studied this episode and is likely to publish his results, I shall describe it only to the extent that is necessary for an understanding of subsequent developments. My account is based on the following sources: Chinese official documents, especially memorials from Foochow officials, in IWSM-HF, II, 15b-20, 23b-39; III, 8-11, 12b-14b, 15b-16, 20-24, 38-38b, 41-45b; IV, 1-1b, 6b-7, 13-16, 18b-22b, 24b-27; 34-35; also additional memorials of Governor Hsü Chi-yü in *Sung K'an Hsien-sheng ch'üan-chi* (Collected Works of Hsü Chi-yü, 1915), Shang, 28a; Hsia, 9a, 16a; Western sources are Stock, *Story of the Fuh-kien Mission*, pp. 15-16; "Journal of Occurences," *Chinese Repository*, XIX (1850), 459-62; "Protestant Missions Among the Chinese," *ibid.*, XX (1851), 525; extracts from letters from American Board Missionaries Richards and Peet in *Missionary Herald*, XLVII (1851), 40, 129; unpublished letters of Oct. 2, 1850, and Dec. 31, 1850, from C. C. Baldwin, ABC, 16.3.3(2), letters 140, 180; letters from Methodist missionaries and other notices in *Missionary Advocate*, VI (1851), 83, 84 and VII (1852), 19.

catastrophe to occur. Both Western and Chinese sources seem to establish that Lin Tse-hsü, whose actions as high commissioner at Canton in 1839 had helped to precipitate the Opium War, and who was resting in his native Fukien in 1850, played a part in precipitating this agitation.[11]

The opponents of missionary residence on Wu-shih-shan sent communications to the foreigners and to the responsible Chinese officials, posted placards in the city, warned of popular violence, and sent memorials to the emperor in an attempt to persuade the missionaries to leave or, failing that, to force the responsible British and Chinese officers to evict them. Antagonism to foreign residence on Wu-shih-shan was strong, but the removal of Jackson and Welton was not the only aim. Some of those who participated in this effort to eject Welton and Jackson were using the fact that the missionaries had been allowed to take up residence on the hill to discredit the Fukien governor, Hsü Chi-yü. Hsü's efforts to learn about the West and to establish satisfactory relations with foreigners in Foochow had brought him the enmity of many Chinese.[12]

The literati and hostile officials employed a number of arguments: Shen-kuang-szu was a place where scholars had studied and assembled; the priests of the temple had no authority to rent it; the treaty right of foreign residence applied to the port but not to the walled city; the treaty required consideration of the feelings of the local people in renting houses to foreigners; the official sealing of the rental documents had been the result of carelessness rather than proper consideration of the matter in the District Magistrate's Yamen; the missionaries' doctrines were

11. Dorothy Ann Rockwell, "The Compilation of Governor Hsü's *Ying-huan chih-lueh*," *Papers on China* (Center for East Asian Studies, Harvard University), XI (1957), 22; the *Chinese Repository*, XIX (1850), 460, reported that a placard attacking foreign residence on Wu-shih-shan was believed to have been written by Lin or issued with his approval; a memorial of September 4, 1850, written by Lin Yang-tsu speaks of a public letter on the subject of foreign residence on Wu-shih-shan written by Lin Tse-hsü, IWSM-HF, II, 24; in a memorial of April 21, 1877 Ting Jih-ch'ang referred to Lin's role in 1850, *Ch'ing-chi wai-chiao shih-liao* (Historical materials on foreign relations in the latter part of the Ch'ing dynasty, compiled by Wang T'ao-fu, edited and published by Wang Liang, Peiping, 1932, to be cited hereinafter as WCSL), XI, 16b.

12. Tu Lien-che, "Hsü Chi-yü," in *Eminent Chinese of the Ch'ing Period*, ed. Arthur W. Hummel (Washington, D. C., 1943-44), I, 309-10. For examples of the attack on Hsü, see memorials of the Censor Ho Kuan-ying, dated Sept. 6, 1857, and Nov. 21, 1850, IWSM-HF, II, 25b-27; III, 20-22.

corrupt and misleading; the residence of the foreigners on Wu-shih-shan was resented by the common people and was likely to produce violence which would harm relations between the people and the barbarians.[13]

When the missionaries refused to give up their position on Wu-shih-shan and the British consulate and the governor of Hong-kong supported them,[14] the Chinese officials, especially Governor Hsü Chi-yü and Governor-General Liu Yun-k'o, were in a most unenviable situation. They were caught between the demands of the foreigners and of the Foochow populace, and serious offense to either could bring disaster. Too vigorous opposition to foreign residence in the city might provoke forceful British action in defense of treaty rights. Too little response to the feelings of the literati, critical officials, and common people might result in mob violence, "the anger of the crowd being difficult to control."[15] Either eventuality would be proof that the officials had not been able to manage things satisfactorily, and might be expected to bring the wrath of the emperor upon them.

The officials proceeded cautiously. They ordered the missionaries to leave but stopped short of actually evicting them. Various pressures were put on the missionaries, quite obviously designed to convince Jackson and Welton that Wu-shih-shan could not be a satisfactory place of residence and work. People in the neighborhood were warned not to listen to the missionaries' preaching or make use of Welton's medical practice. For a time artisans were prohibited from making badly needed repairs at Shen-kuang-szu, and Chinese whom the missionaries had employed to teach in their school and assist in Welton's dispensary were frightened into leaving their work. The priests refused to accept further rent payments from the missionaries, and it appears that hostile crowds damaged the property. The Chinese

13. Among sources cited in note 10, see particularly the memorial of Sun Ming-en, dated Aug. 25, 1850, IWSM-HF, II, 15b-16b; a translation of a placard of the Foochow literati in *Chinese Repository*, XIX (1850), 460-62; memorial from Liu Yün-k'o and Hsü Chi-yü, dated Sept. 1, 1850, IWSM-HF, II, 17-19b.

14. IWSM-HF, II, 18; III, 9; letters of Aug. 1, 1850, and Sept. 2, 1850, written by Judson D. Collins of the Methodist mission, *Missionary Advocate*, VI (1851), 84.

15. IWSM-HF, III, 9b.

officials blocked Welton's effort to secure a location for a dispensary at the foot of Wu-shih-shan.[16]

A major source of future difficulty, especially the incident of 1878, is to be found in the failure to settle this dispute of 1850 in either a clear-cut or a mutually satisfactory fashion. The foreigners did not clearly establish their right to have premises in the city, and the Chinese did not succeed in bringing about their removal. In what has all the earmarks of a face-saving arrangement, the foreigners were finally persuaded to leave Shen-kuang-szu. But they did not leave the city, or even Wu-shih-shan, but agreed to take up residence in two outbuildings of another Wu-shih-shan temple known as Tao-shan-kuan. Tao-shan-kuan was very close to the British consulate, and a British officer of the consulate had previously lived there. Shen-kuang-szu would again be available to the literati for study and meetings, but the whole question of whether the foreigners should be allowed to live in the city or on Wu-shih-shan had not really been solved.[17]

Although Welton and Jackson had managed to stay on Wu-shih-shan, the work of the C.M.S. mission was very discouraging for more than a decade after 1850. Continued opposition to their presence on the hill was only part of the trouble. None of the missionaries who came to the mission before 1862 was able to settle down to more than six years of work; one by one they were transferred, or returned home, or died in the field. Although Welton's medical work was quite popular until he went home, not to return, in 1856, the seeds of the gospel fell on quite stony ground. During the first decade of the mission there were no converts, and discouragement with the Foochow field became so great that for a time the society in London considered giving it up.[18]

A turning point finally came, however, and from 1861 or 1862 the outlook for the mission began to improve rapidly. Eighteen

16. IWSM-HF, II, 28-28b; III, 8-9b, 41, 43-45; IV, 19-19b; 22-22b; Judson D. Collins' letter of Aug. 1, 1850, *Missionary Advocate*, VI (1851), 84; C. C. Baldwin's letter of Oct. 2, 1850, ABC, 16.3.3(2), letter 180; "Protestant Missions among the Chinese," *Chinese Repository*, XX (1851), 525.

17. IWSM-HF, III, 45-45b; IV, 1-1b, 6b-7, 13-14, 15b, 19-20; C. C. Baldwin's letter of Dec. 31, 1850, ABC, 16.3.3(2), letter 140.

18. Stock, *Story of Fuh-kien Mission*, pp. 17-19, 24, 32, 51, 324-25; Frank L. Norris, *Handbooks of English Church Expansion: China* (London, 1908), p. 32; *Missionary Herald*, LIV (1858), 60 and LV (1859), 296.

sixty-one saw the first baptisms and the opening of a chapel in premises acquired the previous year. In the years that followed the mission opened additional chapels and places of work in Foochow and vicinity, and the number of baptisms mounted rapidly until by 1876 the mission had 1648 Chinese Christians under its care in Foochow and, more importantly, nearby outstations. The number of converts was 2,323 in 1877, "about 3,000" in 1878, and 3,556 in 1880.[19]

Among the factors that contributed to the success of the mission in this period were the Tientsin treaties of 1858, which provided toleration for Christianity and gave the missionaries the right to travel into the interior. These treaty provisions opened the way for the establishment of outstations in the vicinity of Foochow, and it was there that most of the successes of the C.M.S. and other missionary societies were won. Of the 1648 C.M.S. converts up to 1876, all but thirty-two were in the outstations. The reports of the C.M.S. and other missionaries contain frequent remarks as to the greater willingness of rural people, as compared with the inhabitants of the city, to receive Christianity. In 1875 the senior missionary complained that Foochow "still shows not the slightest interest in the message of salvation."[20]

Another important factor in the growth of the C.M.S. work in Foochow was the arrival, in the spring of 1862, of the Reverend John R. Wolfe, the most important missionary at the Foochow mission in the nineteenth century. Archdeacon Wolfe played an important part in the events of 1878, and his intolerance, single-mindedness, irascibility, and lack of sensitivity to Chinese feelings were part of the situation that exploded in the incident of that year. In the meantime, however, Wolfe's zeal for the cause, his tireless efforts over a long period, and his ability to develop successful methods all contributed greatly to the growth of the

19. Norris, *Handbooks*, pp. 32, 82, 83; Stock, *Story of Fuh-kien Mission*, pp. 31, 32, 40, 42, 51, 260, 261. Reports of progress of the mission appeared in the *Church Missionary Review*, published beginning in 1849 under this and other titles by the Church Missionary Society, cited hereinafter as CMS; by 1876 and 1877 reports of the Foochow mission were very enthusiastic; see particularly CMS, XXVII (1876), 304 and XXVII (1877), 204-209, 309-10, 417.

20. CMS, XXVII (1876), 304; XXVIII (1877), 204-205, 309-10.

mission. Another missionary related that Wolfe would push ahead energetically without consideration of the limits on his appropriations, leaving the board at home with no alternative but to back him up.[21] He was quick to take advantage of the opportunity, mentioned above, to open outstations, and the C.M.S. had seventy of them by 1876. And it was after Wolfe's arrival that the mission began to conduct its work rather largely through Chinese helpers.[22]

Wolfe and missionaries of other societies working in Foochow agreed in attributing the success of the C.M.S. to the use of Chinese evangelists.[23] Other missionaries complained that some of these Chinese workers were only recent converts and that they had been taken from other missions, but there was no denying the success of their work.[24] The Chinese workers were especially important in the opening of stations in villages and towns outside of Foochow, where the procedure, according to Wolfe, was "first to send a Native teacher, who living quietly among his countrymen, removes prejudice, explains the objects of the mission, and the motives that have led to its establishment, and thus smooths the way for the visits of the European missionary."[25]

The success of the C.M.S., beginning in the sixties, was achieved in the face of continuing opposition to the presence of the missionaries and obstruction of their work. The reports of all of the Foochow missions are an almost continuous story of difficulties in obtaining the use of buildings and land, damage or destruction of mission buildings, and attempted intimidation and even physical injury of converts, Chinese evangelists, and missionaries. In 1864 mobs largely destroyed a C.M.S. chapel as well as

21. S. F. Woodin of the American Board, ABC, 16.3.5(2), letter of April 18, 1878.
22. Reports of the Foochow mission in CMS for the years after 1862 deal rather largely with Wolfe and his work. See "Fuh-Kien: Further Remarkable Progress," CMS, XXVIII (1877), 309-10; "In Memoriam, Venerable Archdeacon John Richard Wolfe," *Chinese Recorder*, XLVII (1916), 695-702; Stock, *Story of Fuh-Kien Mission, passim.* For a Chinese official's view of Wolfe, see WCSL, XIV, 16b. S. F. Woodin of the American Board mission wrote that other members of Wolfe's mission "generally had trouble" with him, ABC 16.3.5.(2), letter of April 18, 1878.
23. CMS, XXII (1871), 25; Norris, *Handbooks,* pp. 82-83. For data on particular Chinese workers see Stock, *Story of Fuh-Kien Mission,* p. 47; CMS, XXVIII (1877), 204; CMS, XXXII (1881), 245.
24. Feb. 17, 1868, letter by C. Hartwell, ABC, 13.3.5(1), letter 132; views of S. F. Woodin appear in ABC 16.3.5(2), letter of April 18, 1878.
25. CMS, XXVII (1876), 705.

properties of the American Methodist mission.[26] In 1871, when rumors were circulating widely that foreigners were poisoning wells with "magical powder," several chapels were destroyed and the Reverend J. E. Mahood (who had joined Wolfe in 1869) was attacked and nearly lost his life.[27] The C.M.S. missionaries frequently sought the help of the British consul, and there were several incidents serious enough to become the subject of representations by the British Minister to the authorities in Peking.[28] The help provided by the British authorities did not always satisfy the missionaries, however; Wolfe frequently complained that the British government was not firm enough in demanding Chinese respect for the missionaries' treaty rights.[29]

Among the missionaries of all the Foochow missions there was an interesting unanimity in the beliefs that the common people were not unfriendly and that it was the literati who were hostile and were the source of all varieties of difficulty. Behind the obstructionism of the officials or the violence of the mob, the missionaries could always see the plotting and goading of the literati.[30] Wolfe even reported, on "good authority," the existence of an association of literati "whose express object is to oppose the progress of the religion of Jesus, and, if possible, root it out of this literary city."[31] Most of the Christian converts were from the lower classes. In reporting on his visit to Foochow in 1876, the Bishop of Hongkong said that Wolfe "had not a half a dozen literary men among all his converts"; the Bishop complained that

26. Stock, *Story of Fuh-kien Mission*, pp. 32-33; S. L. Baldwin (Methodist missionary in Foochow), "Persecution in China," *Christian Advocate*, XXXIX (1864), 107; a long dispatch on this incident, dated Feb. 5, 1864, from Foochow Consul A. L. Clarke to Minister Anson Burlingame, is in the National Archives, Washington, D. C. (Legation Archives, Vol. XLII, No. 232, Consular Records: Foochow, Swatow, 1861-69, pp. 33-41).

27. Stock, *Story of Fuh-Kien Mission*, p. 53; CMS, XXVIII (1877), 205-206; *Chinese Recorder*, IV (1871), 109-11.

28. For a few examples, see *Chinese Recorder*, I (1868-69), 49, 192; II (1869-70), 116, 176, 264; CMS, III (1852), 210-11; XVIII (1867), 288; XIX (1868), 172, 183, 348-49, 352; XX (1870), 380; XXVII (1876), 615-16; *Missionary Herald*, LXIV (1876), 62; *Christian Advocate*, XXXIX (1864), 107; *Ch'ing-chi chiao-an shih-liao* (Historical materials concerning missionary cases in the latter part of the Ch'ing Dynasty, Peiping: Palace Museum, 1937), I, 27-29, 59-63, 71-74, 80-81.

29. Stock, *Story of Fuh-kien Mission*, p. 252; CMS, XX (1869), 318-20; CMS, XXVII (1876), 615-16.

30. See, for example, CMS, XX (1869), 318-20; XXVII (1876), 556; XXVIII (1877), 205, 206, 667; *Chinese Recorder*, IX (1878), 396-98.

31. CMS, XVIII (1867), 217.

the Chinese converts and the chapels were dirty and that wor-
shipers ate peanuts and "attended to the necessities of babies" in
the church during services."[32] One of the most striking things
about all of the Protestant missionary work in Foochow was the
failure either to make converts among the literati or to establish
any real acquaintance or understanding with them. What happened, rather, was that the hostility of the literati for the missionaries, based on cultural pride, was soon paralleled by a missionary hostility toward the literati, based on the conviction that
the latter were obstacles to the Lord's work. Communication between the missionaries and the Chinese upper class (including
scholars and officials) remained largely official; it was often conducted by the consul, who had his own reasons for irritation and
frustration. Much of it was with reference to treaty rights,
which the missionary considered of fundamental importance but
which the literati could not see as a substitute for Confucian
principles.

Despite continuing Chinese resentment at its presence on Wu-
shih-shan, the mission was able to keep, enlarge, and transform
its property there. The original buildings were substantially
altered; after one of them burned in 1870, the mission replaced it
with a two-storied, Western-style structure. In 1871 a new building went up on land, contiguous to the original property, that
had been acquired in 1866. In all of this, troublesome problems
and disputes arose. There was talk of the mission having encroached beyond the boundaries of the land it had rented and of
having destroyed an historic landmark. Several of Wolfe's arrangements for acquiring additional property, or for improving
the mission's tenure on land already held, fell through when the
Chinese authorities disputed the right of the temple priests and
others with whom he was dealing to enter into the arrangements.
On the eve of the Wu-shih-shan incident of 1878 mission use of
the Wu-shih-shan property was based on rental agreements of
1866 and 1867 with, respectively, the government authorities and
the "directors" of the Tao Shan Kuan temple. Events of 1877,
1878, and 1879 would make it clear that the missionaries and the
Chinese had quite different views as to the permanence of C.M.S.

32. CMS, XXVIII (1877), 208, 209.

tenure. But between 1850 and 1877 there had been no serious Chinese effort to evict the mission. The Wu-shih-shan issue had continued to simmer, but it had not boiled over.[33]

In his report to the Church Missionary Society for the year 1877 Wolfe warned that:

There has been a deep and bitter hatred shown toward us everywhere by the haughty gentry and official classes. Here and there we have found a friendly mandarin, but, as a rule, the hostility and opposition from these classes have been very great, and have exceeded anything that we have known in the years that are past. These gentry, backed up and supported as they are by the mandarins, have opposed us at every step, and have caused us a great deal of trouble and anxiety during the year. A retrograde policy, with respect to intercourse with foreigners, has been inaugurated here, and vigorously pursued by the present Viceroy, who is most bitterly inimical to foreigners, and I fear matters are becoming serious.[34]

In writing these lines Wolfe must have been thinking, among other things, of the effort of the new governor-general, Ho Ching, and the retiring Fukien governor, Ting Jih-ch'ang, to try to bring about the removal of the C.M.S. mission from Wu-shih-shan to buildings in the Nantai suburb outside of the city walls.

Just why this effort came at this time is not clear. Perhaps the rapid growth of the mission in previous years made its presence even more intolerable than it had been. In the documents having to do with the events of 1877 and 1878 there is much more talk than previously about *feng shui. Fengshui* (literally, "wind and water"), often translated as "geomancy," is based on the belief, to use Professor Latourette's words, "that in every locality forces exist which act on graves, buildings, cities, and towns, either for the welfare or ill of the quick and the dead," and in practice it involved location and erection of buildings in such a way that natural forces would act beneficially

33. The whole history of property arrangements, buildings, and disputes over the same was brought out quite fully in the course of legal action brought by the Chinese against Wolfe and the C.M.S. in the spring of 1879. See the published proceedings, *The Wu Shih Shan Trial; report of the case of Chow Chang Kung, Lin King Ching, &c., versus Rev. John R. Wolfe,* Hongkong, 1879, especially pp. 4-9, 28-37, 41-46, 48-52. (This source will be cited hereinafter as WSS.)

34. CMS, XXIX (1878), 499.

rather than adversely.[35] The argument in 1877 was that the high Western-style buildings erected by the foreigners had an adverse effect on the *feng-shui* of the area. In the seventh moon (August 9—September 6) of 1877 an inscription was carved on a rock near the British consulate stating that sale or rental of properties on Wu-shih-shan to foreigners was prohibited because of *feng-shui*.[36] To what extent the officials and gentry of Foochow actually believed in *feng-shui* is not clear and is, perhaps, somewhat beside the point. In April, 1877, Ting-Jih-ch'ang wrote that the common people were furious, that "the anger of the crowd is difficult to oppose," that if there were popular violence the calamity would be difficult for Chinese and foreign officials to handle, and that it was necessary to solve the problem in order to prevent violence.[37]

Prior to his retirement from the governorship of Fukien in 1877 Ting had conversations with the British consul, Sinclair, about the possibility that English missionaries give up their position on Wu-shih-shan in return for the use of buildings outside the city that had been used for, or intended for, the Telegraph Office. Ting reported in April, 1877, that Sinclair was favorable to the proposal, that Wolfe was not opposed, and that it should be possible to get the views of the missionary society in England in about fifty days.[38] It appears from the Chinese documents that the Chinese literati and others were informed of the arrangement and that hopes for missionary evacuation of Wu-shih-shan ran high. When a reply from London did not come for some time, the Chinese officials urged the consul to hasten it. Meanwhile Sinclair informed the Foreign Office of the proposal.[39]

The Church Missionary Society did not agree to the exchange,

35. Kenneth Scott Latourette, *The Chinese, Their History and Culture* (3rd ed.; New York, 1949), p. 651.

36. *North China Herald,* XX (1878), 107. This British newspaper, published in Shanghai, will be cited hereinafter as NCH.

37. WCSL, XI, 16b; WSS, p. 54; *Christian Advocate,* LIII (1878), 693. The main sources of information on this Chinese effort in 1877 are memorials written by Ting Jih-ch'ang, dated April 21, 1877, Dec. 5, 1878, May 13, 1879, WCSL, XI, 16-17; XIV, 26-31b; XV, 23-25. When violence occurred in 1878, as Ting had feared, the English missionaries made little mention of Ting's efforts to prevent it.

38. WCSL, XI, 16-17; XIV, 2b, 6.

39. WCSL, XIV, 2b-3, 6, 10b-11, 26b-27, 29.

though as late as April, 1879, Sinclair was still interested and was awaiting instructions from the Foreign Office.[40] In this situation the Foochow missionaries took a step which made it very clear that Ting Jih-ch'ang's proposal had not broken the impasse that had begun in 1850: they began construction of a large new building on Wu-shih-shan. Four months later this building precipitated the Wu-shih-shan incident.

Looking back on the failure of Ting Jih-ch'ang's proposal, one is impressed with the fact that the failure to agree on a course of action cannot be explained simply in terms of the immediate facts of the case. Much of the real difficulty sprang from differences in basic assumptions and attitudes that the two sides brought with them as they reacted to the Wu-shih-shan problem, and from the fact that both sides were convinced that they were in the right. At least some Westerners regarded Ting Jih-ch'ang as a reasonable and able official, and he had been active in Chinese adoption of Western technical knowledge.[41] One gets the impression from his memorials that he was making a sincere effort to arrive at a satisfactory settlement. But he went to work in a quite Confucian way. He was less concerned about absolute requirements of law or treaty than he was with what would be reasonable in the particular situation. Confucian considerations of harmonious social relations dictated that a potential source of conflict should be removed. The attitudes of the missionaries were shaped by very different assumptions. They were sure they were doing the Lord's work, and the Lord had need of their presence in the city of Foochow. Their Western cultural background gave priority to the rule of law and to the importance of respect for legal rights, and they were outraged at a Chinese effort to deny their treaty right to reside in the walled city. A meeting of minds was not achieved, and on August 30, 1878, the violence which Ting Jih-ch'ang had feared took place.

What finally caused the long simmering Wu-shih-shan problem to boil over was the decision of the mission to erect a multi-

40. WCSL, XIV, 10-11, 26b-27.
41. See biography of Ting by Fang Chao-ying in Hummel, *Eminent Chinese of the Ch'ing Period,* II, 721-23. When Ting was called back to Foochow in 1878 to deal with the Wu-shih-shan trouble, the foreign *Foochow Herald* was pleased at the assignment, according to NCH, XXI (1878), 475.

story building on Wu-shih-shan to house a "college" for the training of the Christian workers who played such an important part
in the work of the mission.[42] At first the mission tried to acquire
a new plot of land for the building, but, failing that, it decided to crowd the building into the existing compound,

planning the house to lie against the side of the hill, so that the
second story should be larger than the first, and the third larger than
the second; and also being content with a not very symmetrical-look-
ing structure . . . it turned out that a house could be put up with
forty-eight little rooms, each about seven and a half feet square, for
as many students, and in addition a large dining room and lecture-
room for the European in charge. . . .[43]

The consul, Sinclair, who was awaiting the views of the Foreign
Office on Ting Jih-ch'ang's exchange proposal, was not pleased
with the mission's decision, but he gave a reluctant approval on
April 2, 1878, subject to the condition, agreed to by the Reverend
Mr. Stewart, who had joined the mission in 1876, that the mission
would stop work on the building "at the first symptom of opposition on the part of the gentry."[44]

The protest that Sinclair had feared did not come immediately. According to the missionaries there was no objection until
the outer walls and the roof were completed, some three months
after building had commenced. Then, at the instigation of the
Chinese authorities, Sinclair requested that work should be suspended because of opposition that had arisen. But in spite of
his earlier promise to the consul, Stewart refused to halt work
on the interior of the building until it was near enough completion for the students to move in.[45] Only then did he agree to
suspend work, and he went off to Sharp's Peak for a vacation.
He subsequently explained that

this was not a private matter, but one affecting our whole mission
work all over the country; if I stopped work in this Treaty port, to
please a few of the Literati, who disliked foreigners and the spread

42. The erection of the building was under the charge of R. W. Stewart (WSS,
p. 53). For his account of the building see CMS, XXX (1879), 29-35.
43. CMS, XXX (1879), 29-30.
44. WSS, p. 53, gives letters on subject from Stewart to Sinclair and from
Sinclair to Stewart.
45. WCSL, XIV, 11; CMS, XXX (1879), 30-31.

of Christianity, all over the country the same thing would be tried, and with the action of the Missionary here as a precedent, it would be impossible to hold our ground.[46]

Chinese and Western sources agree that it was the literati, led by a *chu jen*, Lin Ying-lin, who had objected to the new building, arguing that the multi-storied structure would adversely affect the *feng shui* and that in building it the mission had encroached on land outside of the boundaries of the property covered by the rental agreements.[47]

Tension rose during the summer. After June the Chinese refused to accept further rent money for the Wu-shih-shan property.[48] Early in August the *North China Herald* reported that the literati had tried to organize a popular demonstration, and later in the month the same paper said that "the literati have gone so far as to name a day on which it is proposed to carry out the demolition" of the property.[49] Meanwhile discussion of the scheme for exchanging the property for the telegraph building was resumed, and on August 29 an American Methodist missionary wrote that "the officers are trying hard to get the English mission out of the city. They are trying to get us to persuade the missionaries to accept a compromise before there is too much excitement among the people. . . . The officers claim to be hardly driven by the 'literati.' "[50]

The explosion finally came on August 30, 1878, the day when an officer of the British consulate and several Chinese officials (including the Prefect and the Magistrates of the two Districts of Foochow) came to the C.M.S. compound to investigate whether the new building "really encroached on someone else's land." The circumstances of the investigation as described by the missionaries[51] were not pleasant. When the officials arrived

46. CMS, XXX (1879), 30.
47. WCSL, XIV, 2b-3.
48. WSS, pp. 32-33, 78.
49. NCH, XXI, (1878), 132, 154.
50. *Christian Advocate,* LIII (1878), 693.
51. There are several accounts by missionaries, or reflecting the missionary point of view: that of Stewart, CMS, XXX (1879), 29-35; Wolfe's account, CMS, XXIX (1878), 760-62; that of the *Chinese Recorder,* X (1879), 155-58; the *Foochow Herald* version, reflecting the missionary point of view, was reprinted in NCH, XXI (1879), 269-71. Another important Western account is that of the American consul, De Lano, which was forwarded with Dispatch No.

at eleven in the morning they were followed, or accompanied, by a crowd of fifty or sixty people made up, according to the missionaries, not of near neighbors, with whom they got along very well, but of people whom they had not seen before, and who, presumably, had been hired by the hostile literati. The crowd not only entered the compound but began pushing into Stewart's house. The officials claimed to be helpless to do anything about the crowd, and when Wolfe tried to keep more people from entering, two or three of them struck him on the head and chest. Then the investigation of the disputed ground took place in the presence of "the howling mob and the angry gentry." The hostile gestures of the officials were said to have excited the mob, which became more and more violent, destroying property and pulling up trees and shrubs. The Chinese version was somewhat different. It, too, spoke of a crowd but indicated that the officials restrained it and persuaded it to leave so that the investigation could take place.[52]

The missionary and Chinese accounts also differ on the results of the investigation. Stewart reported that "the Mandarins seemed to be of the opinion that our right to the place was indisputable," and Wolfe added, "This rather upset them, and they were evidently much enraged."[53] Subsequently, however, the Chinese governor-general memorialized to Peking that "The site of the building definitely encroached. The missionary could not contradict this, but he said that the surrounding wall had been built a long time already, and how was it that it had not been objected to earlier."[54]

When the investigation was completed, the officials left, leaving a "Mr. Ho," who called himself a legal adviser to the Chinese government, to protect the missionaries from the mob, but Ho left about five minutes later,[55] and for several hours, as Stewart put it, "the missionaries had the mob all to themselves."[56] According to Wolfe, Ling (the *chu-jen,* Lin Ying-lin) "came several

---

61 of October 28, 1878, from the American Minister to the Secretary of State, *Foreign Relations of the United States,* 1879, pp. 183-89.

52. WCSL, XIV, 3, 11.
53. CMS, XXX (1879), 32; XXIX (1878), 761.
54. WCSL, XIV, 11.
55. NCH, XXI (1878), 269-70.
56. CMS, XXX (1879), 32.

times and excited the mob, and evidently did not seem pleased that they had abstained so long from mischief," but finally with the help of a few friendly Chinese and "by good humour and coaxing," the missionaries persuaded the larger part of the crowd to leave.[57]

Late in the afternoon, according to the missionary accounts,[58] the British consul, having heard of what had transpired, arrived on the scene. About this time the crowd reassembled, and Sinclair sent a request for protection to the governor-general. About six o'clock some mandarins arrived with forty unarmed soldiers, but not a hand was raised to arrest anyone, and Stewart claimed on unidentified "good authority" that the governor-general had told the mandarins to "Let the people do as they like."[59] The crowd then proceeded to wreck the new college building and an older building and then set fire to the college, which was largely destroyed. The mandarins made no effort to disperse the crowd, according to the missionaries, and the soldiers joined in the destruction which went on all night long.

The governor-general, Ho Ching, reported that the crowd was infuriated by Wolfe's insults and abuse and by the discovery that there were young Chinese women in one of the buildings in the compound. The crowd could not be stopped, but the Chinese officials managed to prevent the fire from spreading by having the soldiers remove the roof, doors, and windows of a nearby building. He acknowledged that the instigators and participants in the destruction had not been apprehended or arrested, claiming that this would have been impossible under the circumstances.[60] Subsequently Ting Jih-ch'ang memorialized that the officials present had not called a stop to the destruction or seized a single culprit.[61]

For some days after the events of the thirtieth it was not at all clear that violence had ended. Inflammatory placards, posted in the city, threatened further destruction of mission property. On the thirty-first Stewart agreed to Sinclair's suggestion that

57. CMS, XXIX (1878), 761.
58. See sources cited in note 51 above.
59. CMS, XXIX (1878), 761; XXX (1879), 32.
60. WCSL, XIV, 11-11b.
61. WCSL, XIV, 31.

Captain Namier of H.M.S. *Nassau,* which had arrived in the river below Foochow, be asked to provide a guard of "Blue Jackets." When it developed, however, that the river was too shallow to allow the *Nassau* to come up to Foochow to land the men, Captain Napier and the consul insisted that the governor-general put a Chinese guard around the mission premises and issue a proclamation forbidding further violence. He did so, apparently with some reluctance, and the threats in the placards were not carried out.[62]

Against the long background of resentment of the foreign presence on Wu-shih-shan, the unwillingness of the missionaries to accept Ting Jih-ch'ang's proposal for an exchange of properties and their decision to build the college were too much for the patience of the officials and literati in Foochow. It appears, however, that what happened on August 30 was not just an explosion but a desperate effort, led by the literati and not prevented by the officials, to obtain by violence what official negotiation had not achieved—the removal of the foreigners from Wu-shih-shan. The effort was successful, for a year after the incident the C.M.S. finally agreed to leave the disputed premises.

During the months immediately after the violence of August 30, however, it was not at all clear that the missionaries would have to leave. Not only the consul, Sinclair, but also the acting British Minister in Peking, and then the Minister himself, Thomas Wade, came to their defense,[63] and it would not have been at all surprising if the British government had demanded Chinese recognition of the mission's right to use the Wu-shih-shan property in the future as part of the settlement of the "outrage" of August 30.[64] At the very least, Chinese negotiations to bring about the withdrawal of the mission from Wu-shih-shan were now burdened with a whole new set of immediate issues. Had the Chinese mob's action been provoked by the wrong-doing and intransigence of the missionaries, or was it an "outrage" for which the Chinese should make reparation? What steps would the

62. CMS, XXX (1879), 33, 34; NCH, XXI (1878), 269-71.
63. WCSL, XIV, 6-7b; *Ch'ing-chi chiao-an shih-liao,* I, 98-104; NCH, XXI (1878), 474.
64. Chinese fears of such a development appear in the Chinese documents, WCSL, XIV, 15, 15b.

Chinese side have to take to prevent a recurrence of mob action? What reparation would have to be made? Would the Chinese participants in the events of August 30, including the literati, have to be punished?

From the point of view of Chinese officials, the situation was an alarming one.[65] The missionaries were more infuriated than frightened; believing that to give in at this time would be an admission that they had been in the wrong, they stood stubbornly on their claimed right to be on the hill.[66] On the other hand, the Chinese documents make it clear that there were limits to the actions which Chinese officials would dare to take in order to come to terms with the missionaries or the British government. They were caught in a most unenviable position in which it appeared that they could not satisfy the foreigners without offending the literati, or vice versa, and one of the big questions was whether they would be able to extricate themselves from their dilemma.[67] It is not surprising that the matter was taken up by high Chinese officials in Peking, that the advice of Li Hung-chang, governor-general of Chihli and commissioner of the Northern ports was sought,[68] and that the throne ordered Ting Jih-ch'ang, the official who had tried to bring about the exchange of properties in 1877, to return to Foochow to help settle the matter.[69]

That the situation did not result in a victory for the missionaries or in continued deadlock is largely explained by two important developments. The British government, while demanding redress, did not give strong support to the missionaries in their determination to stay on Wu-shih-shan and rebuild their college there. This attitude of the British government, in turn, made it possible to *separate* the settlement of the incident of August 30 from the more fundamental question of the continued use of Wu-shih-shan.[70]

65. This fact is apparent in many of the Chinese documents dated after August 30. See particularly the views of Li Hung-chang and Ting Jih-ch'ang in WCSL, XIV, 14b-15b, 28b-30.
66. See Stewart's letter dated July 31, 1879 in NCH, XXIII (1879), 163-64.
67. See particularly Ting Jih-ch'ang's December 5, 1878, memorial, WCSL, XIV, 28b-30.
68. WCSL, XIV, 2-6, 12-15b.
69. WCSL, XIV, 14b.
70. That this is what Ting Jih-ch'ang was hoping for is suggested in his memorial

So far as the incident itself was concerned, the British officials did not hesitate to take a strong stand. They condemned the mob action and insisted upon punishment of Chinese participants, compensation for the losses which the mission had sustained, and the issuing by the Chinese governor-general of a public proclamation condemning the mob action and prohibiting any recurrence of it.[71]

The Chinese compliance with these demands was not all that the British side hoped for. The payment of compensation to the missionaries for property loss and damage was not a serious problem,[72] but the Chinese officials were more inclined to find scapegoats than they were to round up the real instigators of the trouble.[73] Lesser Chinese officials were dismissed for having allowed the incident to happen.[74] In response to the demand that participants and instigators be punished, a few of the common people ("wretched coolies," said the *North China Herald*),[75] who may or may not have been guilty,[76] were arrested, tried, and punished.[77] But the Chinese officials were definitely worried about the reaction that might result from the arrest of any of the literati, especially Lin Ying-lin.[78] As late as February 7, 1879, there were reports that no action had been taken against Lin,[79] though a memorial of April 13, 1879, indicated that he would be prohibited from wearing the insignia of his rank for three years.[80] The proclamation issued by the governor-general, in response to British demand, condemned the burning of the college and

of December 5, 1878, WCSL, XIV, end of page 29b. The desirability of separating the issues arising from the incident from the question of long-term tenure is suggested in NCH, XXII (1879), 412.

71. WCSL, XIV, 6-7b; NCH, XXI (1878), 474.

72. WCSL, XIV, 11b, 15; XV, 14; *Chinese Recorder*, X, (1879), 392.

73. In one of his memorials Ting Jih-ch'ang made the point that if they could find someone to confess to being the instigator, then there would be no question that Lin Ying-lin was at fault. WCSL, XIV, 30b.

74. WCSL, XIV, 12.

75. NCH, XXII (1879), 118.

76. According to the *North China Herald* the arrest of innocent people infuriated the populace, and the Chinese officials defended themselves by blaming the British. NCH, XXI (1878), 568.

77. WCSL, XIV, 13, 13b; XV, 13b-14.

78. The problem of what to do with Lin Ying-lin runs through the Chinese documents; see, for example, WCSL, XIV, 12b, 13b, 14, 15, 30-31.

79. The *North China Herald* reported on numerous occasions that Lin and the "real culprits" had not been arrested, NCH, XXI (1878), 315, 495, 568, 591; XXII (1879), 118.

80. WCSL, XV, 14.

warned against further incidents but also scolded the missionaries for having usurped land which they had no right to use.[81] Although there was dissatisfaction with the Chinese performance, it was not great enough to cause the British government to take the strong measures that would have been necessary to get complete compliance with its demands.

What is especially significant, however, is that the British officials did not demand Chinese acquiescence in continuing mission use of Wu-shih-shan. In September the acting British Minister asked that uncertainties as to boundaries of the mission property should be investigated jointly by Chinese officials and the British consulate,[82] and before long it became evident that on the issue of continued use of Wu-shih-shan the British government was more interested in getting the matter settled in such a way as to prevent further difficulty than it was in giving strong support to the missionaries.[83]

In efforts to settle the question of continued use of Wu-shih-shan two main approaches were evident. One was quite Western, that of testing the mission's rights to the property through legal proceedings. The other, which would seem to have been more Chinese, was that of trying to bring about a mutually acceptable compromise through negotiation. Curiously enough, British officials took the lead in the unsuccessful efforts to negotiate and compromise, and the Chinese advocated the Western-style legal proceedings that finally paved the way for the removal of the mission from Wu-shih-shan.

The English Minister, Thomas Wade, who was in Foochow from March 22 until April 1, 1879, led the effort for compromise. Wade first suggested that the missionaries give up the idea of rebuilding the college on the old site and that in return for a long-term lease on the Wu-shih-shan property they agree to use it only as a place of residence, moving their schools and the college to the

81. English translation published in NCH, XXI (1878), 519.
82. WCSL, 14, 7-7b; NCH, XXI (1878), 474.
83. The missionaries complained at this lack of support from the British government, CMS, XXX (1879), 442-43. The American consul in Foochow, De Lano, commented that "unhappily the English Missionaries here do not receive the support and sympathy of their consul, and of this the crafty natives are ever ready to take advantage." Dispatch No. 248 of Oct. 20, 1879, from De Lano to Charles Payson, U. S. Archives, Foochow Papers, Vol. V.

suburb. The Chinese refused this proposal, arguing that continued foreign residence at Wu-shih-shan would make for future
trouble. There was also discussion of the possibility of exchanging the Wu-shih-shan property for a piece of ground in another
part of the city; but even though Wade thought the latter property was desirable—good enough, he said, to locate a consulate
there—the mission refused it on the grounds that it was unhealth-
ful. Wade also attempted to get agreement to a face-saving
arrangement resembling the exchange of Shen-kuang-szu for Tao-
shan-kuan in 1850; he suggested that the British consulate give
up its Wu-shih-shan premises and that the mission be allowed to
lease them in return for surrendering the disputed ground. Again
it was the mission that frustrated Wade's efforts.[84]

The Chinese were impressed with Wade's sincerity. They
seem to have been responsive to his suggestion that it would be
better to reach agreement by reconciling differences than to settle
the problem by judicial proceedings in which someone would
win and someone would lose. Ting Jih-ch'ang praised Wade's
efforts in memorials to Peking and reported that Wade was angry
with the missionaries for their unwillingness to compromise.[85]

After the failure of Wade's attempts at compromise, the Chinese decided to proceed with a suit against the mission
which they had been contemplating for some months. Wade
agreed that this was the only course that remained.[86] By this
time the missionaries and the British officials were so estranged
that the former objected to having Consul Sinclair hear the case,
and a Judge French had to be brought from Shanghai to Foochow to preside over the hearings.[87]

Several of the Chinese literati brought the suit, acting as
"directors of the Tao Shan Kuan temple"; technically the Chinese
officials were not parties. It appears, however, that the officials
were really the "prime movers."[88] The directors entered several
pleas, but the obvious purpose of the legal action was simply to

84. WCSL, XV, 15, 17b, 23b-24b; NCH, XXII (1879), 367; WSS, p. 34.
85. WCSL, XV, 15, 17-17b, 23b.
86. WCSL, XV, 17b.
87. Dispatch No. 121 of March 15, 1879, from Vice Consul F. D. Cheshire
to Chester Holcombe, Chargé d'Affaires, National Archives (in volume marked
"Legation Archives: Consular 1879, Amoy No. 284, Newchwang").
88. NCH, XXII (1879), 295.

prepare the way for eviction of the missionaries from Wu-shih-shan by establishing one of two claims: (1) that the agreements by which the mission rented the property were void or that the mission had forfeited its rights under them; or (2) that the terms of the agreements permitted the Chinese to terminate them.[89]

The proceedings, which ran from April 30 to May 10, 1879, attracted much attention and were published in full by the *Daily Press* of Hongkong.[90] The Chinese charged the mission with misuse of the property, with encroachment on land it had not rented, with having tried to make its tenure permanent by improper arrangements with temple priests and others. The most important witness in the trial was Wolfe. His testimony, which makes up a large part of the published proceedings, must have been disappointing to his friends and supporters. He seemed evasive, and he frequently denied recollection of matters at issue.[91]

Of the seven pleas of the plaintiffs only one was granted by the court in the decision given on July 18, 1879,[92] and this fact was taken by some as a basis for concluding that the judgment was in favor of the missionaries. The *Chinese Recorder* made the point that "so far as the charges that affected the character and integrity of the missionaries are concerned, the judgment is clear in their favor, and completely exonerates them from the aspersions that were so freely cast upon them." It pointed out that the Chinese had not been able to establish wrongful dealings; in particular, the court had not judged the missionaries guilty of encroaching on land they had not leased.[93]

For all practical purposes, however, the real victors were the Chinese. The crucial decision of the court had to do with a provision of the agreement of 1867 by which the Chinese had agreed not to rent the property to any other party as long as the missionaries continued to pay rent. The court ruled that this provision

89. WSS, *passim.*
90. See note 33 above. NCH, XXII (1879), 517, reported that officials were arranging publication of the proceedings in Chinese. See also NCH, XXII (1879), 439.
91. WSS, pp. 40-52.
92. WSS, pp. 74-80.
93. *Chinese Recorder*, X (1879), 310-13. See also NCH, XXIII (1879), 69, 70, 129.

did not prevent the directors of the temple from terminating the arrangement on three months' notice if the temple itself had *bona fide* need for the property.[94]

Subsequent events followed directly from the court's decision. The Chinese proceeded to exercise the right, established in the court's decision, to recover the disputed property. For a time the mission considered the possibility of appealing Judge French's decision, but it finally decided to leave Wu-shih-shan and to take a lease (on terms favorable to the mission) on the Telegraph Office property in the suburb. After two years of tension, violence, negotiation, and litigation, the mission now accepted precisely what it had refused in 1877.[95]

A quarter of a century had not sufficed to overcome Chinese hostility, especially that of the literati and officials, to missionary presence and activity on Wu-shih-shan. The pride of the Chinese in their own culture had remained strong, and the literati had remained unimpressed with both the religion of the missionaries and their insistence that the treaties gave them the right to acquire property, reside, and preach the gospel on Wu-shih-shan. They remained convinced that it was unreasonable for the missionaries to court violence and disorder—the opposite of the Confucian ideal of social harmony—by pressing their rights in the face of hostility. The missionaries, on the other hand, with their belief in their treaty rights and their conviction that they were doing the Lord's work, could see the Chinese plea for reasonableness as nothing less than a demand that they surrender their rights and endanger their calling.

The crucial element in this victory for the Chinese and defeat for the missionaries was the flexibility of both the Chinese and British officials, which was in marked contrast to the rigidity of the literati and the missionaries. The British officials were more receptive than the missionaries to the Chinese plea for reasonableness; while demanding satisfaction for the mob action of August, 1878, they were willing to work for compromise on the question of continued use of Wu-shih-shan. Then, when the

94. WSS, pp. 79-80.
95. *Chinese Recorder*, X (1879), 313, 392; NCH, XIII (1879), 179, 249, 295, 325; CMS, XXX (1879), 633-34, 739-42; XXXI (1880), 437-38.

missionaries refused to compromise in the spirit of Confucianism, the Chinese officials were agile enough to use Western judicial procedures, provided in the treaties, to achieve their ends, and the missionaries were finally undone by this Chinese appeal to a Western consular judge.

The missionaries' departure from Wu-shih-shan and their acceptance of the Telegraph Office premises removed a serious specific irritant in relations between the missionaries and the Chinese. But, important as the Wu-shih-shan issue had been, it cannot be concluded that its settlement amounted to a solution of the basic problem in Foochow. A continuing history of difficulty and incidents after 1879 shows that the gulf between the missionaries and the Chinese literati remained. The Wu-shih-shan issue was not as much a cause of trouble as it was a result and an important symbol of misunderstanding and antagonism.

A *Century of* War and Peace *(1863-1963)*

THEODORE ROPP

The Reader's Companion to World Literature suggests a "basic separation" of novels "into fantasy, love, and adventure," and possible variant or subclassifications of "epistolary, picaresque, Gothic, and Utopian, . . . Western, detective, and science-fiction, . . . phychological, stream-of-consciousness and even psychoanalytical, . . . religious, sociological, and 'escape,' . . . romantic, sentimental, realistic, naturalistic, and surrealistic."[1] War is not mentioned in this incomplete subject listing; "war books" have attracted little attention from literary historians. Yet war was to become the primary subject of the great novel which Leo Tolstoy began a hundred years ago and was to become an even more important literary subject in the half-century of violence from 1904 to 1954, the half-century after Tolstoy finished his last extensive literary work, *Hadji Murad*.[2] Pacifist as he had become, he was still fascinated by his earlier experience of war and with individuals' reactions to it.

This essay does not deal with Tolstoy's philosophy of history or with his imaginative reconstruction of its "seamless web" from numerous acutely observed individual incidents. These suggestions deal only with certain of Tolstoy's attitudes toward war, attitudes which can be seen in the reactions of many later authors in the era in which war was to play its most significant historic role. They may not be out of place in a work honoring a scholar whose "greatest gifts" lie in communicating "the ideas and the humane values" undergirding that "synoptic history" which "is the ultimate achievement of historians." They may help historians of that era or of what Carl von Clausewitz called the

1. Ed. Calvin S. Brown (New York, 1956), pp. 318-19.
2. Trans. Louise and Aylmer Maude (London, 1935).

"veritable chameleon" of war, to see "the relations of things to each other and separate the important from the trifling."[3]

Most war books may be classified as "realistic sociological adventure." They deal with a classic theme—the individual facing death and danger. But death and danger do not come from divine, but from social, forces. Tolstoy planned a novel of family life among the Russian gentry. War and his philosophy of history forced their way into his tale and utterly transformed it. For war provides the most dramatic examples of the conflicts between the two basic aspects of the life of Everyman: "the personal life, which is free in proportion as its interests are abstract, and the elemental life of the swarm, in which a man must inevitably follow the laws laid down for him."[4] In the century since Tolstoy began his work the internal social and political problems created by the Liberal and Industrial Revolutions were often handled without violence. The passions aroused by nationalism and heightened by war were less easily compromised. Clausewitz had accurately predicted this trend in the unfinished Book VIII of his own masterpiece, which was found among his papers after his death in 1831, three years after Tolstoy was born. "Since the time of Bonaparte," Clausewitz had commented, "war . . . has approached much nearer to its real nature [absolute violence]. . . . The cause was the participation of the people in this great affair of state." Because of this the bounds that statecraft had placed on war "are not easily built up again; . . . whenever great interests are in question, mutual hostility will discharge itself in the same manner as it has done in our time."[5]

The first significant feature of modern war books—their realistic depiction of combat—is related to the second—the "participation of the people." For the first time large numbers of literate men had been conscripted into, or had volunteered to serve in the ranks. The experiences of even greater numbers of such men in the wars of 1854 to 1954 were to be reflected in a growing realism in both professional military literature and in the

3. *On War*, trans. O. Matthjis Jolles (New York, 1943), p. 568.
4. *War and Peace*, trans. Constance Garnett (New York, n. d.), p. 570. This theme of the individual's struggle to keep his spirit alive and the absence of an explicit political viewpoint were responsible for Soviet official criticism of Victor Nekrasov's routine *Front-Line Stalingrad*, trans. David Floyd (London, 1962).
5. *On War*, pp. 583-84.

treatment of war in the visual arts. The destructiveness of these wars led, third, to the realization that war is the most dangerous of modern social evils, an idea which became the common coin of *Realpolitik* as early as 1954. By 1962 the United States Army's *Field Service Operations: Regulations* defined general war as "a specialized category of conflict, . . . when no other course offers a chance of attaining national objectives," and limited war as one in which "the essential objective . . . will be to terminate the conflict . . . in a manner best calculated to prevent its spread to general war."[6]   In 1951, a century after Tolstoy set out for his first war in the Caucasus, General of the Army Douglas Mac-Arthur stated flatly, "Sooner or later, if civilization is to survive, . . . war must go."[7]

"Realistic" description of a discontinuous social phenomenon such as war depends on the experiences of both author and public. In the relatively peaceful late nineteenth century adventure and costume dramas continued to dominate war literature. The increasing number of books by men in the ranks—many of them of the "as told to" variety, photography, and the careful observations of artists such as Frederic Remington or Vassili Verestchagin were used chiefly to add realistic detail, like that demanded by twentieth-century movie or television producers. Verestchagin alluded to this pseudo-realism in discussing the works of a French artist who used photographs to add authenticity to his commissioned paintings of one of the Zulu Wars. "The artist . . . turned out several lively pictures in which there are a great many men attacking; . . . much blood; much gunpowder-smoke; . . . Frenchmen dressed up in British uniforms, and instead of Zulus, the ordinary Parisian negro-models, reproduced in various more or less warlike attitudes."[8]   Realistic descriptions of combat are not

6. Headquarters, Department of the Army (Washington, 1962), pp. 6, 9.
7. U. S. Congress. Senate. Committee on Armed Services, *Military Situation in the Far East* (Washington, 1951), Part I, p. 149.
8."1812" *Napoleon in Russia*, intro. R. Whiteing (New York, 1899), p. 25. Cf. H. Eric Solomon, "Studies in Nineteenth Century War Fiction" (unpublished doctoral dissertation, Harvard University, 1958); Susanne Howe, *Novels of Empire* (New York, 1949); Charles Edmund Carrington, *The Life of Rudyard Kipling* (Garden City, 1955); J. M. S. Tompkins, *The Art of Rudyard Kipling* (London, 1959); Robert Speaight, *The Life of Hilaire Belloc* (London, 1957). There is no study of G. A. Henty, who served in the hospital commissariat in the Crimea and organized Italian hospitals in 1859 before becoming a full-time journalist and novelist.

light entertainment. C. S. Forester's Horatio Hornblower versions of Frederick Marryat's adventure novels have been more popular than his classic novel of the First World War,[9] and the pseudo-realism of Erich Maria Remarque's *All Quiet on the Western Front* was chiefly responsible for its acceptance abroad as *the* German classic of that same war.[10]

If violence is the essence of war, long-sustained violence is one precondition for an extensive realistic war literature. Even Napoleonic battles were relatively short and episodic. In Stendhal's famous description of Waterloo—from which Tolstoy later claimed that he had learned most about war[11]—battle had still been only the "culminating point" (another of Clausewitz's terms) of those alternating periods of tension and rest in the marches, voyages, fevers, hardships, and dangers that had been the soldier's lot since the dawn of history. In the classic rankers' accounts of the Peninsular War—or in lower-deck accounts of life in the close-packed wooden hells of sailing-ship warfare—combat is almost lost in a host of other details. And novels—or pseudo-scientific "projections" of the "reconstitution and recovery" phases—of a general nuclear war are surrealistic because of the similarly brief periods into which quite unimaginable violence may be concentrated.[12]

This essay deals only with the "realistic" treatment of war in the century in which it most clearly revealed its "nature." By this standard the most realistic war literature of the nineteenth century came out of the later Napoleonic, Crimean, American Civil, and Russo-Turkish Wars, and the fall and winter campaigns of 1870, in which large numbers of literate men were held in combat in conditions and over periods of time normally re-

---

Studies of the artists and photographers of the American Civil War lack general background. The pseudo-realistic combination of official nationalism and photography can be seen indirectly in so recent a work as Oskar Regele, *Feldzeugmeister Benedek. Der Weg nach Königgrätz* (Vienna, 1960).

9. *The General* (Boston, 1936). Cf. Christopher Lloyd, *Captain Marryat and the Old Navy* (London, 1939); Oliver Warner, *Captain Marryat, a Rediscovery* (London, 1953).

10. Trans. A. W. Wheeler (Boston, 1929).

11. *Paul Boyer chez Tolstoï* (Paris, 1950), p. 40.

12. Cf. Henry Curling (ed.), *The Recollections of Rifleman Harris* (London, 1929); B. H. Liddell Hart (ed.), *The Letters of Private Wheeler* (Boston, 1951); John Howell (ed.), *The Life and Adventures of John Nicol, Mariner* (New York, 1936).

garded as "insupportable" by eighteenth-century states and armies. For the same reasons the Russian campaigns in Asia against well-armed and tenacious "semi-civilized" opponents produced many of the most realistic accounts of colonial or guerrilla warfare.

Most military theorists of the period after 1871 convinced themselves and the public that the next great Continental European war would be comparatively short, like the Seven Weeks War of 1866 or the German campaign that had overthrown the Second French Empire. The greatest single surprise of the First World War—for professional and citizen soldiers alike—was to be its length. This was the shock that was to produce the greatest of all war literatures. The English poet Wilfred Owen's comment on Tennyson—so often unjustly cited as the nineteenth century's worst war poet—reveals this as the main source of his own realism. "Did he hear the moaning at the Bar . . . at dawn, noon, and night, eating and sleeping, walking and working? . . . Tennyson, it seems, was always a great child. So should I have been, but for Beaumont Hamel. (Not before January 1917 did I write the *only* lines of mine that carry the stamp of maturity.)"[13]

Owen was then twenty-five. What he, and many writers of his war, did not live to realize was that their work was to be added to a considerable body of realistic war literature, and that their experiences had been strikingly similar to those of Tolstoy between his twenty-third and twenty-seventh birthdays. Tolstoy had gone to the Caucasus to test himself. This traditional theme—war as a test of maturity—was the basis of his first war story, *The Raid*.[14] The new element, in a tale that applied Stendhal's realism to the romantic scenes of Pushkin and Lermontov, was the realism with which Tolstoy was beginning to treat fear in combat. "My state at the time of danger," he had written in his *Diary*, "opened my eyes. I loved to imagine myself [as one of Stendhal's heroes] entirely cold-blooded and calm in danger. But in the affair of the 17th and 18th [O. S., February,

13. *Poems,* ed., with memoir and notes, by Edmund Blunden (London, 1949), p. 26.
14. Trans. Andrew MacAndrew (New York, 1961).

1852, a shell had struck the wheel of the gun he was aiming] I was not so."[15]

The problem of fear in battle was not systematically examined until the middle of the nineteenth century. Ardant du Picq, seven years older than Tolstoy and another veteran of the Crimea, was to be the first professional soldier to try to find out what happens in battle to "the nervous, easily swayed, moved, troubled, distrait, excited, restless being . . . who is the fighting man from general to private." The Jominis—here he was substantially correct about the vast literature of the post-Napoleonic era—"speak . . . for the heads of states and armies, but they never show me . . . a battalion, a company, a squad in action." Du Picq's curiosity—he had sent a questionnaire to his fellow officers —seemed unmilitary. The articles and notes that eventually became his classic *Battle Studies* did not become influential until their publication six years after he died of wounds in 1870.[16] Klemens Meckel, the brilliant staff officer who headed the German military mission to Japan in 1885, was criticized for his realistic *Summer Night's Dream*, published anonymously in 1888.[17] And the two most famous and most imitated American war writers, Stephen Crane and Ernest Hemingway, never went beyond this theme of the individual's reactions to fear in combat.

The second element in Tolstoy's treatment of war is his defense of the ordinary fighting man against the massive incompetence of Russian society. This is the burden of *Sebastopol* and of his draft "Memorandum on the Negative Aspects of the Russian Soldier and Officer." "By virtue of my oath and still more because of my feeling for humanity, I cannot be silent about . . . the destruction of millions of people and of forces of worth and

15. Ernest J. Simmons, *Leo Tolstoy* (2 vols.; New York, 1946-1947, reprint 1960), I, 95.

16. Trans. John N. Greely, Robert C. Cotton (New York, 1921), pp. 40-41, 5-6. Edward S. Farrow, *Military Encyclopedia: A Dictionary of Military Knowledge* (2d ed., 3 vols.; New York, 1895) has no entry for morale. The key essays in William Trotter, *Instincts of the Herd in Peace and War* (2d ed.; London, 1919) date from 1908-1909.

17. Trans. Capt. Gayne (Kansas City, 1908). It was bound with the then anonymous classic by Ernest Swinton, *The Defence of Duffer's Drift* (London, 1904). Cf. Giuseppe Cesare Abba's realistic *Diary of One of Garibaldi's Thousand*, trans. E. R. Vincent (1880, London, 1962) and Fritz von Hoenig's critical and criticized *Untersuchungen über die Taktik der Zukunft* (Berlin, 1890).

honor to the fatherland."[18] The same spirit can be seen in Du Picq, in Edward Bruce Hamley's anonymous letters to *Blackwood's Magazine*, in his *War in the Crimea*,[19] and in the "lions led by donkeys" literature of the First World War. Their common theme is the fighting man's quarrel with the rear echelons: with inadequate training, poor equipment, corrupt and/or incompetent superiors, and a government and/or public that neglected him in peacetime and expected the impossible in war. This theme reflected the citizen army's need for more and better equipment and transport for more extensive and sustained operations—a need illustrated in the campaigns of both Napoleons—and the soldier's demand that he be treated as a citizen. Both were essential to Colmar von der Goltz's *Nation in Arms*. A belief that the next war would be short came to seem essential to the citizen's whole-hearted participation. "Experience in the short wars of our day . . . even works injuriously upon courage. . . . In the ranks 'veteranism' has lost its former significance. . . . Only the young . . . advance into battle with joy and lightheartedness."[20]

This essentially nationalistic theme was to become important in various nationalist movements, insofar as increased national strength would result from better leadership and economic and social reform. The explanation of the process by which the later Marshal Lyautey's anonymous *Du rôle social de l'officier,* of 1891,[21] led to the belief that only the army could reform France is an important task for historians. This is equally true of the process by which military "honor" came to be compatible with political assassination and, finally, random terrorism. The first victims were writers or artists who seemed to be weakening the state by destroying confidence in the army, and the tides of nationalist extremism might be traced by listing works that were suppressed or censored, or artists who were imprisoned, exiled, or murdered.

The Brazilian writer Euclides da Cunha was shot down by a soldier in 1909, when he was allegedly expanding *Rebellion in*

18. Simmons, *Tolstoy,* I, 124. *Sebastopol,* trans. Frank D. Millett, intro. Philip Rahv (Ann Arbor, 1961).
19. London, 1891. *The Story of the Campaign of Sebastopol* (Edinburgh, 1855).
20. Trans. Philip Ashworth (London, 1887), pp. 17-18.
21. Pref. General Juin (Paris, 1946).

the Backlands, published in 1902,[22] the only war book that can be compared with *War and Peace.* Da Cunha had resigned his army commission, but had accompanied the Saõ Paulo battalion as a newspaper correspondent on the expedition which put down the Canudos rising in 1896-1897. Like *War and Peace* and *Simplicius Simplicissimus,*[23] *Rebellion in the Backlands* eludes classification. Emile Zola's *The Debacle,* published in 1892, Stephen Crane's *The Red Badge of Courage,* which came out two years later, and Jules Romains's and Arnold Zweig's multi-volume epics of the First World War failed to meet these standards.[24] That war may have been too "enormous" for any single artist, or the prose epic may subtly lead to artistic overexpansion. The other volumes of Tolstoy's trilogy were never more than sketched in a literary career that extended for another forty years.

Tolstoy's final conviction that war was the greatest of all social evils may be even more important today than his later advocacy of non-resistance as the only weapon against it. Isaiah Berlin's conclusion that "Tolstoy's sense of reality was . . . too devastating to be compatible with any moral ideal which he was able to construct out of the fragments into which his intellect shivered the world" may be true only of that "desperate old man, beyond human aid,"[25] who died in the stationmaster's house at Astopovo. That Tolstoy may be less significant today than the soldier who convinced himself in 1855 that the expansion of Christianity had already made the world—and Tolstoy was a Westernizer in his view of other civilizations—more Christian than the official leaders of Christianity realized.

"This is the idea," he wrote in his *Diary* in terms which he repeated in a more analytical passage in *The Kingdom of God Is*

22. Trans., with introduction and notes, by Samuel Putnam (Chicago, 1944).
23. Christoffel von Grimmelshausen, *The Adventures of a Simpleton,* trans. Walter Wallich (London, 1962).
24. Cf., Helen LaRue Rufener, *Biography of a War Novel, Zola's La Débâcle* (New York, 1946); Rudolf Pfeiffer, *Les hommes de bonne volonté von Jules Romains: Individuum und Kollektiv im unamimistischen Roman* (Winterthur, 1958). *Men of Good Will* was translated in 14 volumes (New York, 1934-1946). *The Case of Sergeant Grischa,* trans. Eric Sutton (New York, 1926) is the best of Zweig's trilogy.
25. *The Hedgehog and the Fox: An Essay on Tolstoy's View of History* (New York, 1953), pp. 81-82. Cf. W. K. Hancock, *Four Studies of War and Peace in This Century* (Cambridge, 1961); Stephen King-Hall, *Power Politics in the Nuclear Age* (London, 1962).

within You thirty-eight years later, "the founding of a new religion corresponding to the development of mankind: the religion
of Christ, but purged of all dogma and mysteriousness, a practical religion, not promising future bliss but realizing bliss on
earth. . . . One generation will bequeath the idea to the next, and
some day fanaticism or reason will achieve it."[26] This does describe the Judeo-Christian-rationalist civic religion of contemporary Western civilization. A century later it is possible to hope
that it may triumph over the parochial nationalisms, liberalisms,
and socialisms with which historians of that century have been
concerned. The Hobbesian view of the great journalist C. E.
Montague, who had enlisted as a private at forty-seven and wrote
in 1922, "The party of order and decency . . . is really bluffing
a much larger party of egoism and greed that would bully and
grab if it dared,"[27] turned out to have been wrong at least for
the next generation.

This approach demands a reinterpretation of the literature
and art of the First World War to reveal the strength that this
"practical religion" drew from that experience and to see the
period between the World Wars as a Long Armistice in which
"the party of order and decency" was only temporarily defeated.
The generation of the First War may be too close to that tragedy
to see its significance. Even the sensitive historical novelist Bryher takes too parochial a view. "The English took the First
World War far more deeply and seriously than they did the
Second. . . . There was more fluidity in 1939. People knew what
to expect and took it as a necessary evil, like going to school.
The real British revolution took place on August 4, 1914, and
none of the survivors have got over it."[28] No people had prepared
for total war. The strength of the Tolstoyan majority over the

26. Simmons, *Tolstoy,* I, 126. After "eighteen centuries . . . every man of
our world recognizes . . . the law of Christ. Some . . . consider that salvation
will come [with] . . . the second advent. . . . Others, . . . through the Church.
. . . Others, . . . [by] progress . . . [to] freedom, equality, and fraternity. . . . A
fourth section, . . . when through a violent revolution men are compelled to
adopt community of possessions, absence of governments, and collective . . .
industry—that is, by the materialization of one side of the Christian teaching."
The Kingdom of God and Peace Essays, trans. and intro. by Aylmer Maude (London, 1936), pp. 236-37.
27. *Disenchantment* (London, 1922), p. 17.
28. *The Heart to Artemis: A Writer's Memoirs* (New York, 1962), p. 165.

next forty years could be the only realistic interpretation of what is properly named the "Resistance" and of a movement for unity that no longer depends on the aging veterans of the First World War.

The task of rescuing Tolstoy from the Tolstoyans involves a similar reinterpretation of Ivan S. Bloch's *The Future of War in Its Technical, Economic, and Political Relations,* published in 1898.[29] This work is a landmark in both military and pacifist literature, but its arguments rested on theories derived from the short European wars of 1859 to 1871. Nobody foresaw the courage with which citizen soldiers would face the *Storm of Steel* from rapid-fire weapons as "terrible in effect" as they were "simple in manipulation,"[30] or with which other citizens would endure invasion, blockade, bombardment, and quite unimaginable atrocities. Bloch's vision of the revolutions that would follow a military stalemate and a general financial collapse was limited to Verestchagin's fear of "a downright religion of despair."[31] Nobody could be expected to see the special role of the veteran after a long war between nations in arms or the resilience that its very length would give these nations. As William James told the American Philosophical Association in 1906, psychologists had no "topography of the limits" of "The Energies of Men," or of those "various keys for unlocking them in diverse individuals, [which] dominate the whole problem of individual and national education."[32]

The public was then less impressed by Verestchagin's realistic "All Quiet at Shipka" than by his allegorical "Apotheosis of War," with its pyramid of skulls and flock of carrion crows. Though Bertha von Suttner was shocked when Verestchagin admitted that war could be like hunting " 'uncommonly large game,' "[33] the integrity that led him to his death in the Russo-Japanese War

29. Trans. of Vol. VI of the original by R. C. Long (New York, 1899).
30. Ernst Jünger, trans. Basil Creighton, intro. R. H. Mottram (New York, 1927). Mottram's classic was *The Spanish Farm Trilogy* (London, 1929). The quotation is from Colmar von der Goltz, *The Conduct of War,* trans. G. F. Leverson (London, 1908), p. 190.
31. "*1812,*" pp. 40-41.
32. *Essays on Faith and Morals,* ed. Ralph Barton Perry (New York, 1949), p. 236.
33. *Memoirs of Bertha von Suttner: The Records of an Eventful Life* (2 vols.; Boston, 1910), II, 14.

made him considerably more than a "highly gifted stage manager."[34] He was one of the few artists of this period who could claim that he painted war "exactly as I have seen it."[35] Few Tolstoyans could admit, with Tolstoy, that men could be fascinated by war, or the force of William James's analysis in *The Moral Equivalent of War,* published in 1910, the year in which both men died. "Showing war's irrationality and horror is of no effect. . . . The horrors," at least when they are only vicariously experienced, "make the fascination. War . . . is life *in extremis.*"[36]

Bloch gave his fortune to an anti-war museum of modern weapons. Two years before he died, Bryher's parents took her to the Paris Exhibition of 1900. "We turned into . . . Krupp's exhibit of long, burnished guns. My mother hurried me out. My father explained that it was wrong to spend money and labor upon tools of war, . . . but nothing in the Exhibition interested me more, . . . the normal reaction of any child toward the models, say, in a science museum."[37] None of the Tolstoyans sensed this or the closely related appeal of war as a kind of bloody chess. Both these old themes became more pronounced with the Industrial Revolution and the possibility and necessity of more detailed war planning, though novels or memoirs of omniscient commanders or staff officers sold better after 1871 and 1945 than after 1918. While Tolstoy's theory of history is a massive protest against the Napoleonic "cult of personality," the intellectual appeal of military "science" is still strikingly evident. William James's "moral equivalent of war" included the "intellectual refinement . . . [of] the sciences of production" as one challenge to which "we must still subject ourselves collectively, . . . unless, indeed, we wish . . . to invite attack whenever a . . . military-minded enterprise gets formed."[38]

34. Christian Brinton, "Introduction," in Alexandre Benois, *The Russian School of Painting* (New York, 1916), p. 131.
35. "*1812,*" p. 32. The realism of the professional literature on which Bloch based some of his conclusions came from two wars—Crimean and Russo-Turkish —which were most like the First World War. Cf. Alexander V. Verestchagin, *At Home and in War, 1853-1881: Reminiscences and Anecdotes,* trans. Isabel F. Hapgood (New York, 1888). Another brother, Sergei, was killed at Plevna.
36. *Essays on Faith and Morals,* p. 312.
37. *The Heart to Artemis,* p. 25.
38. *Essays on Faith and Morals,* p. 323. A familiar example of computer war-

The literature of the First World War was surveyed in two books published in 1930. Twenty-four years later Edmund Blunden correctly called Cyril Falls's *War Books, A Critical Guide,* "one of the most remarkable displays of precise criticism in our day." Captain Falls, who was then working on the British official history, had participated in "the real war," that tremendous siege that had been the "peculiar" military event of a "period that cannot recur."[39] *Armageddon: The World War in Literature,* a sensitive anthology by the American writer Eugene W. Löhrke, defined war books more narrowly.[40] These two books and Blunden's pamphlet, *War Poets,* published in 1958,[41] provide the essential "synoptic" framework for any large-scale study of twentieth-century war literature.

The parallels between these works and those of Tolstoy are apparently unconscious. The first problem, Blunden feels, "was primarily one of reporting" combat. Next came the realization "that freedom has been eclipsed, and that men have become mechanisms knowing that they are mechanisms."[42] The final stage was Wilfred Owen's attempt to universalize the sacrifices of men in "the swarm" by reaching out to the enemy. In his unfinished "Strange Meeting," Owen rejected "I was a German conscript, and your friend" and "I am the German whom you killed, my friend," for the Tolstoyan "I am the enemy you killed, my friend."[43] If few writers reached this stage at that time, few young men, in Blunden's words, had Owen's "profound interest in the great subjects of the world's destiny."[44] Another critic thinks that Owen and Siegfried Sassoon, who had so influenced him, were "more read than any others by practising [English] poets" during the Second World War. Owen "created the terms within which the despair, the common understanding, the nerv-

---

gaming literature is Herman Kahn, *On Thermonuclear War* (Princeton, 1960). It is science-fiction, not science.

39. "Douglas Grant's War Book," *The Times Literary Supplement* (cited hereinafter as *T.L.S.*), Aug. 6, 1954, p. iii. Blunden's classic is *Undertones of War* (London, 1928).

40. New York. William K. Pfeiler, *War and the German Mind: The Testimony of Men of Fiction Who Fought at the Front* (New York, 1941), is good, but dated, and attempts no international comparisons.

41. *Writers and Their Work* (London).

42. *Ibid.*, p. 27.

43. *Poems*, p. 126. The loaded word "conscript" also vanished.

44. *War Poets*, p. 36.

ous excitement and the occasional peace of the ordinary soldier could be most naturally expressed"[45]

Before he returned to France for the offensive in which he was killed a week before the Armistice, Owen began a Preface and listed *"Motives"* of that *"outcry"* that sums up realistic war literature. "This book is not about heroes. . . . Nor is it about deeds, or lands, nor anything about glory, honour, might, majesty, dominion, or power, except War. . . . All a poet can do to-day is warn. That is why the true Poets must be truthful." His motives included: "How the future will forget the dead in war. The unnaturalness of weapons. Madness. Heroic Lies. Inhumanity of war. Indifference at Home." These were grouped under *"Protest."* *"Description,* Grief, Foolishness of War, The Soul of Soldiers" were grouped under "Philosophy."[46]

War and Peace was published between 1867 and 1869. The First World War was the half-way mark of that novel's century. The time is surely ripe for reconsidering a body of literature that is now substantially complete, a fact underlined by the deaths of Ernest Hemingway, William Faulkner, and E. E. Cummings, to mention American writers only. Henry Williamson, who was only nineteen when he fought on the Somme, has moved into the postwar era in his Philip Maddison series.[47] Critics are recognizing the effects on such disparate writers as Ezra Pound, T. S. Eliot, and D. H. Lawrence of their failure to participate in the greatest experience of their generation.[48] The current rash of First World War costume dramas may indicate no more than American Civil and Second World War market saturation and the futility of pretending to think about the "unthinkable." These works are balanced by more serious historical and artistic studies

45. "Wilfred Owen against the Background of Two Wars," *T.L.S.*, August 28, 1953, p. xxvii.
46. *Poems*, pp. 40-41.
47. His best war book is *The Wet Flanders Plain* (London, 1929). After a Second Great War the anti-militarism of *The Patriot's Progress* (London, 1930) gave way to the poignant *Love and the Loveless* (London, 1958). His epic is merging into those of the Long Armistice, such as that begun by Richard Hughes in *The Fox in the Attic* (New York, 1962).
48. They "wrote, from the start, as . . . sifters, collectors, absorbers of other men's experiences." "Wilfred Owen against the Background of Two Wars." Cf., Harry T. Moore (ed.), *The Collected Letters of D. H. Lawrence* (2 vols.; New York, 1962).

and reprints that show a renewed interest in the First World War as a turning point in the history of Western civilization.[49]

The literature of the Second World War is thin and derivative. One cannot be more naked and more dead. Theodor Plievier and C. S. Forester, who dealt with both wars, show little development.[50] John W. Aldrich's "What Became of Our Postwar Hopes?" does not ask whether "the classic war novels" of the Second War had anything new to say, except to an American public that had read few of the European classics of the First War, or why Bill Mauldin, one of the few "untutored" observers of the Second War, was also one of the best.[51] The best books on this war and its aftermath deal with subjects that were barely explored for the First War: naval and aerial combat, the sufferings of the civilian populations, the relations of conqueror and conquered, and guerrilla warfare—another aspect of those relations. Some of these works—the most important deal with the long and bitter French wars in Indochina and Algeria—may survive.[52]

The greatest single work of the Second World War comes from one of the greatest writers of the First War, Ernst Jünger. His diary, *Strahlungen,* completes a "journey of the soul" that began with the realistic observation of combat, through a nationalism that made him one of the intellectual heroes of National Socialism, to a final position like that of Tolstoy and Owen.[53]

49. More of Jaroslav Hasek may soon be translated. *The Good Soldier: Schweik,* trans. Paul Selver (Garden City, 1930; London, 1951) is heavily cut. Significant reprints were Lawrence Stallings (ed.), *The First World War: A Photographic History* (New York, 1933, 1962), and David Jones, *In Parenthesis* (London, 1937; New York, 1962).

Romain Rolland, *Journal des années de guerre 1914-1919; notes et documents pour servir à l'histoire morale de l'Europe de ce temps* (Paris, 1952) is a key source. For various war artists see the lead review articles, *T.L.S.,* July 29, 1960, pp. 473-75; June 9, 1961, pp. 349-50; Feb. 23, 1962, pp. 113-15.

50. Plievier's best war book is still *Des Kaisers Kulis: Roman der deutscher Kriegsflotte* (Berlin, 1929).

51. *The New York Times Book Review,* July 29, 1962, pp. 1, 24.

52. Cf. Kelley F. Cook (ed.), *The Literature of Flight: A Selective Annotated Bibliography of Works on Aviation, 1903-1961* (U. S. Air Force Academy, 1961). On guerrilla warfare three of the best English works are Lindsay Rogers, *Guerilla Surgeon* (London, 1957); Arthur Campbell, *Jungle Green* (London, 1953); and, for atmosphere, Lawrence Durrell, *Bitter Lemons* (New York, 1957). Outstanding French works are Nguyen Tien Lang, *Les Chemins de la révolte* (Paris, 1955), and François Denoyer, *4 ans de guerre en Algérie: lettres d'un jeune officier* (Paris, 1962). Jean Lartéguy, *The Centurions,* trans. Xan Fielding (New York, 1962) watered down the title from *Les Prétoriens* (Paris, 1961).

53. Tübingen, 1949. Joseph Peter Stern, *Ernst Jünger* (Cambridge, 1953)

War literature may have no future in an era in which all civilized men realize the "insupportability," another of Owen's terms, of total war. But its historical development will continue to be highly significant for critics who hope to illuminate the life of this century and for historians who respect the intellectual integrity and boldness of that historian to whom these studies are presented.

---

is less pretentious than Christian von Krockow, *Die Entsheidung: eine Untersuchung über Ernst Jünger, Carl Schmitt, Martin Heidegger* (Stuttgart, 1958).

Two Centuries of American Interest in Turkey*

SYDNEY NETTLETON FISHER

At the Casablanca Conference in January, 1943, President Roosevelt agreed that Prime Minister Churchill should "play the Turkish hand" for the United States.[1] Four years later, President Truman, in a historic address to the Congress, requested the outlay of a considerable sum to assist the people of Turkey, in addition to those of Greece, "to work out their own destiny in their own way." This apparent about-face on the part of President Truman was believed by most Americans to be such a startling departure that considerable discussion was inevitable.

Much emphasis was given to the Soviet bid for a share in the defense of the Turkish Straits[2] and to Great Britain's inability to bolster Turkey's resistance to Soviet pressures. Indeed, so much stress was placed upon these points that it commonly came to be said that America was the heir of Great Britain in Turkey. This idea became accepted rapidly in official circles, and an Assistant Secretary of State, in discussing this point, said, "I assume that there is not much question as to United States 'heritage of responsibilities in Turkey.' "[3]

* The basis of this essay was a paper, "One Hundred and Seventy-five Years of American Interest in Turkey," read at Boston in December, 1949, at a meeting of the American Historical Association. The author's first interest in this topic came from reading E. D. G. Prime, *Forty Years in the Turkish Empire; or Memoirs of Rev. William Goodell, D.D., Late Missionary of the A. B. C. F. M. at Constantinople* (New York, 1876), which Professor Artz gave him in 1932. Since 1949 the paper has been brought up to date and considerably recast. For some of these changes the author is indebted to the Social Science Research Council for a grant which enabled him to live and travel in Turkey in 1958-1959 and to four graduate students: Keith E. Wagner, Louie Jean Haythorne, Lysle E. Meyer, and James T. Doyle.

1. Cordell Hull, *The Memoirs of Cordell Hull* (New York, 1948), II, 1365-68.
2. Harry N. Howard, *The Problem of The Turkish Straits,* Department of State Publications No. 2752 (Washington, 1947).
3. Letter of George C. McGhee to the author, Washington, D. C., July 29, 1949.

Britain's fear of having her routes to the East disastrously impaired by Russian control of Istanbul and the Straits was the usual cliché advanced to epitomize the so-called Eastern Question of the century and a quarter between the French and the Bolshevik revolutions. Resistance to Russian advance southward was an important underlying factor in the Convention of the Straits in 1841, the Crimean War, the Congress of Berlin, and numerous other diplomatic excursions that have been alternately the joy and the bane of diplomats and historians. In this aspect of the Question, the United States in recent years has taken over the major responsibility and burden from Great Britain, even though Britishers long resident in Istanbul were reluctant to admit the change as permanent and sought to "save face" by referring to America as having grown to be Great Britain's "big brother."[4]

In large measure, however, the British policy to contain Tsarist and Bolshevik Russia had been pursued because of British interests within Turkey. Englishmen were concerned with commerce, finance, shipping, politics, communications, railways, industry, mines, religion, archaeology, ancient history, and even education. From Napoleonic times until 1947, except for momentary lapses such as in the Treaty of Sèvres in 1920 and the period immediately following the First World War, British policy contrived to secure these interests by maintaining an independent and friendly Turkish state and by assuring Turkish control of the Straits.[5] It was a similar and parallel policy that President Truman advocated in his address to the Congress on March 12, 1947. In many ways this was only an official pronouncement of a policy that had been advanced by private American citizens since the eighteenth century.[6] Wendell Willkie recognized this on his world tour in 1942 when he found in Turkey a great reservoir of good will toward the American people—a reservoir, as he described it, that had been filled by countless individual Americans

4. Many letters to the author from British residents of Istanbul, written in the period from 1947 to the mid-1950's.

5. The most recent study of this can be found in J. C. Hurewitz, "Russia and the Turkish Straits: A Revaluation of the Origins of the Problem," *World Politics*, XIV (1962), 605-32.

6. Harry N. Howard, "The United States and the Problem of the Turkish Straits: The Foundations of American Policy (1830-1914)," *Balkan Studies* (Thessalonika, Greece), III, No. 1 (Spring, 1962), 1-28.

"who had no other purpose than to make the whole world richer by fighting against superstition and ignorance in one part of it." He felt that America had "some reason for special pride" in the remarkable development of modern Turkey.[7]

The first interest of Americans in Turkey is not recorded, but at the outbreak of the Revolution Boston already was the colonial center for Turkish products. The first expression of official interest was the Second Continental Congress' listing of the Ottoman Empire in 1776 as one of the nations with which its commissioners might negotiate. In 1786 John Adams discussed with the French Foreign Minister, Vergennes, the idea of a mission to the Porte. When the French Minister informed him of the cost of presents necessary for such an approach, Adams decided no treaty could be worth that much. Later, in 1799, President Adams appointed the American Minister to Portugal, William Smith, as Envoy Extraordinary and Minister Plenipotentiary to the Ottoman Empire. Confirmed by the Senate, Smith received no instructions to go to Istanbul, and his mission was abandoned when news of the French invasion of Egypt arrived.[8]

Meanwhile, American merchants were busily cultivating an interest in Turkey, an area previously denied to them as colonial merchants under the British Navigation Acts. During the Revolution William Lee Perkins, a merchant of Boston, became established in Izmir, and after the war the new Stars and Stripes was a common sight in that harbor. The opium trade from Izmir to Canton was most lucrative, and in some years more than half of the Turkish opium was carried in American ships. The *Grand Turk,* built in Salem in 1782, frequently made the port of Izmir to load gum arabic, carpets, figs, tragacanth, raisins, scammony, and filberts, along with the opium. Sometimes on the return Mocha coffee was sold in Izmir at a profit of 400 per cent. No wonder, when the moral issue of carrying opium to China was raised in Boston or Salem, that many New Englanders advanced the argument that opium was no more harmful to the Chinese than rum was to the Yankees.[9]

7. Wendell Willkie, *One World* (New York, 1943), p. 41.
8. Charles Oscar Paullin, *Diplomatic Negotiations of American Naval Officers, 1778-1883* (Baltimore, 1912), pp. 127-29.
9. Samuel Eliot Morison, "Forcing the Dardanelles in 1810, with Some Ac-

During the Napoleonic wars American traders enjoyed a profitable trade in Turkey. Twenty-four American ships called at Izmir in 1809, and in some years American ships discharged there as much as a million dollars worth of cargo, though little of it was of American origin. The first American ship to call at Istanbul was a man-of-war, the *George Washington,* under the command of Captain William Bainbridge. Arriving in 1800 at Algiers with the annual tribute for the Dey, one of the so-called Barbary pirates, Captain Bainbridge was compelled to carry the Dey's presents to the Sultan. He ran the blockade of the Dardanelles without permission and approached Istanbul on November 9, 1800. When the Porte denied any knowledge of his flag or the United States, Bainbridge reported his ship belonged to the new world that Columbus had discovered. After delivering his cargo and undertaking several excursions in the Straits area, Bainbridge sailed for Algiers on December 30.[10]

The first trader to drop anchor in the Golden Horn, the *Telemachus* of Salem, arrived in 1809 with a cargo of spices, sugar, coffee, frankincense, and myrrh. Since the United States had no commercial treaty with the Ottoman Empire, American ships flew the Union Jack in Turkish waters and traded under the conventions of the British Levant Company. With the Straits closed to British ships in 1810, the *America,* out of Salem, " 'painted exactly like a frigate of twenty guns' with pennant flying at the main and all the parade of a man-of-war," forced the Dardanelles and reached Istanbul with a valuable cargo of sugar, tea, gum arabic, ginger, pepper, indigo, rhubarb, cotton, logwood, frankincense, and myrrh.[11] The Porte was incensed with this act and was quieted only by the willingness of the *America's* companion, the *Calumet* from Boston, to proceed to Odessa for a load of wheat (Istanbul was in very short supply) and thus incidentally to be the first American ship in the Black Sea. Eventually the *America* left to take on a cargo at Izmir, and the *Calumet* sailed with a cargo of sailcloth, cordage, and opium.

---

count of the Early Levant Trade of Massachusetts," *New England Quarterly,* I (1928), 208-25.

10. John Frost, *Lives of the Commodores of the U. S. Navy* (New York, 1843), pp. 364-67; Paullin, *Diplomatic Negotiations,* p. 130.

11. Morison, "Forcing the Dardanelles," pp. 214-20.

The embarrassment of this incident, coupled with the establishment in Izmir of the American trading firm of Woodmas and Offley, led the British Levant Company to terminate the arrangement of extending company privileges to American ships. Duties on goods in American holds suddenly doubled. In 1811, however, David Offley obtained a grant from the Porte for American traders to become "guests of the Sultan" and thus to have the right to import goods on the basis of the tariff schedule accorded to the French.[12] Offley became the first American consul resident in Turkey when he was accepted by the local authorities in 1824.

The profits in the trade with Turkey were so great that they neutralized some of the American sympathy for the Greeks during their Revolution. Four leading Boston merchants refused to serve on the Committee for Greek Relief for fear it would hurt their interests in Izmir, and in commercial circles there was much criticism of Daniel Webster's anti-Turkish speeches. Henry Clay, speaking in the House of Representatives on behalf of the Greeks, said, "A wretched invoice of figs and opium has been spread before us to repress our sensibilities and eradicate our humanity."[13]

In addition to trade there were other indications of interest in Turkey in the early decades of the nineteenth century. The largest privateer out of Salem during the War of 1812 was the *Grand Turk,* and other ships, such as the *Smyrna,* the *Smyriote,* and the *Osmanli,* attest to the appeal of Turkey to the seafaring men of New England. Moreover, after the disappearance of William Morgan of anti-Masonic fame in 1826, New England sea captains reported having talked to him in Izmir, where he supposedly lived and dressed like a native. The first American missionaries to go to the Turkish part of the Ottoman Empire were the Reverend Levi Parsons and the Reverend Pliny Fisk. They went to Izmir but soon left for Jerusalem. The first continuous mission was established when the Reverend William Goodell arrived in Istanbul in 1831.[14]

These varied interests induced President Monroe in 1820 to consider establishing diplomatic relations with the Porte. Some kind of a treaty or convention would be necessary. To this end,

12. *Ibid.,* pp. 211, 221-23.
13. *Ibid.,* p. 224.
14. Prime, *Forty Years,* p. 112.

Luther Bradish "visited" Istanbul in 1820-1821; George B. English and Commodore John Rodgers tried in the years 1823-1825; and David Offley and Commodore William M. Crane negotiated in vain in 1827-1828. Again, in 1829 President Jackson authorized Charles Rhind, David Offley, and Commodore James Biddle to try their hands at concluding a treaty with the Ottoman Empire. Largely the result of Rhind's work, a Treaty of Commerce and Navigation was signed on May 7, 1830. The difficulties had been over the tariff rates to be levied on American merchandise, adverse pressure by Great Britain upon the Porte, and the exorbitant fees demanded by Turkish officials. The treaty as finally drawn granted American goods and nationals "most favored nation treatment," including extraterritorial rights as defined in "Capitulatory Treaties" with France and Great Britain. The Sultan had insisted upon a secret article in the treaty to give him the privilege of obtaining naval timbers and stores in America and assistance in the designing and building of naval ships in American yards.[15] The Senate refused to accept this secret article, but the remainder of the treaty was approved, and Commodore David Porter was sent to Istanbul to ratify it. This was accomplished on October 5, 1831, and Porter remained there first as chargé d'affaires and then as Minister until his death in 1843.[16] By 1831, therefore, the main pattern of American interest in Turkey in the nineteenth century had been drawn. Commerce and missionary activity had become dominant; politics and diplomacy were relatively unimportant.

Within a decade after the arrival of the Reverend Mr. Goodell the work of the mission had expanded greatly. The station in

15. Probably the first published version and public translation of the secret article appeared in An American [James E. DeKay], *Sketches of Turkey in 1831 and 1832* (New York, 1833), pp. 294-95.

16. *Executive Documents, Printed by Order of the House of Representatives at the First Session of the Twenty-Second Congress, Begun and Held at the City of Washington, December 7, 1831; and in the Fifty-Sixth Year of the Independence of the United States*, Vol. VI, Doc. No. 250, pp. 3-94; U. S. Department of State, *Treaties and Conventions Concluded between the United States of America and Other Powers since July 4, 1776* (Washington, 1889), pp. 798-800; J. C. Hurewitz, *Diplomacy in the Near and Middle East: A Documentary Record: 1535-1914* (Princeton, 1956), I, 102-105; Paullin, *Diplomatic Negotiations*, pp. 132-51; An American [David Porter], *Constantinople and Its Environs, in a Series of Letters, Exhibiting the Actual State of the Manners, Customs, and Habits of the Turks, Armenians, Jews, and Greeks, as Modified by the Policy of Sultan Mahmoud* (New York, 1835), I, 43-53.

Izmir was re-established and new ones founded in Bursa, Trabizon, and Erzerum. Soon Goodell was joined by H. G. O. Dwight, William G. Schauffler, Cyrus Hamlin, Dr. Elias Riggs, Herman N. Barnum, and many others; mission stations spread across Anatolia so that by 1869 there were twenty-one major stations served by forty-six American missionaries.[17] Apostasy in Turkey was punishable by death until 1844, but the Ottoman government generally had been moved only when a Muslim converted to Christianity. Therefore, to the consternation of many pious American churchmen, their missionaries worked almost exclusively with the Armenian population. The Russian ambassador kidnaped the missionaries' Armenian teacher and frankly told the Americans that his master, the Tsar of Russia, would never allow Protestantism to set foot in Turkey. Hamlin indignantly replied, "Your excellency, the kingdom of Christ, who is my master, will never ask the emperor of all the Russias where it may set its foot!"[18]

In 1840 Hamlin started a seminary in Bebek, one of Istanbul's suburbs, and within a few years achieved great success. The work of the Americans, however, was never easy, and especially after 1864 the actions of the Ottoman government were such as to place the missions in a state of continuous jeopardy. Nevertheless, the stations and substations, schools, and hospitals numbered about three hundred by 1914. Success among the Armenians led their Patriarch in 1846 to anathematize those succumbing to the Protestant doctrine, an action which expelled those Armenians from their *millet*[19] and canceled their legal rights. The Armenian Evangelical Church became a political necessity and, urged by Sir Stratford Canning, Grand Vizir Rashid

17. Leland James Gordon, *American Relations with Turkey, 1830-1930: An Economic Interpretation* (Philadelphia, 1932), pp. 221-27; James L. Barton, *Daybreak in Turkey* (Boston, 1908), pp. 119-78.
18. Cyrus Hamlin, *Among The Turks* (New York, 1878), p. 34.
19. *Millet* is an Arabic word meaning "nation." It came to be used almost exclusively for identifying religious groups or communities in the Ottoman Empire. Between 1453 and 1914 the Sultan officially recognized the existence of more than a dozen *millets*, each of which had a position of semi-independence within the Empire. There is an extensive literature on the subject; see Sir Harry Luke, *The Old Turkey and the New: From Byzantium to Ankara* (London, 1955), pp. 66-101; Geoffrey Lewis, *Turkey* (New York, 1955), pp. 22-24; Bernard Lewis, *The Emergence of Modern Turkey* (London, 1961), pp. 328-30.

issued a charter to it in 1847; Abdul Mejid gave *millet* status to it in 1850.[20]

Schools became an important part of the mission work, but in 1856 a faction within the A.B.C.F.M. opposed to educational missions gained control. Hamlin left the mission and started an independent college, made possible in 1860 by the philanthropy of Christopher Robert of New York. Turkey did not object to such a college, but Jesuit missionaries and the Orthodox Patriarchs did; consequently, the Porte promised the French and Russian ambassadors that permission would never be given to Hamlin to build on the commanding site overlooking the Bosphorus at Rumeli Hisar, land Hamlin had purchased from Ahmet Vefik Pasha, Ottoman Ambassador in Paris. J. P. Morgan asked Secretary Seward to instruct Minister Morris to act on Hamlin's behalf, but the Grand Vizir gave vague replies. Opening in 1863 in Bebek instead of at Rumeli Hisar, Robert College was formally incorporated by the legislature of the State of New York in 1864. In 1868 Admiral Farragut visited Istanbul and upon Hamlin's suggestion asked every Ottoman official who feted him why permission had not been given to build Robert College at Rumeli Hisar. Farragut's question produced a flurry in Turkish government circles. Fearing American naval intervention in Crete and seeing some connection between Farragut's visit and the fact that Dr. Hamlin's cousin had only recently been vice-president of the United States, the Sultan issued a rescript to the American Legation granting permission to build on the desired spot. It soon became a successful undertaking, and by 1914 Constantinople Woman's College and International College, just outside Izmir, had become highly respected independent institutions in Turkey.[21]

The missions and the colleges were the result of very real American interest in Turkey. Money was collected from every Congregational Church to support the missions, and endowment for the colleges came from many sources. Missionaries and representatives of the college traveled throughout the United States

20. Prime, *Forty Years*, pp. 483-85.
21. Cyrus Hamlin, *My Life and Times* (Boston, 1893), pp. 195-97, 205 ff.; *The Nation*, XXVI (1878), p. 170; George Washburn, *Fifty Years in Constantinople and Recollections of Robert College* (Boston, 1909), pp. 9, 39.

creating new interest in Turkey. The Armenian massacres of 1894-1895 and of 1908-1909 were much publicized by the missions and colleges, and such a storm of protest was raised that soon almost every American knew of Turkey and the "starving Armenians."[22]

Before the treaty of 1830 became effective, the chief commodities involved in Turkish-American trade were opium and raw wool from Turkey and rum and cotton cloth from the States. Direct trade never became significant, and the various American tariffs, beginning with the Tariff of Abominations, made return cargoes difficult to obtain. The combined value of imports and exports exceeded one million dollars only once (1836) before 1850;[23] trade languished, and American residents in Turkey sometimes complained of not seeing the Stars and Stripes in the harbors of Istanbul or Izmir for a whole year.

A new Treaty of Commerce and Navigation, signed in 1862, removed some obstacles to American trade in Turkey, and for the next twenty years Turkey was a good market for kerosene, cotton cloth, rum, firearms, and ammunition. Then, for a dozen years at the close of the century, a British shipping monopoly virtually eliminated American goods. The monopoly was broken in 1899, and American interests expanded so rapidly that an American Chamber of Commerce for the Levant was organized in 1911 with headquarters in Istanbul.[24] By this time "Turkish blend" cigarettes had become popular in the United States, and tobacco was climbing to top spot in imports from Turkey. Representatives of the American tobacco companies assumed important positions in the American colonies of Istanbul and Izmir.

The portion of the Monroe Doctrine indicating that the

22. William E. Strong, *The Story of the American Board: An Account of the First Hundred Years of the American Board of Commissioners for Foreign Missions* (Boston, 1910), pp. 196-226, 385-412. In addition to the works of Goodell, Washburn, and Hamlin, there were countless books by missionaries and ministers of the gospel who visited the Ottoman Empire. One typical example is the Rev. Walter Colton, *Land and Lee in the Bosphorus and Aegean, or Views of Constantinople and Athens* (New York, 1860). Divinity schools, colleges, Chautauquas, and lyceums had lecture series on missions to popularize them, the lectures later appearing in book form, e.g., Edward A. Lawrence, *Modern Missions in the East: Their Methods, Successes, and Limitations* (New York, 1895), pp. 109-329.
23. Gordon, *Relations with Turkey*, pp. 46-47.
24. *Ibid.*, pp. 49-53, 120.

United States would not take any part in purely European affairs was the guiding principle of American diplomacy in Turkey before the First World War. During the Crimean War the American government maintained a strict neutrality, although most Americans favored Turkey and her allies, probably because of the slanted reporting from London and the favorable attitude of Americans in Istanbul.[25] Every American envoy was instructed to observe meticulously this hands-off aspect of the Monroe Doctrine. In 1865 the United States for this reason declined to participate in a sanitary conference in Istanbul. In 1885, when the ten-oared caiques of the great ambassadors were almost flying from embassy to embassy on the Bosphorus on account of the Bulgarian annexation of Eastern Rumelia, Minister Samuel S. Cox called at the Porte to emphasize the American policy of non-intervention.[26] Ambassador William W. Rockhill, at the time of the Turco-Italian War, had to inform the Young Turks that the United States would not serve as mediator because of the Monroe Doctrine.[27] However, Americans in private capacities took part in the diplomacy of the Eastern Question. Dr. Washburn played a positive role in the public revelations of the Bulgarian troubles of the 1870's, and Eugene Schuyler, American Consul General in Istanbul, took an important part in drafting the articles adopted by the Ambassador's Convention of 1877 in Istanbul.[28]

After the Young Turk Revolution, "dollar diplomacy" became evident in Turkey. Isolated cases of this type had appeared since 1830. Henry Eckford, an engineer from New York, obtained a contract in 1831 from the Ottoman government to superintend the construction of the Turkish navy.[29] In the 1880's Leland Stanford was offered a concession to build the railroad that later became the Anatolian Railway of Berlin to Baghdad fame. Stanford declined, but other American entrepreneurs sought the concession with mineral rights and land grants. Failing to obtain it

25. "Russia and the Porte," North American Review, LXXVIII (1854), 524.
26. Samuel S. Cox, Diversions of a Diplomat in Turkey (New York, 1887), pp. 638-40.
27. Paul Varg, Open Door Diplomat (Urbana, Illinois, 1952), p. 116.
28. William L. Langer, European Alliances and Alignments, 1871-1890 (New
29. Prime, Forty Years, p. 121; Porter, Constantinople, I, 13.
York, 1931), p. 106.

for lack of capital, the adventurers tried to sue Turkish officials to regain the bribes that had been given.[30] In the 1890's the Cramp shipbuilders of Philadelphia built a cruiser for Abdul Hamid II, but they received the contract for it in part so that the Sultan could include in its price certain indemnities due American missionaries from ravages of the Armenian massacres. Minister Oscar Straus, a lawyer, pressed so skilfully for these indemnities that Abdul Hamid suggested the "cruiser arrangement" as a face-saving device, but the Sultan continued to delay final settlement until Lloyd C. Griscom, the American chargé d'affaires, used the visit of the battleship *Kentucky,* commanded by Captain Colby M. Chester, to force the Sultan to sign. At a dinner at Yildiz Palace Abdul Hamid told Captain Chester that he intended to purchase three or four more cruisers should the present one from the Cramps prove successful and that he planned to purchase a large quantity of American rifles in the near future.[31]

Perhaps the most important episode of this period was the affair of the so-called Chester Concession. In 1908 on a visit to Istanbul to investigate railroad building as the representative of the New York Chamber of Commerce and the New York State Board of Trade, Admiral Colby M. Chester applied for a concession for about nine hundred miles of railroad, including mineral and oil rights along the right of way. Ottoman officials and parliamentary committees reacted favorably, and a New Jersey company (the Ottoman American Development Company) was organized to develop the concession when approved formally by parliament. President Taft and Secretary Knox became actively interested and invited officials of the company "to call at the Department" to discuss "a line of action." In 1911 Ambassador William W. Rockhill was transferred from St. Petersburg to Istanbul to press the matter, with definite instructions to prepare for the final struggle against German interests. However, when the company withdrew its caution money and sent no representative to Turkey for the final action, Knox washed his hands of the

30. Cox, *Diversions*, p. 629.
31. Oscar Straus, *Under Four Administrations* (Boston, 1922), p. 142; Lloyd C. Griscom, *Diplomatically Speaking* (New York, 1940), pp. 162-71; Alfred L. Dennis, *Adventures in American Diplomacy* (New York, 1928), p. 452.

affair, and Rockhill informed the Grand Vizir that the application was withdrawn. Dollar diplomacy in Turkey was a failure,
and Rockhill wrote to MacMurray in the Department of State,
". . . how the devil are you going to do it if nobody in America, I
mean in the business world, is willing to . . . give me full instruc-
tion as to how I am to act here. . . ."[32]

Another manifestation of American interest in Turkey prior
to 1914 was the number of books and magazine articles dealing
with Turkey that appeared in America. Almost every missionary
wrote a book on his experiences. The publishers guaranteed Dr.
Hamlin $500 for his book, *Among the Turks,* even before it was
written.[33] Minister Cox wrote two books on his short tenure.
General Lew Wallace's novel *Ben Hur* carried the reader to the
East, and the appropriateness of his appointment as Minister to
Turkey in 1881 was hardly questioned, although the reason he
desired the post was to gather material, ideas, and local color for
his novel *A Prince of India.* In the newspapers the diplomacy in
regard to the "Sick Man of Europe" proved to be very adaptable
for cartooning, and magazines such as *Outlook, Arena, Our Day,*
the *North American Review,* and *The Nation* carried frequent
articles on Turkey. The history of the Ottoman Empire was
studied and taught at some of the American universities, and by
1902 Professor Archibald Cary Coolidge, the precursor of Ottoman specialists in the United States, had written a biography
of Suleiman the Magnificent.[34]

The appointments in the diplomatic service to Istanbul also
show the increasing importance of Turkish-American relations.
From 1843 until 1887 American Ministers to Turkey had been
political appointees with no special qualifications for the post.
Affairs of Americans resident in Turkey grew more complex and
confused, and President Cleveland in 1887 chose Oscar Straus,
an outstanding New York lawyer, to straighten out the difficul-

32. Varg, *Open Door Diplomat,* p. 114; Gordon, *Relations with Turkey,* pp.
257-64.
33. Hamlin, *My Life and Times,* p. 505. His book, *Among The Turks,* was
priced at $1.50 when it first appeared.
34. Roger Bigelow Merriman, *Suleiman The Magnificent, 1520-1566* (Cambridge, Mass., 1944), pp. v-vii. Professor Merriman states in the preface that
he found Coolidge's unpublished manuscript in the Widener Library, reworked
it, added three chapters, and brought it out under his own name.

ties. At the time *The Nation* wrote, "At such a crisis it is most desirable that the United States should be represented there . . . by somebody who, in intelligence as well as in character, will do credit to the American name, and maintain American influence."[35] Other than Straus, who served three separate terms, there were such capable men as Leishman, who became ambassador in 1906, Rockhill, G. Bie Ravndal, and Henry Morgenthau, Sr.

When war broke out in 1914, Ambassador Morgenthau informed the Turkish government that America would pursue a policy of non-intervention, and this principle was officially followed until April 20, 1917, when Turkey severed diplomatic relations with the United States.[36] Even after the diplomats left Istanbul, many missionaries and educators remained at their posts.[37] Luther Fowle of the Mission Board joined the staff of the Swedish Legation and looked after American interests. However, the Armenian massacres of 1915-1916 horrified the Americans and produced such a reaction in the United States that it became impossible for the Senate even ten years later to ratify a treaty with Turkey.

After America's entry into the First World War President Wilson, in discussing Turkish problems, seemed to believe that Istanbul and the Straits should be internationalized (a view that quickly became advertised as "sound time-honored American doctrine"), Armenia should become a state, and other portions of Turkey should be administered by various of the Allies.[38] A slightly different view was presented in Point XII of the Fourteen Points, which stated, "The Turkish portions of the present Ottoman Empire should be assured a secure sovereignty . . . and the Dardanelles should be permanently opened as a free passage to the ships and commerce of all nations under international guarantees."

35. XLIV (1887), 260.
36. Henry Morgenthau, *Ambassador Morgenthau's Story* (New York, 1919), pp. 123-46; Henry Morgenthau, *All In A Life-Time* (New York, 1922), pp. 174-210.
37. Caleb Frank Gates, *Not To Me Only* (Princeton, 1940), pp. 207-27; Lynn A. Scipio, *My Thirty Years in Turkey* (Rindge, N. H., 1955), pp. 90-157.
38. Harry N. Howard, *The Partition of Turkey: A Diplomatic History, 1913-1923* (Norman, Okla., 1931), pp. 218-42.

Soon after the Mudros Armistice of October, 1918, which ended the hostilities between Turkey and the Allies, Americans and American interests rushed to resume and expand their work in Turkey. The autumn of 1919 saw the return of many missionaries and teachers, who believed that their opportunities would be much enlarged. Perhaps the most outstanding expression of American interest was the Near East Relief, which collected, over a period of nine years, more than $100,000,000 from the American people. Headquartered in Istanbul, this organization established camps, orphanages, hospitals, and trade schools and gave assistance to destitute people, not only in Turkey but throughout the Middle East.[39]

Commerce began to boom almost immediately. In 1919, and again in 1920, the value of American imports from Turkey reached nearly $40,000,000, more than double what they had been before the war. Exports to Turkey zoomed to $42,000,000 in 1920, an increase of almost 1100 per cent over the best prewar year. In 1920 the Guaranty Trust Company of New York opened the first American bank in Turkey, and it was followed the next year by a branch of the American Express Company. Many people were led to believe that America would remain the leading country in Turkish foreign trade.[40]

Meanwhile, the Paris Peace Conference was considering Turkey. Wilson's general thesis was that Istanbul and the Straits should be internationalized but that a Turkish sovereign state about the size of New Mexico should be left to the Sultan in Anatolia. Many of Wilson's advisers believed that "American interests in Turkey were largely sentimental, and largely limited to Armenia." Under these circumstances and buffeted by British and French pleas, Wilson was unable to maintain his adamant stand against the Greek occupation of Izmir, and the battleship *Arizona* and five destroyers helped to cover the Greek landing forces.[41]

In the settlement of the Turco-Greek War and the recognition

39. C. Luther Fry, "Turkey," *The Near East and American Philanthropy: A Survey Conducted under the Guidance of the General Committee of the Near East Survey*, ed. Frank A. Ross, C. Luther Fry, and Elbridge Sibley (New York, 1929), pp. 143-76.
40. Gordon, *Relations with Turkey*, pp. 65-66, 146.
41. Howard, *Partition of Turkey*, p. 234.

of the Turkish Republic, Americans participated in various ways. Admiral Mark L. Bristol, the American High Commissioner in Istanbul, helped so much that Turks in later days suggested a statue should be erected there in his honor, and Asa Jennings, a Y.M.C.A. secretary, achieved notable success when he arranged a truce of several days to enable thousands of Greeks to evacuate Izmir before the occupation by Kemal's army in 1922.[42] Secretary Hughes, in sending "unofficial observers" to the Lausanne Conference convened in 1922 to negotiate a new treaty between Turkey and the Allies, stated that the United States was interested in demilitarizing and preserving the freedom of the Straits, in ending capitulations only in principle, in protecting the minorities and the American educational, philanthropic, and religious institutions, and in preserving the open door for American enterprises.[43] Only on the last point was there very much debate, for Britain was supporting the exclusive claims of the Turkish Petroleum Company. Only after the Turkish Nationalist government had granted to the revived Chester group a concession similar to the one sought by that group in 1911 did the British accept the open door policy in Turkey. This new Chester Concession called for an expenditure of $300,000,000 to build about 2,600 miles of railroad, half of which was to be completed in two years. Exploitation of oil along the right of way was the trump card. But this Chester bubble soon broke,[44] and the American adventurers "did not leave too good a flavor" behind them.[45] A separate Turco-American Treaty was signed at Lausanne, but the Senate rejected it, and Admiral Bristol stayed on as a pseudo-ambassador. Diplomatic relations were fully resumed by a *modus vivendi* in 1927, and Joseph C. Grew, one of the American

42. Jennings remained popular among the Kemalists. The author met him at an international educational conference at Elsinor, Denmark, in 1929, where Jennings was the adviser and close companion of the Turkish Minister of Education.

43. Joseph C. Grew, *Turbulent Era: A Diplomatic Record of Forty Years, 1904-1945* (Boston, 1952), I, 475-526.

44. Howard, *Partition of Turkey*, pp. 299-301, 311-12; Gordon, *Relations with Turkey*, pp. 270-82; Grew, *Turbulent Era*, I, 527-85; *New York Times*, April 17, 1923, p. 2; April 22, 1923, Sec. VIII, p. 1; April 29, 1923, p. 2; Oct. 15, 1923, p. 1; July 20, 1925, p. 2.

45. Letter of Luther Fowle to the author, Istanbul, May, 1949.

observers at the Lausanne Conference, went to Turkey as Ambassador.[46]

Within a short time after the Declaration of the Republic in
1923, laws were passed prohibiting the teaching of religion in
schools. This act presented the American missions with difficulties, but the American Board voted to maintain its schools
and hospitals. International College in Izmir closed in the 1930's,
and the buildings and land were sold to the Turkish government
and later used as NATO headquarters. The enrollment at Robert
College and Istanbul (Constantinople) Woman's College, however, doubled from the prewar figures, and by 1928 50 per cent of
the students were Muslim Turks.[47] In 1932 the two colleges were
united, administratively, to form the Istanbul American College
under the presidency of Dr. Paul Monroe.

After the cancellation of the Chester Concession in 1923,
American business firms were more cautious in extending their
commitments in Turkey. The oil and tobacco companies maintained their establishments, but few new companies expanded
into Turkey. With the development of cellophane and skinless
weiners and sausages, the demand for sheep casings, which had
been an important Turkish export, almost vanished. The Ford
Motor Company built a small assembly plant in Istanbul, but it
must have been a total loss, for it never assembled a score of
cars. In 1930 an American group loaned $10,000,000 to the Turk-
ish government in return for a match concession, but in 1938
payments on these bonds were suddenly shifted from dollars to
Turkish liras, which were not exchangeable for hard currencies.
The American Export Line opened offices in several Turkish
ports, and ships called somewhat regularly in the 1920's and
1930's, and during the winter months of those years numerous
cruise boats would stop for twenty-four or forty-eight hours in
Istanbul for the American tourists to see the sights and to do a
little bargaining in the bazaars.[48]

46. Grew, *Turbulent Era*, I, 586-605.
47. Gates, *Not To Me Only*, p. 324.
48. Gordon, *Relations with Turkey*, pp. 60-69, 146, 285-86; Robert W. Dunn,
American Foreign Investments (New York, 1926), p. 169; O. K. D. Ringwood
and J. K. Birge, "American Interests in Turkey," *Foreign Policy Report*, XX
(1944), 208; *New York Times*, Feb. 9, 1930, Sec. IX, p. 14; July 6, 1930, Sec.
III, p. 3.

In this period between the two World Wars, news and information about Turkey grew increasingly voluminous in America. Despite the unfavorable stories emanating largely from Armenian and Greek sources, great interest was stirred by the developments in the Turkish Republic. Many articles on Turkish regeneration under Kemal Atatürk appeared in *Outlook,* the *National Geographic, Current History,* the *Christian Herald,* the *Missionary Review,* the *Literary Digest, Foreign Affairs, Life,* and many others. In 1924 Eliot Grinnell Mears brought out a large volume, *Modern Turkey,* in which chapters by different authorities considered a wide variety of subjects, including education, capitulations, the Turkish press, the Kemalist movement, and agriculture.[49] Another book, perhaps more significant in indicating the depth of American interest, was a sociological work entitled *Constantinople To-Day,* in which the various chapters dealt with civic administration, orphanages, industrial life, widowhood, adult delinquency, and other topics, each written by a distinguished American long resident in Istanbul.[50]

Probably the greatest contribution to American friendly understanding of Turkey came from the wide circulation of the works of Halide Edib, one of the first Turkish graduates of Constantinople Woman's College and often billed as the modern Turkish Joan of Arc. Titles of other books indicate the American interest: *Allah Dethroned, Unveiled Ladies of Stamboul, The Turkish Transformation,* and *The Turkey of Atatürk.*[51]

But the trade figures in the years between the wars were a great disappointment to the earlier enthusiasts. The Turkish

49. Eliot Grinnell Mears, *Modern Turkey: A Politico-Economic Interpretation, 1908-1923 Inclusive, with Selected Chapters by Representative Authorities* (New York, 1924).

50. Clarence Richard Johnson (ed.), *Constantinople To-Day, or The Pathfinder Survey of Constantinople: A Study in Oriental Social Life* (New York, 1922). Anyone familiar with the history of Americans in Istanbul in the first quarter of this century will find the list of contributors significant: Caleb F. Gates, Clarence R. Johnson, Fred Field Goodsell, William W. Peet, Elizabeth Dodge Huntington, Laurence S. Moore, C. C. Davis, Anna Welles Brown, G. Gilbert Deaver, Mabelle C. Phillips, Charles T. Riggs, and Floyd H. Black.

51. Halide Edib [Adivar], *Shirt of Flame* (New York, 1924); *Memoirs of Halide Edib* (New York, 1926); *Turkish Ordeal* (New York, 1928); *Turkey Faces West* (New Haven, 1930); Lilo Linke, *Allah Dethroned* (New York, 1937); Demetra Vaka, *Unveiled Ladies of Stamboul* (Boston, 1923); Henry E. Allen, *The Turkish Transformation* (Chicago, 1935); Donald E. Webster, *The Turkey of Atatürk* (Philadelphia, 1939).

tariff and exchange restrictions of 1929, the Fordney-McCumber and Hawley-Smoot tariffs, and the world-wide depression reduced trade to a mere trickle. The branch of the Guaranty Trust Company never showed a profit, and it was closed in 1922. The American Express Company hung on for another decade.[52]

To increase Turkish-American trade Ambassador John Van A. MacMurray was instructed early in 1937 to discuss the possibilities of a trade agreement with Turkey. The Turks gave a favorable reply, and they were "immensely flattered" when a delegation was sent the next year to Ankara to negotiate. But everything proceeded slowly and then stalled until after Atatürk's death in November, 1938, when Numan Menemencioglu, the Foreign Minister, indicated that he would like to get on with the agreement in a hurry.[53] The trade agreement was concluded in 1939, and the unique exchange formula added to it satisfied both governments, for it had the "superficial appearance of multilateralism" consistent with Hull's Reciprocal Trade Program while in reality it recognized the Turkish necessity of bilateralism. The outbreak of the Second World War made it impossible to estimate the trade value of the agreement, but it did give the Turks an indication of American interest in Turkey, as one of its chief provisions tended to make the Turkish economy more independent of restrictive bilateral trading arrangements such as the one that had been concluded with Germany.[54]

The spread of the war into Greece in 1940-1941 raised American interest in Turkey to a high point. Newspaper articles and the spate of public lectures on Turkey's probable role in the war

52. *New York Times,* Jan. 1, 1922, Sec. VII, p. 4; Grew, *Turbulent Era,* II, 859; Gordon, *Relations with Turkey,* pp. 161-89.

53. Letter of Norman Burns to the author, Washington, D. C., Sept. 9, 1949. At the time of the negotiation, Norman Burns (presently President of American University of Beirut) was an officer of the Tariff Commission and one of a two-man team sent to Ankara to negotiate the agreement. See also Burns's unpublished report, prepared for Henry Grady, *Recent Turkish-German Trade Relations,* in the Department of State files. Also, letters of Norman Burns to A. M. Fox, United States Tariff Commissioner, Ankara, April 19, 1938, and Norman Burns to Howard S. Piquet, United States Tariff Commissioner, Ankara, May 22, 1938; May 27, 1938; May 31, 1938; June 15, 1938; June 28, 1938; Istanbul, July 13, 1938; July 27, 1938; Aug. 9, 1938.

54. Letter of Norman Burns to the author, Washington, D. C., Sept. 9, 1949; United States Tariff Commission, *Trade Agreement between the United States and the Republic of Turkey *** Digests of Trade Data with Respect to Products on Which Concessions Were Granted by the United States together with Other Pertinent Information* (Washington, 1939).

were an indication of widened public concern.[55] Early in 1941 MacMurray was instructed to dangle before the Turks the possibilities of lend-lease. After Pearl Harbor the United States exerted many pressures to induce Turkey to continue her "benevolent neutrality." Turkish posts on the Aegean were convenient for Americans to raid German bases on the Greek Islands. Airfields were built and used by American forces. Istanbul became an important American espionage center. Untold millions were spent on chrome and other materials in the preclusive buying program in Turkey. In lend-lease goods American interest in Turkey amounted to about $125,000,000.[56]

But this was not all. American interest led to involvement in internal Turkish affairs. In 1942 the British American Coordinating Committee was created in Ankara to license informally, yet very effectively, all Turkish imports from sources under Allied control.[57] At Cairo Roosevelt rather bluntly informed President İnönü that the Turkish capital tax "had better be called off if Turkey hoped to maintain good relations" with the United States. At Casablanca, Quebec, Moscow, Tehran, and Cairo, American desire that Turkey should enter the war was lacking, for General Marshall opposed a Balkan campaign. Threats and "practice" blockades, however, led the Turks to prohibit chrome exports to Germany, and late in June, 1944, Ambassador Steinhardt was instructed to request Turkey to sever economic and diplomatic relations with Germany. Later he was authorized to tell the Turks that the United States would do all "within reason to alleviate the economic disturbances that a break in relations might produce." These conversations were effective, and Turkey severed relations with Germany on August 2, 1944.[58]

Throughout the war the historic problem of the Straits was recognized and American officials at Moscow, Tehran, Yalta, and

55. There was a great demand everywhere for individuals with some experience in Turkey to lecture and write popular pieces on that country. Professors Edgar J. Fisher, Albert H. Lybyer, J. K. Birge, and Walter L. Wright, Jr., and many others with knowledge of Turkey were called upon from California to Florida to Minnesota to speak on many occasions.

56. Hull, *Memoirs*, II, 929; Eleanor Bisbee, *The New Turks: Pioneers of the Republic, 1920-1950* (Philadelphia, 1951), p. 194.

57. Confidential letter to the author, dated December 3, 1949, from an American official who was active in Ankara as one of the chief operators of BACC.

58. Hull, *Memoirs*, II, 1279-80; 1297, 1301, 1312, 1365, 1368-75.

Potsdam always insisted that the question should come before an international conference in which Americans would participate. In 1945 at the London Conference of Foreign Ministers, Secretary Byrnes opened the Straits question and the Big Three governments agreed to offer suggestions looking to the revision of the Montreux Convention. On November 2, 1945, the United States sent notes to the Montreux signatories stating her position on the question and her willingness to join in a multilateral guarantee of the freedom of the Straits. The Soviet proposals, presented on August 7, 1946, seemed to envisage a bilateral arrangement whereby Turkey and the Soviet Union would fortify and control the Straits. Before the year was out, eight notes on the question had been made public, with Turkey, the United Kingdom, and the United States strongly opposing the Soviet bid for control over the Straits.[59]

In 1911 the Charykov "trial balloon" set off by the Russians concerning the Straits had been very similar to the proposals of Stalin in 1946. In 1911 Ambassador Rockhill reported the Charykov move in full to the Department of State and received from Secretary Knox the succinct reply, "Your despatch has been read with interest, and note has been taken of the apparent attitude of the Governments of Russia and Turkey towards this question."[60] In 1947 President Truman went personally before the Congress to ask for authorization of American assistance to Turkey in resisting Russian pressure, and the Congress quickly gave the authorization.

In the fifteen years since the inauguration of this special aid to Turkey and her inclusion later among the ECA countries, her admission to NATO, and the formation of CENTO under American aegis, the transformation of Turkey has been amazing. The

59. James F. Byrnes, *Speaking Frankly* (New York, 1947), pp. 77-78, 128, 294, 300-303; Grew, *Turbulent Era*, II, 1470-73; Bisbee, *New Turks*, pp. 199-209; Altemur Kilic, *Turkey and the World* (Washington, 1959), pp. 114-33. The texts of the notes and other relevant materials can be found in Harry N. Howard, *The Problem of the Turkish Straits*.

60. Letter of P. C. Knox to William W. Rockhill, Washington, D. C., Jan. 5, 1912, Department of State files; Edward R. Stettinius, Jr., *Roosevelt and the Russians: The Yalta Conference* (New York, 1949), pp. 44, 267-69, 349; Stephen G. Xydis, "The 1945 Crisis over the Turkish Straits," *Balkan Studies*, I, No. 2 (Autumn, 1960), 65-90; Cyril E. Black, "The Turkish Straits and the Great Powers," *Foreign Policy Reports*, XXIII (1947), 174-82.

American impact began almost immediately in 1947, and within two years, as a wise American who had had long experience with Turkish people remarked, "America has cast a spell over the Turks." In 1949, before Turkish participation in the Korean War, he continued, "No one could have been rash enough five or six years ago to predict the present state of American-Turkish cooperative relations, and one would hardly dare predict now what the situation will be five or six years hence."[61] The American infiltration has taken the form of goods, methods, books, ideas, and people. Turks educated in American schools in Turkey or in America have played a significant role in this movement.[62] English has become the popular second language, and bookstores are full of American and English publications. In demand, particularly, are books about Turkey in English. Translations into Turkish are common, and they run from Edgar Rice Burroughs to Ernest Hemingway.

Over the last fifteen years the United States has given to Turkey more than $3,000,000,000 in the form of military supplies and assistance, commodities of almost every sort from flour, butter, and frozen turkeys to antibiotics, and even outright free dollar credits. No totaling of these grants should ever be attempted, for no one knows what price tag should be put on missile bases, submarines, and the unending variety of military hardware. Since the end of the Second World War and the beginning of the continual emanation of bombastic Soviet pronouncements toward Turkey and the Straits, the primary American interest has been the preservation of Turkish independence. Furthermore, America has desired Turkey as a military observation and forward post with respect to the Soviet Union. American radar units, airfields, depots, army bases, and naval stations dot Turkey from one end to the other, and American armed forces teams have been located in the most remote parts of Anatolia to instruct Turkish military in the use of new weapons and techniques. The ill-fated U-2 incident is enough to call to mind American involve-

61. Letter of Harold L. Scott to the author, Istanbul, May, 1949.
62. Even at the highest levels: Kasim Gulek, a Robert College graduate of the class of 1926, was Secretary General of the Republican People's party, and Adnan Menderes, the Democrat Prime Minister from 1950 to 1960, was graduated from International College in Izmir.

ment in Turkey. The educational role of the American military in Turkey was not without some effect upon the Turkish military in their *coup* in 1960.

The first corollary to the direct military interest was an intense American concern for Turkish transport and communications. The United States Bureau of Public Roads had given encouragement to Turkish government feelers as early as 1946 and with the Truman Doctrine aid went forward in larger amounts, $5,000,000 out of the first $100,000,000.[63] Since then, roads have been improved east and west, north and south, so that one can now drive in a day from Kayseri to Istanbul or from Ankara to Iskenderum and from Istanbul to the Bulgarian frontier in four hours, whereas in 1936 it took two days. One now drives on the highway, rather than along side of it. Assistance with telephone, telegraph, and radio facilities has paralleled road work, and several years ago startled Turkish workmen watched American technicians crawl inside locomotive boilers to scrape off the scale to raise the efficiency and lower the incidence of repairshop detail.

The United States has given considerable attention to industrial development in Turkey. The more showy form has come in branch establishments such as General Electric, Mobil Oil, and Squibb; in Ankara a usual activity for a visitor is to go out to the edge of the city to see the Minneapolis-Moline Türk Traktör Fabrikasi.[64] Equally important has been the technical assistance in developing a wide range of industries under Turkish owner-

63. Winifred N. Hadsel, "U. S. Aid to Turkey," *Foreign Policy Reports,* XXIII (1947), 182-84; Herbert J. Cummings, "Turkish Highway Program—An Interim Economic Appraisal," *Foreign Commerce Weekly,* XLV, No. 8 (Nov. 19, 1951), 3-4, 31-32; Robert W. Kerwin, "The Turkish Roads Program," *The Middle East Journal,* IV (1950), 196-208; Vedat Eldem, "Turkey's Transportation," *Middle Eastern Affairs,* IV (1953), 324-36.

64. Samuel Goldberg, "Turkey Re-Orients Policy toward Foreign Capital," *Foreign Commerce Weekly,* XL, No. 1 (July 3, 1950), 3-5, 39-40; William Diamond, "The Industrial Development Bank of Turkey," *The Middle East Journal,* IV (1950), 349-52; Peter G. Franck, "Turkey: Problems and Progress," *The Middle East Journal,* III (1949), 333-36; Ömer Celal Sarc, "Economic Policy of the New Turkey," *The Middle East Journal,* II (1948), 430-46; Osman Okyar, "Economic Framework for Industrialization: Turkish Experiences in Retrospect," *Middle Eastern Affairs,* IX (1958), 261-67; Alfred Michaelis, "The Economy of Turkey: An Account of Postwar Developments," *Middle Eastern Affairs,* IV (1953), 278-89; International Bank for Reconstruction and Development, *The Economy of Turkey: An Analysis and Recommendations for a Development Program* (Baltimore, 1961).

ship and management. Americans have also shown an interest in labor problems in Turkey; labor attachés have been sent, and CIO representatives have visited Turkey to aid in the training of potential labor leaders. The Hilton hotel on the Istanbul skyline overlooking the Bosphorus is the most obvious American contribution to the city. Moreover, it is one of the sights for Turkish tourists from the provinces to see when they come to the city, and its style of architecture has been copied far and wide throughout the country.

Philanthropic endeavors continue unabated. Istanbul American College has erected a new engineering building (1960-1962) and has developed a new humanities curriculum (1959) to integrate Eastern and Western cultures more effectively. Mission schools and hospitals remain, and the Admiral Mark L. Bristol Hospital in Istanbul continues its outstanding work, staffed by American trained Turkish doctors. American scholars with Fulbright, Ford, Rockefeller, Social Science Research Council, American Council of Learned Societies, or other grants have gone to Turkey in large numbers to study or to give educational and scientific assistance in Turkey from library to architectual training. For a number of years the head of the Middle East Technical University (in part an UNESCO project) in Ankara was an American, and many American advisers were attached to its faculty. Other Americans have gone to Turkey to dig into her past, helping Turkish archaeologists in such spots as Troy, Gordion, and Sardis.

These interests and connections have brought a great many Americans to Turkey, so many that an American who has lived in Turkey off and on since 1931 remarked recently that it was no fun living in Ankara any more as there were too many Americans. Since over 700 American children were going to an American-dependent school there in 1959, the point seems well taken. Americans have come to and gone from Turkey with great frequency in the last decade. In view of the great differences in living standards and customs, in addition to the almost complete lack of preparation most of them are given, it is a remarkable fact that a vast majority return to the United States with a fondness for and an abiding interest in Turkey and her people.

In view of the rapid influx of Americans and American products and ideas the lack of ill-feeling is noteworthy. At first, some Turks charged that most of the American aid and much of the attention was coming to strengthen the front line against the Soviets, or, as the saying went, "Buying Turkish blood with surplus American dollars."[65] But the aid became too massive and too enveloping to resist for long. Even the casualties suffered in the Turkish participation in Korea under American direction did not raise a storm of protest, perhaps because of the pride in the valor and showing of Turkish troops and the American praise for Turkish gallantry under fire. Later, when many Turks grew restless under the rigidity of Menderes' rule, which might have ended in the economic crisis of 1958 had not America quickly advanced grants and credits of $300,000,000, rumors circulated that the United States favored the "dictatorship" in Turkey; assertedly Ambassador Fletcher Warren, who had served as ambassador in a half-dozen Central and South American Republics and was therefore assumed to be an expert in maintaining dictators in office, was sent to Turkey to keep Adnan Menderes in control. With American sergeants driving flashy new cars, enjoying a pay rating often above that of a Turkish colonel, and bringing in goods without customs duties or control, some Turks bitterly recalled former Ottoman days of the foreign postoffices and the capitulations.

But, whatever the present motives for American interest in Turkey may be, the activities and connections of the last fifteen years have been so varied and so penetrating that there is no thought of going back to the former modest role. True, Americans are not establishing themselves in Turkey as did the British, French, Dutch, Italians, and others in the eighteenth and nineteenth centuries, and American families do not seem to be settling in a manner that would foreshadow a residence there for generations as did the Europeans heretofore. Few American companies have American representatives living in Turkey, and there is not a heavy investment of private capital. Times, in these respects, have changed. Even should political trends shift or military and scientific developments be such that certain con-

65. Letter of Middleton Edwards to the author, Istanbul, May, 1949.

temporary American interests in Turkey vanish, American concern and interest in Turkey and her people would persist.

The world has grown more compact, and the peoples know more about each other. In 1881 when Caleb Gates left for Mardin, Turkey, his family and friends in Chicago thought he was leaving for another world.[66] In 1912 the Scipios in journeying from Nebraska to Istanbul were going to a spot few had ever visited, and their families in Indiana were appalled at the idea.[67] But in 1961 Dr. Scipio on a motor trip to California met people at a motel in Missouri who had lived in Turkey for a number of years and the very next night at a motel in western Oklahoma found another family that had lived there, too. And Americans, who have never been there, have a favorable attitude toward Turkey and the Turks. Part of this may have come from dispatches from Korea during the fighting, for the Turkish soldiers distinguished themselves there for bravery. No small role was played by the skilful direction of the Turkish Information Office in New York by Nuri Eren, who was successful in obtaining an excellent press for Turkey.

In the end, however, there remains the interest of people in the United States for Turkey and her people. Over the long pull of history it has been men like Goodell, Hamlin, Gates, Albert H. Lybyer, Walter Livingston Wright, Jr., Laurence S. Moore, the Dodges, and the Grosvenors who have nurtured and fostered American concern for Turkey. It was neither the railroad adventurers nor the Chesters. How wrong was President Taft in 1911 when he instructed Ambassador Rockhill "that the Embassy's energies [were to] be constantly directed to the real and commercial rather than the academic interests of the United States in the Near East."[68] It would seem that an old note was struck anew when in the last week of August, 1962, Vice President Johnson and Foreign Minister Feridun C. Erkin signed an accord under which a fifty-member American Peace Corps contingent would arrive within a few weeks to scatter to Turkish provincial towns to teach English and work on Turkish farms.[69]

66. Gates, *Not To Me Only*, pp. 14-16.
67. Scipio, *My Thirty Years*, pp. 49-51.
68. Varg, *Open Door Diplomat*, p. 114.
69. Turkish Information Office, *News from Turkey*, XV, No. 35 (Aug. 30, 1962), 1; No. 37 (Sept. 13, 1962), 2.

The names of the towns to which they go—Bandirma, Bolu, Bursa, Adapazari, Cankiri, Corum, Karabük, and Kütahya—cannot but remind "old Turkish hands" of the towns where the mission stations were situated. No matter what Peace Corps men and women may accomplish in their "mission" in Turkey, it is likely that most will return to the United States with a soft spot in their hearts for Turkey and the Turkish people. This has been the pattern over the years that now span two centuries.

Carpetbaggers Reconsidered

RICHARD N. CURRENT

The story of the post-bellum South is often told as if it were a morality play or a television melodrama. The characters personify Good or Evil, and they are so clearly identified that there is no mistaking the "good guys" and the "bad guys." One of the villains, who deserves the boos and hisses he is sure to get, is the carpetbagger. As usually portrayed, this contemptible Yankee possesses as little honor or intelligence as he does property, and he possesses so little property that he can, quite literally, carry all of it with him in a carpetbag. He is attracted southward by the chance for power and plunder that he sees when the vote is given to Southern Negroes and taken from some of the Southern whites by the Reconstruction Acts of 1867. Going south in 1867 or after, he meddles in the politics of places where, as a mere roving adventurer, he has no true interest. For a time he and his kind run the Southern states. At last, when the drama ends, Good has triumphed over Evil, and the carpetbagger has got his come-uppance. But he leaves behind him a trail of corruption, misgovernment, and lastingly disturbed race relations.[1]

That picture may seem an exaggeration, a caricature. If so, it nevertheless has passed for a long time as a true, historical likeness, and it continues to pass as such. A standard dictionary defines *carpetbagger* as a term of contempt for Northern men who went south "to seek private gain under the often corrupt reconstruction governments."[2] Another dictionary, based on "historical principles," contains this definition: "One of the poor

1. This paper was presented, in an earlier form, at the annual dinner of the Mississippi Valley Historical Association in Chicago on December 28, 1959. Thanks are due to the Research Council of the University of North Carolina at Greensboro for a grant assisting part of the research on which the essay is based.
2. *Webster's New International Dictionary of the English Language* (Springfield, Mass., 1934), p. 410.

northern adventurers who, carrying all their belongings in carpetbags, went south to profit from the social and political upheaval
after the Civil War."[3] A recent textbook refers to "the Radical
carpetbaggers who had poured into the defeated section after
the passage of the First Reconstruction Act of March, 1867."[4]
The prevailing conception, then, is that these men were late
arrivals who waited till the Negro was given the suffrage and
who then went off with their carpetbags, cynically, to take advantage of the colored vote.

Even those who hold that view concede that "a few were
men of substance, bent on settling in the South,"[5] and that some
of them took up residence there before the passage of the Reconstruction Acts. With respect to men of this kind, however, the
question has been raised whether they should be considered
carpetbaggers at all. Many of the Northerners active in Mississippi politics after 1867, the historian of Reconstruction in that
state observes, had arrived as would-be planters before 1867. "It
is incorrect, therefore, to call them 'carpet baggers,'" this historian remarks. "They did not go South to get offices, for there
were no offices for them to fill. The causes which led them to
settle there were purely economic, and not political."[6] Thus the
brothers Albert T. and Charles Morgan, when they moved from
Wisconsin to Mississippi, "came not as carpetbaggers," for they

3. Mitford M. Mathews (ed.), *A Dictionary of Americanisms on Historical
Principles* (Chicago, 1951), p. 273.

4. Richard Hofstadter, William Miller, and Daniel Aaron, *The United States:
The History of a Republic* (Englewood Cliffs, N. J., 1957), p. 404. The use of
the carpetbagger stereotype in recent historical writing could be illustrated at
length. Nash K. Burger and John K. Bettersworth, *South of Appomattox* (New
York, 1959), p. 124, speak of Congress having instituted "military reconstruction" in 1867 and go on to say: "It was now that the era of carpetbag and
Negro rule flourished unabated in the South. When carpetbaggers arrived from
the North to control the Negro. . . ." J. G. Randall, *The Civil War and Reconstruction* (Boston, 1937), p. 847, says the carpetbaggers went south to "make
money and seize political power." The revised edition of this work, by Randall
and David Donald (Boston, 1961), omits this passage but substitutes no other
definition or description of the carpetbaggers. In the preface to the best-selling
novel by Harold Robbins, *The Carpetbaggers* (New York, 1961), there is an
eloquent description, from the stereotyped view, of men who "came to plunder."
The title is figurative, and the novel itself has nothing to do with Northerners in
the postwar South.

5. William A. Dunning, *Reconstruction Political and Economic, 1865-1877*
(New York, 1907), p. 121.

6. James W. Garner, *Reconstruction in Mississippi* (New York, 1901), p. 136.
But Garner is inconsistent. See the next note.

brought with them some $50,000, which they invested in plant-
ing and lumbering enterprises (and lost).[7] And the much better-
known figure Albion W. Tourgée, who moved from Ohio to North
Carolina, was perhaps no carpetbagger, either, for he took with
him $5,000 which he put into a nursery business (and also lost).[8]

Now, suppose it could be demonstrated that, among the
Northern politicians in the South during Reconstruction, men
essentially like the Morgans and Tourgée were not the few but
the many, not exceptional but fairly typical. Suppose that the
majority moved to the South before 1867, before the establishment of the "corrupt reconstruction governments," and hence for
reasons other than to seek private gain or political power under
such governments. One of two conclusions must follow. Either
we must say that true carpetbaggers were much fewer and less
significant than has been commonly supposed, or we must seek
a new definition of the word.

In redefining it, we should consider the actual usage on the
part of Southerners during the Reconstruction period. We may
learn something of its denotation as well as its connotation if we
look at the way they applied it to a specific person: the one-time
Union army officer Willard Warner, of Ohio and Alabama.

Warner might seem, at first glance, to exemplify the late-
comer rising immediately in Southern politics, for he completed
his term in the Ohio legislature and was elected to the United
States Senate from Alabama in the same year, 1868. But he was
not really a new arrival. He had visited Alabama and, with a
partner, had leased a plantation there in the fall of 1865. He
bought land in the state the next year, and he spent most of the
spring and summer of 1866 and most of the autumn and winter of
1867-1868 on his Alabama land. He intended to make an economic career in the South (and indeed he was eventually to do
so).[9]

At first, Warner had no trouble with his Alabama neighbors.
"A Northern man, who is not a fool, or foolish fanatic," he wrote

7. Frank E. Smith, *The Yazoo River* (New York, 1954), pp. 153, 156. Garner,
forgetting his own words of caution, refers on pp. 309-10 to "the well-known
'carpet-bagger,' Colonel A. T. Morgan."
    8. Ethel S. Arnett, *Greensboro, North Carolina* (Chapel Hill, 1955), p. 400 n.
    9. Warner to John Sherman, April 15, June 21, 1866; Dec. 9, 19, 1867; Jan.
10, 1877, John Sherman MSS, Library of Congress.

from his plantation in the spring of 1866, "may live pleasantly in Alabama, without abating one jot of his self-respect, or independence."[10] At one time or another, as he was to testify later, the leading Democrats of the state, among them the ex-Confederate General James H. Clanton, came to him and said: "General, when we talk about carpetbaggers we want you to understand that we don't mean you; you have come here and invested what means you had in property here, and you have the same interest here that we have."[11]

The Alabamans changed their attitude toward Warner when he was elected to office with Negro support. Afterwards (1871) General Clanton himself explained:

If a man should come here and invest $100,000, and in the next year should seek the highest offices, by appealing to the basest prejudices of an ignorant race, we would call him a political carpet-bagger. But if he followed his legitimate business, took his chances with the rest, behaved himself, and did not stir up strife, we would call him a gentleman. General Warner bought land; I fixed some titles for him, and I assured him that when men came there to take their chances with us for life, we would take them by the hand. But we found out his designs. Before his seat in Ohio got cold, he was running the negro machine among us to put himself in office.[12]

Another Alabama Democrat, from Huntsville, in the area where Warner had bought land, elaborated further upon the same theme in testifying before a congressional committee, as follows:

Question: You have used the epithets "carpet-bagger" and "scalawag" repeatedly . . . give us an accurate definition. . . .

Answer: Well, sir, the term carpet-bagger is not applied to northern men who come here to settle in the South, but a carpet-bagger is generally understood to be a man who comes here for office sake, of an ignorant or bad character, and who seeks to array the negroes against the whites; who is a kind of political dry-nurse for the negro population, in order to get office through them.

Question: Then it does not necessarily suppose that he should be a northern man?

Answer: Yes, sir; it does suppose that he is to be a northern man, but it does not apply to all northern men that come here.

10. Warner to Sherman, April 15, 1866.
11. *Testimony Taken by the Joint Select Committee to Enquire into the Condition of Affairs in the Late Insurrectionary States: Alabama* (41st Congress, 2d session, House Report No. 22, part 8, Washington, 1872), I, 34.
12. *Ibid.*, p. 233.

Question: If he is an intelligent, educated man, and comes here for office, then he is not a carpet-bagger, I understand?

Answer: No, sir; we do not generally call them carpet-baggers.

Question: If he is a northern man possessed of good character and seeks office he is not a carpet-bagger?

Answer: Mr. Chairman, there are so few northern men who come here of intelligence and character, that join the republican party and look for office alone to the negroes, that we have never made a class for them. . . . They stand *sui generis*. . . . But the term "carpet-bagger" was applied to the office-seeker from the North who comes here seeking office by the negroes, by arraying their political passions and prejudices against the white people of the community.

Question: The man in addition to that, under your definition, must be an ignorant man and of bad character?

Answer: Yes, sir; he is generally of that description. We regard any man as a man of bad character who seeks to create hostility between the races. . . .

Question: Having given a definition of the carpet-bagger, you may now define scalawag.

Answer: A scalawag is his subservient tool and accomplice, who is a native of the country.[13]

So far as these two Alabamans were concerned, it obviously made no difference whether a Northerner came before 1867 or after, whether he brought with him and invested thousands of dollars or was penniless, whether he was well educated or illiterate, or whether he was of good or bad character in the ordinary sense. He was, by definition, a carpetbagger and a man of ignorant and bad character if he, at any time, encouraged political activity on the part of the Negroes and thus arrayed the blacks against the whites, that is, the Republicans against the Democrats. He was not a carpetbagger if he steered entirely clear of politics or if he consistently talked and voted as a Democrat or Conservative.

This usage was not confined to Alabama; it prevailed throughout the South.[14] To speak of "economic carpetbaggers," as historians sometimes do, is therefore rather hard to justify on a historical basis. Politics—Republican politics—was the distinguishing mark of the man whom the Democrats and Conserva-

13. Testimony of William M. Lowe, *ibid.*, pp. 887-88.

14. In the text and footnotes of this paper more than seventy so-called carpetbaggers are mentioned by name. All are illustrations of this usage.

tives after 1867 dubbed a carpetbagger, and they called him by
that name whether or not he had gone south originally for
economic rather than political reasons. To speak of "Negro
carpetbaggers" is also something of an anachronism. Colored
men from the North did go south and enter politics, of course,
but in the Reconstruction lexicon (with its distinction among
carpetbaggers, scalawags, and Negroes) they were put in a category of their own. Northern-born or Southern-born, the Negro
was a Negro to the Southern Conservatives, and they did not
ordinarily refer to him as a carpetbagger. From contemporary
usage, then, we derive the following as a non-valuational definition: the men called carpetbaggers were *white Northerners who
went south after the beginning of the Civil War and, sooner or
later, became active in politics as Republicans.*

With this definition at hand, we can proceed to make at least
a rudimentary survey of the so-called carpetbaggers as a group,
in order to find out how well they fit the traditional concept with
respect to their background. Let us consider first the state and
local office-holders. There were hundreds of these people, and
many of them left too few traces for us now to track them down.
Studies have touched upon the subject in some of the states, and
though fragmentary, these studies at least suggest that most of
the men under consideration do not conform to the stereotype.

In Arkansas the carpetbag governor (1868-1872) Powell Clayton had owned and lived on a plantation since 1865. Many years
later he was to gather data showing that the overwhelming
majority of the so-called carpetbaggers, who were in office when
he was, had arrived in Arkansas before 1867, and that the small
minority who came as late as 1867 "did so when the Democrats
were in full power, and before the officers to be elected or appointed, together with their salaries and emoluments, had been
fixed by the [Reconstructed] State Constitution." Clayton adds:

With a very few exceptions, the Northern men who settled in Arkansas came there with the Federal Army, and . . . were so much impressed with its genial climate and great natural resources as to cause
them . . . to make it their future home. A number, like myself and
my brother William, had contracted matrimonial ties. Many of them
had been away from home so long as practically to have lost their

identity in the States [from which they had come]. . . . These were the reasons that influenced their settlement in Arkansas rather than the existence of any political expectations.[15]

That, of course, is *ex parte* testimony, from one of the carpetbaggers himself. Still, he supports his conclusion with ample and specific evidence.

And, with respect to some of the other states, Southern historians have tended toward similar conclusions. In Alabama, says one of these historians, "Many of the carpet-bag politicians were northern men who had failed at cotton planting."[16] In Florida, says another, about a third of the forty-six delegates elected in 1867 to the state constitutional convention were white Republicans from the North. "Most of the Northerners had been in the state for a year or more and were *bona fide* citizens of the commonwealth." "As a class," they were "intellectually the best men among the delegates."[17] In Mississippi, says a third, "The genuine 'carpet baggers' who came after the adoption of the reconstruction policy were comparatively few in number." The vast majority of the so-called carpetbaggers in Mississippi were men who had arrived earlier as planters.[18]

Information is not available regarding all the carpetbag officeholders in all the reconstructed states. What is needed, then, is information about a representative sample of such officeholders. A sample could be made of the carpetbag governors, of whom the total was nine. Eight of the nine arrived in the South before 1867. Two were officers of the Freedmen's Bureau, two were civilian officials of the federal government, and four were private enterprisers—two of them planters, one a lawyer, and the other a minister of the gospel. The single late-comer, Adelbert Ames of Massachusetts and Mississippi, first appeared

15. Powell Clayton, *The Aftermath of the Civil War in Arkansas* (New York, 1915), pp. 298-306. These facts did not, and do not, exempt Clayton and his colleagues from the "carpetbagger" epithet. Thus, for example, Thomas S. Staples, *Reconstruction in Arkansas, 1862-1874* (New York, 1923), pp. 276-77, writes of Clayton: "Though a carpetbagger, he claimed to be identified with local interests by virtue of the fact that he had purchased a plantation in Jefferson County and had decided to become a permanent resident of the state."
16. Walter L. Fleming, *Civil War and Reconstruction in Alabama* (New York, 1905), p. 718 n.
17. William W. Davis, *The Civil War and Reconstruction in Florida* (New York, 1913), pp. 476-77.
18. Garner, *Reconstruction in Mississippi*, pp. 136, 414 n.

in Mississippi as a regular army officer and as a military governor, not as an adventurer in search of a political job.[19]

A larger sample consists of the entire body of white Northerners who during the Reconstruction period were elected as Republicans to represent Southern constituencies in either branch of Congress. Altogether, there were about 62 of these men, 17 in the Senate and 45 in the House of Representatives. It is impossible to be absolutely precise in listing these congressional carpetbaggers. There were a few borderline cases where, for example, a man was born in the South but raised or educated in the North, and it is hard to know whether he should be classified as a Northerner or not.

Of the 62 senators and congressmen, practically all were veterans of the Union army. That is not surprising, and it does not alter the accepted stereotype. More surprising, in view of the carpetbagger's reputation for "ignorant or bad character," is the fact that a large proportion were well educated. About two-thirds of the group (43 of the 62) had studied law, medicine, or engineering enough to practice the profession, or had attended one or more years of college, or had been school teachers. Of the senators alone, approximately half were college graduates.

19. R. K. Scott of South Carolina and M. L. Stearns of Florida were Freedmen's Bureau agents. Harrison Reed of Florida was a federal tax commissioner (1863) and a United States postal agent (1865). W. P. Kellogg of Louisiana was collector of the port of New Orleans. H. C. Warmoth of Louisiana was a lawyer, Joseph Brooks of Arkansas was a minister, and Powell Clayton of Arkansas and D. H. Chamberlain of South Carolina were planters.

Ames, a regular army officer, became provisional governor of Mississippi in 1868 and military commander of the district in 1869. He was elected United States Senator and served from 1870 to 1874; he was elected governor and served from 1874 to 1876. Though a late-comer to Mississippi, he at times considered establishing a permanent residence in the state. He wrote his wife, October 26, 1872: "I think I will get a house and home for us on the Gulf at Pass Christian or some other point near there. And for business we will go into raising oranges." On November 9, 1872, he bought a house for $6,100 in Natchez, a town that had appealed to his wife. The dangerous and disagreeable aspects of life for a Republican Northerner in Mississippi caused him to change his mind about living permanently there, even before he lost out in politics. See *Chronicles from the Nineteenth Century: Family Letters of Blanche Butler and Adelbert Ames*, compiled by Blanche Butler Ames and privately issued by Jessie Ames Marshall (Clinton, Mass., 1957), I, 403, 416.

Rufus B. Bullock, governor of Georgia from 1868 to 1871, has been called a carpetbagger but does not fit in the category as defined according to the most common contemporary usage. Though a white Republican Northerner, Bullock had settled in the South before the war and had served in the Confederate army. See C. Mildred Thompson, *Reconstruction in Georgia: Economic, Social, Political, 1865-1872* (New York, 1915), p. 217.

Seemingly the academic and intellectual attainments of the carpetbaggers in Congress were, on the whole, at least as high as those of the other members of Congress, whether from the North or from the South.

Still more significant is the fact that nearly five-sixths of the entire carpetbag group—50 of the 62—had arrived in the South before 1867, before the passage of the Reconstruction Acts, before the granting of political rights to the Negro. Of the 50 early arrivals, only 15 appeared on the Southern scene as Treasury Department employees, Freedman's Bureau officials, or members of the postwar occupation forces (and at least a few of these 15 soon left the government service and went into private enterprise). Thirty-five of the 50 were engaged in farming or business or the professions from the time of their arrival or soon after.

As for those other 12 of the 62—the 12 who did not begin to live in the South until 1867 or later—more than half (at least 7) took up some private occupation before getting public office. Their comparatively late arrival does not, in itself, signify that they moved south merely for "office sake."[20]

If, then, the 62 carpetbag Congressmen and Senators make up a representative sample, we must conclude that a majority of the carpetbaggers, taken as a whole, do not conform to the

20. Following is the list, by states, of the carpetbag congressmen and senators as defined and selected for this study (each senator is indicated by an asterisk): *Alabama*—A. E. Buck, C. W. Buckley, J. B. Callis, T. Haughey, F. W. Kellogg, B. W. Norris, G. E. Spencer*, W. Warner*. *Arkansas*—P. Clayton*, S. W. Dorsey*, J. Edwards, J. Hinds, A. McDonald, B. F. Rice*, L. H. Roots, W. W. Wilshire. *Florida*—H. Bisbee, S. B. Conover*, A. Gilbert*, C. M. Hamilton, T. W. Osburn*, W. J. Purman, A. S. Welch*. *Georgia*—J. W. Clift, C. H. Prince. *Louisiana*—C. B. Darrall, J. S. Harris*, W. P. Kellogg*, J. E. Leonard, J. McCleery, J. Mann, F. Morey, J. P. Newsham, L. A. Sheldon, G. A. Sheridan, G. L. Smith, J. H. Sypher, J. R. West*. *Mississippi*—A. Ames*, H. W. Barry, A. R. Howe, G. C. McKee, H. R. Pease*, L. W. Perce, G. W. Wells. *North Carolina*—J. C. Albott*, J. R. French, D. Heaton. *South Carolina*—C. W. Buttz, L. C. Carpenter, S. L. Hoge, J. J. Patterson*, F. A. Sawyer*, B. F. Whittemore. *Tennessee*—L. Barbour, W. F. Prosser. *Texas*—W. T. Clark. *Virginia*—R. S. Ayer, J. Jorgensen, J. H. Platt, C. H. Porter, W. H. H. Stowell.

There were also several Northerners elected as Democrats to represent Southern constituencies in Congress. These Democrats have not been included in the list. Information on the carpetbag Congressmen and senators has been derived from the *Biographical Directory of the American Congress* (81st Congress, 2d session, House Document No. 607, Washington, 1950) and from standard biographical encyclopedias and other sources.

See also C. Mildred Thompson, "Carpet-baggers in the United States Senate," *Studies in Southern History and Politics, Inscribed to William Archibald Dunning* (New York, 1914), pp. 159-76. Miss Thompson does not undertake the some sort of analysis of backgrounds as is attempted here.

traditional view, at least so far as their backgrounds are concerned. With comparatively few exceptions, the so-called carpetbaggers had moved south for reasons other than a lust for offices newly made available by the passage of the Reconstruction Acts. These men were, in fact, a part of the multitude of Union officers and soldiers who, during or soon after the war, chose to remain in or return to the land they had helped to conquer.

To thousands of the young men in blue, at and after the war's end, the South beckoned as a land of wondrous charm, a place of almost magical opportunity. "Northern men are going to do well in every part of the South. The Southern men are too indolent to work and the Yankees are bound to win." So, for example, a cavalry sergeant wrote from Texas to his sister back home in Ohio in 1866. "I have some idea that I will not remain in Ohio long, and maybe I will locate in the sunny South," he continued. "What think you of roses blooming in open air in November, and the gardens glorious with flowers."[21]

Here, in the South, was a new frontier, another and a better West. Some men compared the two frontiers before choosing the Southern one, as did the Morgan brothers, who first looked over Kansas and then decided upon Mississippi. Albert T. Morgan afterwards wrote that the former cry, "Go West, young man," had been changed to "Go South, young man," and in 1865 the change was "already quite apparent, in the purpose of those of the North who were seeking new homes."[22] Many years later Albion W. Tourgée recalled the hopes and dreams with which, in the fall of 1865, he had settled as a badly wounded veteran in Greensboro, North Carolina:

He expected the future to be as bright and busy within the conquered territory as it had been along the ever-advancing frontier of the West. . . . He expected the whole region to be transformed by the power of commerce, manufactures, and the incursion of Northern life, thought, capital, industry, and enterprise. . . . Because he thought

21. John A. Gillis (Victoria, Texas) to "Sister Hattie," Nov. 21, 1866, Sherman MSS. There are, in the Sherman MSS, a number of other letters in which Northerners described the attractions of the South. See, for example, the letters to Sherman from W. P. Dumble (Nashville), June 23, 1865; J. Y. Cantwell (Decatur, Alabama), Dec. 11, 1865, and Jan. 23, 1866; J. Davis, Jr. (Macon, Georgia), Jan. 31, 1866; and John Friend (Fernandina, Florida), March 12, 1866.
22. Albert T. Morgan, *Yazoo; or, On the Picket Line of Freedom in the South* (Washington, 1884), p. 25.

he bore a shattered life he sought a milder clime. He took his young wife with him, and they builded their first home-nest almost before the smoke of battle disappeared. . . . His first object was restored health; his next desire, to share the general prosperity.[23]

Once they had been released from the army, thousands of other Union soldiers and officers returned to the South with similar dreams of prosperity and a pleasant life. For the moment, land was cheap and cotton dear. Labor was abundant, and the Negroes were expected to work more willingly for their liberators than for their late masters. So the veterans turned south. At the end of 1865 a newsman from the North learned that, in Alabama alone, there were already five thousand of them "engaged in planting and trading." Even more than the uplands of Alabama, Tennessee, and Georgia, the Mississippi Valley was proving an "attraction to adventurous capital," this traveling reporter found. "Men from the Middle States and the great West were everywhere, buying and leasing plantations, hiring freedmen, and setting thousands of ploughs in motion."[24] No impecunious wanderers were these, but bringers of "adventurous capital." They paid cash for lands or leases, for wages, for supplies. At a time when the South was languishing for money, these newcomers provided it, put it into circulation, and thus gave the economy a lift.[25]

Most of those who thus adventured with their capital were to lose it. They failed for several reasons. At cotton planting the Yankees were novices, unused to local conditions and deluded in their expectations of the Negro as a free worker, or so the Southerners said.[26] Actually the Southerners as well as the Yan-

23. Albion W. Tourgée, *An Appeal to Caesar* (New York, 1884), pp. 55-67. The conception of the carpetbagger as a frontiersman is borne out by David H. Overy, Jr., "The Wisconsin Carpetbagger: A Group Portrait," *Wisconsin Magazine of History*, XLIV (1960), 15-49. Overy writes, p. 15: "During the Civil War, Wisconsin soldiers on duty in the South discovered a new frontier."

24. John T. Trowbridge, *The South . . . A Journey through the Desolated States* (Hartford, 1866), pp. 380, 448.

25. See, for example, Staples, *Reconstruction in Arkansas,* pp. 86-87. Staples says that there was much suffering in Arkansas during the winter of 1865-1866 because of the money scarcity. Money came "for the most part" from partnerships of Southern merchants and planters with Northern capitalists. "New comers from the North brought in more or less cash, which was thrown into immediate circulation through the purchase of lands and initial supplies." Fleming, *Reconstruction in Alabama,* pp. 717-18, says "Northern energy and capital flowed in" to that state in 1865 and 1866.

26. Fleming, pp. 323-24.

kees ran into economic difficulties during the first few years after the war. "Various causes have arisen to prostrate the people, leaving them nearly ruined," a contemporary observed early in 1867, "among which I may more especially mention the following, which could not have been foreseen or provided against: The too great drouth at one season, which destroyed and blasted their corn; too much rain at another season, which injured their cotton; and then the army worm, which came out of the ground in vast numbers, destroyed what was left." There was, besides, the federal cotton tax, which both Northern and Southern planters denounced as ruinous.[27]

Often, whether as planters or as businessmen, the Northerners faced a special disadvantage—the hostility of the people around them. "The rebels will not buy from a Galvanized Yankee, or Loyal Unionist, nor from a Yankee either," a Unionist Virginian complained late in 1865, "the result being that loyal or Northern merchants are failing all over the South."[28] In many places the Yankees were boycotted if they sympathized with or voted for Republicans. "Only one hundred and one men were found base enough to vote for the Radical ticket," a Memphis newspaper reported in April, 1866. "We have held up the names of a portion of these men and written small pox over their doors in order that our people might shun them."[29]

Discouraged and disillusioned after a year or two in their new homes, large numbers of the Yankees abandoned them and returned to the North. Others, of whom some were successful and some were not, remained in the South. Of those who remained, many turned to state and local politics as Republicans in 1867 or after. These comprised the majority of that class of men who eventually came to be known as carpetbaggers.

Before 1867 the Northerners in the South possessed only limited opportunities in politics. As Republicans, they could not

27. James E. Yeatman (St. Louis) to John Sherman, Feb. 1, 1867, Sherman MSS. Sherman received other letters from Northern planters in the South who protested against the federal cotton tax. See, for example, R. N. Barr (Claiborne, Alabama) to Sherman, July 19, 1867.

28. Augustus Watson (Fredericksburg) to Thaddeus Stevens, Dec. 9, 1865, Stevens MSS, Library of Congress.

29. Memphis *Avalanche*, April 22, 1866, clipping enclosed in letter of William Wilder to Stevens, Stevens MSS.

hope to be elected to office. As newcomers, they often found it difficult even to vote, because of the residence requirements. The Georgia constitution, as remade after the war, extended the residence requirement in that state from six months to two years. "Now it is generally admitted," a Northern settler in Georgia protested, "that this change . . . has been effected to prevent loyal men who were obliged to leave here during the war and those who have come here since the war from having any voice in choosing the officers of the State and representatives to Congress."[30] Of course, the newcomers could seek federal jobs, and many of them did so, but again they faced something of a handicap, for they understood that President Johnson preferred "Southern citizens" when "suitable persons" among them could be found.[31]

To the Northern settlers remaining in the South the congressional acts of 1867 suddenly brought political opportunity and also, as some of them saw it, political responsibility. Tourgée, for one, sought election to the new constitutional convention in North Carolina because, having failed in business and lost the savings he had brought, he needed the money he would be paid as a delegate. But he sought election also because he was concerned about Negro rights and wished to do what he could to protect them.[32] A more prosperous settler, a planter of Carroll Parish, Louisiana, who once had been an Ohio school superintendent, took an active interest in Southern politics for reasons that he explained, in April, 1867, to Senator John Sherman:

On the closing of my services as a Soldier, I became a member of the firm of Lynch, Ruggles & Co., which was organized in Circleville, Ohio, for the purpose of buying lands in the South and planting. We have located at this point, which is 40 miles above Vicksburg, have purchased lands, have organized most efficient labor forces, & our investment now is on a scale which makes us on *that* account deeply interested in every effort made to bring peace to the South. . . .

I . . . respectfully ask your advice as to the proper course to be

30. Frank S. Hesseltine (Savannah) to Stevens, April 26, 1866, Stevens MSS.
31. W. B. Woods (Mobile) to John Sherman, Jan. 28, 1866, Sherman MSS. A. C. Bryant (Stevenson, Alabama), seeking Sherman's aid in obtaining a federal job, wrote, June 15, 1866: "It is hard for a Northern man to get a position here as the people feel naturally a strong prejudice against them & they are so poor themselves that they *go for everything in sight.*"
32. Roy F. Dibble, *Albion W. Tourgée* (New York, 1921), pp. 34-41.

pursued by Northern men in the South who sympathize with Congress in the present crisis. . . . I have never held a civil office and never intended to, if I can avoid it; but we have a large force at work, have their confidence, and now as they are voters, they look to our advice, and I want to give it as wisely as possible. Other Northern men are similarly situated. . . .[33]

The position of some of these other Northern men was later recalled by C. M. Hamilton, a Pennsylvanian who had gone to Florida in 1864, as a Freedmen's Bureau agent, and had become after 1867 one of the most prominent carpetbaggers of that state. In 1871 he told a congressional committee investigating the Ku Klux Klan:

. . . when the reconstruction acts first passed Congress, the Yankees, as we are called, most of us soldiers who were in the South, rather stood back, did not really feel at that time that they [we] had any particular right to interfere in politics, or to take part in them. But the reconstruction laws were passed; reconstruction was necessary; . . . the democratic party of the South adopted the policy of masterly inactivity . . . ; there was a new element here that had been enfranchised who were without leaders. The northern men in the South, and there were but a handful of them in this State, who had been in the Army, took hold of this matter of reconstruction, and they have perfected it so far as it has been accomplished.[34]

These Northerners, already in the South in 1867, felt they had a right and a duty to be where they were and to do what they did. They were Americans. They had fought a war to keep the nation one. South as well as North, it was *their* country. They had chosen to live in the Southern part of it. This was now their home, and they had a stake in its future as well as the future of the country as a whole. Their attitude should be quite understandable—as understandable as the feeling of the majority of Southern whites.

Naturally, the native Conservatives and Democrats resented the Northern Republicans and reviled them with such epithets as "aliens," "birds of passage," and "carpetbaggers." As applied to most of the men, however, these were not objective and

33. John Lynch to Sherman, April 20, 1867, Sherman MSS.
34. *Testimony Taken by the Joint Select Committee to Enquire into the Condition of Affairs in the Late Insurrectionary States: Florida* (42d Congress, 2d session, House Report No. 22, part 13, Washington, 1872), p. 289.

descriptive terms. The Union veterans who settled in the South were impelled by a variety and a mixture of motives: restlessness, patriotic idealism, the desire to get ahead, and what not. But so were the pioneers at other times and places in the United States. So were the Southerners themselves who moved westward or northward during the Reconstruction period. At that time the newer states of the Southwest (such as Alabama, Mississippi, and especially Arkansas) were filled with fairly recent arrivals from the older states of the Southeast. And at that time there were more Southerners residing in the North than Northerners in the South.[35] The latter were no more "birds of passage" than the former. Perhaps the frontiersman has been too much idealized for his propensity to rove. Certainly the carpetbagger has been too much condemned for the mere act of moving from one part of the country to another.

Even if all this be conceded, there remain of course the other elements of the carpetbagger stereotype—the charges of misgovernment, corruption, and racial disturbance.

With regard to the charge of misgovernment and corruption, it is hard to generalize about the carpetbaggers as a class. Nevertheless, a few tentative observations may be made. First, the extent and duration of "carpetbag rule" has been exaggerated. In six of the eleven ex-Confederate states (Texas, Tennessee, Alabama, Georgia, Virginia, North Carolina) there was never a carpetbag governor; there was never a majority of carpetbaggers among the Republicans in or out of office; certainly there was never anything approaching carpetbagger domination of state politics. In all those states the Republicans held power only briefly if at all, and they held it, to the extent that they did so, by means of their strength among Negroes and scalawags. In the other five states (Arkansas, Mississippi, Louisiana, Florida, South Carolina) there were carpetbag governors part of the time, but even in these states the carpetbaggers could maintain themselves only with Negro and native white support. Second, the extent of illegal and illegitimate spending by the carpetbag gov-

35. Tourgée, *An Appeal to Caesar*, pp. 150, 176-77. Tourgée's tables are taken from an article by E. W. Gilliam in the *Popular Science Monthly* for February, 1883. They include in "the South" all fifteen of the prewar slave states and also West Virginia.

ernments has been exaggerated—if spending for schools, transportation, and other social and economic services be considered legitimate.[36] Third, the improper spending, the private use of public funds, was by no means the work of carpetbaggers alone, nor were they the only beneficiaries: heavily involved also were native whites, including Conservatives and Democrats as well as scalawags.[37] Fourth, probably the great majority of the carpetbaggers were no more corrupt than the great majority of contemporary officeholders throughout the United States.[38]

Consider the carpetbag governors, who are generally mentioned as the most conspicuous examples of dishonesty. One of them, Joseph Brooks of Arkansas, did not succeed in exercising uncontested power, for either good or evil, and was soon ousted. Two of the governors, R. K. Scott of South Carolina and W. P. Kellogg of Louisiana, are rather difficult to defend. Four others —Powell Clayton of Arkansas, Harrison Reed and M. L. Stearns of Florida, and H. C. Warmoth of Louisiana—were loudly accused but never really proved guilty of misusing their offices for private profit.[39] Only one of the four, Warmoth, seems actually to have made much money while in Reconstruction politics, and he made a fortune. While governor, he admitted that there was "a frightful amount of corruption" in Louisiana. He explained, however, that the temptation came from the business interests who offered bribes, and he insisted that the Republicans, black as well as white, had resisted bribery as well as had the Demo-

36. W. E. Burghardt DuBois, "Reconstruction and Its Benefits," *American Historical Review*, XV (1910), 781-99.

37. Jonathan Daniels, *Prince of Carpetbaggers* (Philadelphia, 1958), pp. 23, 289-99, and *passim*, eloquently shows the involvement of others besides the Northerner Milton S. Littlefield in the fraudulent financing of North Carolina railroads. With regard to Mississippi, Garner writes, p. 323: "The only large case of embezzlement among the state officers during the post-bellum period was that of the Democratic state treasurer in 1866."

38. The period of Reconstruction in the South, it must be remembered, was the time of scandals in the Grant administration, in the Shepherd government of Washington, D. C., in the Tweed Ring in New York City, and in state and local government elsewhere.

39. "It was never proved that he got any of the bonds," writes Dixon Y. Thomas with regard to the charge that Powell Clayton stole Arkansas railroad securities. *Dictionary of American Biography* (New York, 1928-58), IV, 187-88. "These charges were specific and definite enough, but the trial did not develop any substantial proof of the allegations," opines Davis with regard to embezzlement charges against Reed. *Reconstruction in Florida*, pp. 631-34.

crats.[40] It might be more true to say that Louisiana corrupted Warmoth (if indeed he was corrupted) than to say that Warmoth corrupted Louisiana. The other two carpetbag governors, Adelbert Ames of Mississippi and D. H. Chamberlain of South Carolina, were economy-minded and strictly honest.[41]

There remains the charge that the carpetbaggers disturbed the relations between the races in the South. Of course, the carpetbaggers did so. Their doing so was the basic cause of the animus against them. This is the reason why the honest ones among them, the men like Ames and Chamberlain and Warner, were as thoroughly hated and as strongly opposed as were any of the Yankee scoundrels. Most of the Southern whites opposed the granting of political rights to the former slaves. The carpetbaggers encouraged the Negroes to exercise such rights. Thus the carpetbaggers upset the pattern of race relationships, the pattern of Negro passivity, which most white Southerners considered ideal.

The party struggle in the postwar South amounted to something more than ordinary politics. In some of its aspects it was equivalent to a continuation, or a renewal, of the Civil War.

On the one hand, Southern Conservatives thought of themselves as still fighting for home rule and white supremacy—in essence much the same war aims as the Confederacy had pursued. Carpetbaggers, on the other hand, saw their own basic objective as the reunification of the country, which had been incompletely won at Appomattox, and as the emancipation of the Negroes, who had been but partially freed by the adoption of the Thirteenth Amendment.

On both sides the methods frequently were those of actual, though irregular, warfare. The Ku Klux Klan, the White League,

40. *New York Tribune*, March 14, 1872, clipping in the Warmoth MSS, Southern Historical Collection, University of North Carolina.

41. Garner, *Reconstruction in Mississippi*, pp. 229-36, 297-305, 320-23, concedes that, as governor, Ames made many good appointments and on the whole administered the state honestly and economically. Chamberlain was attorney-general of South Carolina before becoming governor. A letter attributed to him and written while he was attorney-general might be viewed as incriminating him in corruption. However, a South Carolina Democrat has written: "No stolen money was ever traced to him, and he positively denied any participation in the proceeds of public rascality." As governor, he was not even accused of corruption or extravagance. See Henry T. Thompson, *Ousting the Carpetbagger from South Carolina* (Columbia, S. C., 1926), pp. 36, 92-93, 101-102, and *passim*.

the Red Shirts, and the various kinds of rifle companies were military or semi-military organizations. So, too, were the state militias, the Union Leagues and Loyal Leagues, and the other partisan institutions of the carpetbaggers and their Negro allies. The carpetbaggers served, so to speak, as officers of front-line troops, deep in enemy territory, "on the picket line of freedom in the South." The embattled Republicans undoubtedly suffered much heavier casualties than did their foes.

True, the Republicans had the advantage of support by the regular United States army, but often that support was more a potentiality than a fact, and at critical moments it failed to materialize. As for the warriors of white supremacy, they had the backing of Northern sympathizers in strength and numbers that would have gladdened the heart of Jefferson Davis in that earlier war time when he was angling for the aid of the Knights of the Golden Circle. The carpetbaggers were divided and weakened by the Republican party schism of 1872, by personal rivalries among themselves, and by jealousies between them and their Negro and scalawag associates. Finally, as some of the carpetbaggers saw it, they were stabbed in the back—abandoned by the government and the people at the North.[42]

The history of this losing campaign has been written almost exclusively from the Southern, or Democratic, or disillusioned Republican point of view: the story of the carpetbaggers has been told mainly by their enemies. Historical scholarship has given its sanction to the propaganda of the victorious side in the Reconstruction War. That propaganda, like most, has its elements of truth, and like most, its elements of distortion and downright falsehood. Not that the carpetbaggers were invariably the apostles of righteousness and truth. We would make little progress toward historical understanding if we merely took the same old morality play and switched the labels of Evil and Good. But surely the time has long since passed when we can, uncritically, accept the "carpetbagger" stereotype.

No doubt men can be found who fit it. No doubt there were political tramps who went south to make cynical use of the

42. See, for example, Morgan, *Yazoo*, p. 487; Tourgée, *An Appeal to Caesar,* pp. 68-69; and Walter Allen, *Governor Chamberlain's Administration in South Carolina* (New York, 1888), pp. 507-20.

Negro vote and who contrived to win both office and illicit gain. But such men were few and comparatively unimportant. Far more numerous and more significant were those energetic and ambitious men who, with or without carpetbags, brought their savings or their borrowings to invest, who eventually got into politics for idealistic as well as selfish reasons, and who in office behaved no better and no worse than most of their contemporaries. Some of these men, like some others of their time, proved corrupt. It would be interesting to know whether, as peculators, the carpetbaggers took out more than a small fraction of the money that, as speculators, they had brought in.

The "Freedom to Control" in American Business History

ROWLAND BERTHOFF

"I am quite willing to open my shop to the trades union men," the Philadelphia shipbuilder John Roach told a Congressional committee in 1883, "and I have done it."

I say to the men, 'you may enjoy yourselves with your unions just as you do with your religion or your politics, but while you are in my workshop you must conform to my rules. . . . When you came to seek employment of me, you came in your own individual capacity, you presented yourself on your own individual merits, and it was upon that condition that I hired you. Now, if you have any complaint to make, make it for yourself. I will hear it, and try to treat you fairly; but you must not attempt to take the control of my workshop out of my hands.'[1]

Most American industrial employers of the time shared Roach's attitude toward labor, though few expressed it as volubly as he. Their policy, succinctly stated, had a double theme: the "absolute personal independence of the individual to work or not to work" and "the right of an owner . . . to the entire and exclusive control and management of his works."[2] On one hand, freedom; on the other, control.

The first of these two linked doctrines, the so-called "right to work," need not detain us here. Although long out of favor in the public policy of most states and of the federal government, its recent revival as a political issue has made it familiar today. The second doctrine, the employer's complete freedom to con-

1. U. S. Senate Committee [on Education and Labor], *Report on the Relations between Labor and Capital* (1885), I, 1004.

2. Declaration of principles of the National Association of Builders, 1887, in U. S. Industrial Commission, *Report* (1901), VII, 842; arbitration decision of William Elwell, Mauch Chunk, Pa., 1871, in Massachusetts Bureau of Statistics of Labor, *Twelfth Annual Report* (1881), p. 35.

trol all aspects of his business, is all but forgotten. Indeed, it may hardly seem credible that businessmen once commonly made so sweeping an assertion of right. But as a glance at any history of American labor relations in the late nineteenth century reveals, employers almost invariably advanced just this claim during labor disputes. Such continual reiteration, precisely because it reduced the doctrine to a shop-worn platitude, suggests that businessmen saw in their practical situation some urgent necessity for their unchallenged control. So important a bromide bears closer study.

In the middle of the twentieth century we are used to economic control by powerful "countervailing" institutions, notably corporations, labor unions, and governmental agencies.[3] The lack of any system of effective control a century ago begins to seem like a curious aberration in the course of American history —an explosion of individualistic free enterprise unlike anything before or since that time.[4] Earlier in the nineteenth century the old mercantilistic assumption had still prevailed that, at whatever point the public interest required, government had the right and duty to regulate commerce and industry as well as to foster their growth. The Hamiltonian program of subsidies, protective tariffs, and monopoly privileges for business had involved parallel controls, best exemplified by the central Bank of the United States, whose fiscal regulation assisted orderly expansion but curbed excessive speculation. The destruction by Andrew Jackson of this still rudimentary instrument of control made the 1830's a vital turning point in American economic history. Although for the rest of the nineteenth century the federal and state governments continued to subsidize various business enterprises with tariffs, land grants, and other privileges, the new entrepreneurs were left free from effective public regulation.[5]

But "the law of free development," as even a sympathetic critic observed toward the end of the century, was easily abused.

3. John Kenneth Galbraith, *American Capitalism: The Concept of Countervailing Power* (Boston, 1952), pp. 115-93.

4. For a general theory of this and related matters, see Rowland Berthoff, "The American Social Order: A Conservative Hypothesis," *American Historical Review,* LXV (1960), 495-514.

5. Bray Hammond, *Banks and Politics in America: From the Revolution to the Civil War* (Princeton, 1957), *passim.*

It permitted great fortunes to be made "by sharp practice, by chicanery, by circumventing the laws, by monopolizing the national heritage, by gambling on the stock exchange, by making 'corners' in food products, by wrecking railways, by watering stocks. . . ."[6] With enterprise freed and competition unrestrained, the often-expressed anxiety of the time lest liberty descend to license came perilously close to fulfilment. Indeed, the ease of obtaining public sanction for free private enterprise, under the new "general charter" laws, made some corporation charters all too literally licenses for the abuse of liberty. At the height of business competition in the 1860's and 1870's the lack of effective control over costs, production, and prices, either by government or by businessmen themselves, produced a plunging business cycle, a high rate of failures, reckless waste of resources, and uneasy labor relations. As John Roach observed in 1883, ". . . capital is very timid, and there are few persons who know the excitement and fear that exists among capitalists to-day . . . owing to the unsettled condition of things and this feeling which is working up between capital and labor."[7] Where might a means of stabilization be found?

In recent years historians have come to recognize that the trust movement—the consolidation of big business which began about 1870—was intended to be just such a means. So too was the concurrent movement to organize labor. Although in the prevailing individualism of that time both the trusts and the unions were feared as monopolistic conspiracies against the public welfare, to modern eyes they stand revealed as progenitors of the more systematic economic, social, and political order of our own day.[8]

In the latter half of the nineteenth century, however, when the construction of this new order was still in its early stages, it was far from clear that trusts or unions promised this result or even that such a result would be desirable. Until after 1900, therefore, businessmen groped for some more immediately prac-

6. George Frederic Parsons, "The Labor Question," *Atlantic Monthly*, LVIII (1886), 99.

7. Senate Committee [on Education and Labor], *Report . . .* (1885), I, 1013.

8. Thomas C. Cochran and William Miller, *The Age of Enterprise: A Social History of Industrial America* (New York, 1942), Chaps. vii, xi.

ticable method of imposing order upon industry. Herein lay the importance of the doctrine of their own absolute freedom to control. "Now," a student of this doctrine explained as early as 1871, "the employer, not having the power to control the price of either the raw or the wrought material, or to stop competition, or to monopolize the trade, has but one other resort left, and that is to strike at the wage-rate."[9] Labor was at least one element in his cost account that the employer might essay to control.

Given the chaotic circumstances of the time, the employers' doctrine—"the venerable axiom that ownership and control go together, and that they cannot be separated without a fatal invasion of property rights"—was no simple dogma.[10] Practical conditions made it not only complex but often confused. Whenever either employers or unionists argued in terms of theory abstracted from their practical circumstances, they were likely to exhibit more fervor than logical consistency.

Today it might seem that for them to speak of a freedom to control—a liberty to restrict liberty—unduly strained the ordinary meaning of words. At that time, however, the idea of liberty from restraint, as a moral absolute derived from a lengthy national experience with individualism, then at its height, appealed so strongly to Americans that they could quite plausibly apply it to almost any situation.[11] In practice the industrial employer's freedom to control meant his prerogative virtually to decide for himself the terms of employment; the workingman was free only in that he could choose to accept these conditions, usually by a merely tacit "contract," or else exercise his "right not to work." Any claim by employees to a collective share in setting wages and other working conditions would be, as one industrialist put it in 1902, an "insupportable interference with the discipline and ordinary management of our business."[12] By this principle the boundary between the rights of the employer and those of the employee were drawn so as practically to obliterate the latter. From the perspective of our own generation, which has drastical-

9. Massachusetts Bureau of Statistics of Labor, *Report* (1871), p. 42.
10. Parsons, "The Labor Question," p. 101.
11. See Oscar and Mary Handlin, *The Dimensions of Liberty* (Cambridge, Mass., 1961), pp. 9-22.
12. George F. Baer, in *Scranton Republican*, Sept. 4, 1902.

ly redrawn that line, the essence of this ostensibly libertarian doctrine does appear to have been control rather than any species of freedom.

One source of confusion was a certain incompatibility between the employer's practical control and his nominal allegiance to the classically liberal law of supply and demand. That wages could be controlled the trade unions themselves agreed when they maintained that labor was not a "commodity" entirely governed by the impersonal vagaries of economic law. Employers confidently retorted that on the contrary labor was just like any other commodity in the market. "Under the fixed laws of trade, of supply and demand," Joseph Medill of the *Chicago Tribune* intoned in 1883, "the employer has really little more control over prices . . . than over the winds and the weather," and if prices could not be raised, neither could wages.[13]

And yet many an employer appealed to the inexorable workings of economic law virtually in order to justify his own right to determine, free from interference by his employees, precisely what "natural" wage level they could be induced to accept. Employers insisted that their own superior understanding of economic law made the managing of wage rates and other labor costs the inalienable right of property. Particularly when a trade union itself invoked supply and demand in an effort to raise wages, the employer was apt to brush aside arguments of labor scarcity and his own needs and simply to assert his exclusive right of management. Thus the president of Western Union blamed the telegraph operators' strike of 1883 on

the conviction on the part of the operators that there was a limited number of them to be had, and that . . . they . . . could dictate their own terms. . . . I believe it was of the first importance to the company to remove that conviction and beat the strike. . . . The company could never agree that they should have, or should believe themselves to have, power to dictate their own salaries.[14]

The danger of an artificial "labor monopoly" was frequently alleged by employers, mindful perhaps of popular murmuring

13. Senate Committee [on Education and Labor], *Report* . . . (1885), II, 992. Cf. Thomas C. Cochran, *Railroad Leaders, 1845-1890: The Business Mind in Action* (Cambridge, Mass., 1953), pp. 173-83.

14. Testimony of Norvin Green, in Senate Committee [on Education and Labor], *Report* . . . (1885), I, 892.

against the beginnings of the trust movement in business. The real object of the trade unions, so a New York coal dealer said in 1887, was clear enough: "It is speculation. They aim to control all the labor of the country ('get a corner on labor'), break up competition and then put the price very high, the same as is sometimes done with merchandise."[15] Labor would then go on to control not only wages but also prices and output, all of which, if not inevitably fixed by natural economic law, no doubt ought at least to be left to the employer to fix.

More specific objections to union practices—to jurisdictional strikes, apprenticeship quotas, sympathy strikes and boycotts, and the like—involved fewer logical traps. Employers particularly insisted that their right to hire and discharge individuals at will— the open shop—was essential to efficient management. "I don't object to their organization," a Fall River cotton manufacturer quite typically averred during the spinners' strike of 1870, "but do object to their saying who shall and who shall not work. . . . I might as well throw my property away as to submit to their ruling, and I will never do it."[16] The union shop might indeed lead to more interference of this kind than any employer could safely permit. As Charles M. Schwab recalled of his superintendency of the Carnegie steel works at Homestead in the 1890's, before he broke the union:

At one time the labor association took it upon themselves to select their own foremen and to select the men who should succeed them in case of a vacancy. . . . I do not think any commercial business can grow and prosper under such conditions.[17]

An employer could, however, push the principle of property rights farther than necessity or even his own welfare made advisable. By holding too rigidly to his right to control, he might indeed lose control altogether. Some, for instance, rejected arbitration of labor disputes as they did union interference, since both tended "to separate control from ownership, and in effect to transfer the latter by a method of disguised confiscation."[18]

15. New York Bureau of Statistics of Labor, *Fifth Annual Report* (1887), p. 270.
16. Testimony of D. A. Brayton, in Massachusetts Bureau of Statistics of Labor, *Report* (1871), pp. 54, 56.
17. U. S. Industrial Commission, *Report* (1901), XIII, 461.
18. Parsons, "The Labor Question," p. 102.

As George M. Pullman explained in 1894, he could not expose the Pullman Palace Car Company to the judgment of "some man who is not interested" in the business: "Suppose an arbitrator had said, 'Yes, you are able. Go on and pay these additional wages;' it would only be a question of time, of course, when any concern would be bankrupt." Unless competitors were made to pay the same wages, to be sure, the business might fail. But even though Pullman had for years been praised, with considerable reason, as the very model of a benevolent employer, his paternal "principle that a man should have the right to manage his own property" contributed as much as anything to the resentment that boiled over in the strike of 1894.[19] The strike was broken, but it heralded the end of the model company town of Pullman, Illinois.[20]

Employers could never agree whether the danger in labor unions lay in their strength or their weakness. In either case, company discipline was necessary. Thus, so it was often explained, unionists were unwilling or incompetent to exercise control over any aspect of business affairs. A Chicago machinery manufacturer testified in 1900:

I do not believe that the average mechanic is sufficiently a good business man to dictate to his employers how the business should be run. . . . I consider the average laboring mechanic as more or less of an overgrown boy. He wants a guide and a help, and when he is turned loose he gets erratic.[21]

Unions were said to be too weakly organized to hold their members to the terms of a wage contract, and, not being incorporated, they were not legally accountable for contract-breaking. Even when an employer accepted the union shop and trusted the union officers, as a Colorado coal operator said he did, he might find fault with "the individual irresponsibility of the individual miner and the apparent inability of the union to control the miner."[22]

19. U. S. Strike Commission, *Report on the Chicago Strike of June-July, 1894* (1895), p. 556.
20. Almont Lindsey, *The Pullman Strike: The Story of a Unique Experiment and of a Great Labor Upheaval* (Chicago, 1942), *passim*.
21. Testimony of James L. Board, in U. S. Industrial Commission, *Report* (1901), VIII, 42.
22. Testimony of Walter W. Curtis, in U. S. Commission on Industrial Relations, *Report* (64th Cong., 1st sess., Sen. Doc. 415, Aug. 23, 1915), VII, 6535.

On the other hand, when individual workingmen committed acts of violence during strikes, employers were tempted to see behind them the deliberate hand of a powerful labor conspiracy. The "anarchistic labor trusts," so said a spokesman for Southern industry in 1900, "are to-day the greatest menace to this Government that exists [in] their influence for disruption and disorganization of society."[23] Although such talk sounded just as puerile to some contemporaries as the opposite notion that capitalists rejoiced in grinding the faces of the poor, it indicated at least a dim awareness that a species of anarchy, an "individualism gone mad," did infect industrial society in the lack of some kind of stable control.[24]

At a time when it was rank heresy to suggest that government had any right to interfere with business management, there were nevertheless means by which labor relations might be collectively controlled. If the employers in a trade or industry co-operated, whether in a loose trade association or in a unitary trust, they could in fact exercise the control over their labor force that they claimed in theory. Or, if a strong union enforced a uniform scale of wages and working conditions throughout a trade or industry, as the scarcity of its members' craft skills sometimes permitted one to do, no employer would have the unfair advantage of cheap labor. Employers who dealt with a "properly organized" trade union, as one of the machinists' leaders said in 1883, "all go into the market on the same terms."[25] Whichever side it came from, control would take the place of a competition unsettling to management and labor alike. And then, of course, a third arrangement, an agreement between well-organized forces on both sides, would likely prove most effective of all.

All three schemes were tried in the late nineteenth century. Fierce competition in the iron-molding trade in the 1850's and 1860's, to cite a well-known example, led the manufacturers first to pare labor costs to the bone and suppress trade unionism. The

23. Testimony of N. F. Thompson, in U. S. Industrial Commission, *Report* (1901), VII, 756-57.
24. Josiah Strong, *Our Country* (New York, 1885), p. 93; Harry Percy Robinson, "The Humiliating Report of the Strike Commission," *Forum*, XVIII (1895), 523; California Bureau of Labor Statistics, *Ninth Biennial Report* (1900), p. 119.
25. Testimony of William McClelland, in Senate Committee [on Education and Labor], *Report* . . . (1885), I, 682-83.

first joint agreements between the molders' union and the manufacturers' associations in the 1860's proved unstable and temporary, but by the 1890's they had arrived at a system of regular conferences for collective bargaining.[26] There were employers in the industry who were glad to be "governed" to this extent by the union. One of them testified in 1883:

As a general rule we let them do as they please. . . . The prices they demand do not seem to be extortionate as a rule. They seem to want to meet the market generally, but they do not know as the manufacturers know just what the state of the trade is.[27]

The men might propose, but the market and management disposed in most cases.

The joint agreement seemed to be the coming system in other skilled trades and specialized industries. The merger of nineteen firms, half of which had been non-union, into the National Glass Company in 1899 led to prompt recognition of the Flint Glass Workers' Union.[28] The Connecticut hat manufacturers organized an association in 1885 in response to a union request for industry-wide bargaining, in order to do away both with "unjust and unreasonable acts" by labor and with "the starting of independent shops by men without conscience" who would have paid low wages and undercut the market. "The manufacturers surrendered their independence," their association explained, "and the journeymen in return gave them the security of these agreements to protect them against an abuse of the power which was thus placed in their hands."[29] A pottery manufacturer, when taxed with having "given up a part of his liberty" in consenting to deal with trade unions, replied that if formerly "you might be entirely independent, at the same time you were certainly in hot water a good portion of the time. . . . You paid for your independence."[30]

26. Frank T. Stockton, *The International Molders Union of North America* (Baltimore, "Johns Hopkins University Studies in Historical and Political Science," XXXIX, No. 3, 1921), pp. 116-36; Jonathan Grossman, *William Sylvis, Pioneer of American Labor* (New York, 1945), *passim*.
27. Testimony of Thomas M. Miller, in Senate Committee [on Education and Labor], *Report . . .* (1885), II, 19.
28. U. S. Industrial Commission, *Report* (1901), VII, 828-37.
29. Connecticut Bureau of Labor Statistics, *Sixth Annual Report* (1891), pp. 132-78.
30. Testimony of John A. Campbell in U. S. Commission on Industrial Relations, *Report* (1915), III, 2992.

But if a degree of craft-union control sometimes averted labor disorders, employers of unskilled or semi-skilled labor commonly rejected union interference as a source only of disorder. The anthracite mine operators of northeastern Pennsylvania, who employed skilled miners but also a larger number of unskilled laborers and boys, were staunchly anti-union throughout the last quarter of the nineteenth century. And yet for a few years before 1875 some of them welcomed virtual union regulation, not only of wages but of production and prices as well, and after 1900 the entire industry submitted to collective bargaining.

The anthracite industry was chronically bedeviled by excess mining capacity, a surplus of labor, and market prices for coal that were too low, the operators were wont to argue, to permit a comfortable wage scale. As early as the 1840's, hardly twenty years after anthracite mining began, this reckless competition plagued the trade, particularly among the dozens of small, inefficient operators in the Schuylkill or southern coal field.[31] "Hurrah boys!" was the mocking cheer; "Rip it up! Out with it! Get all to market you can, no matter about value, or price, or profits."[32] Although apparently most mine operators failed within a year or two, they were too committed to the new entrepreneurial individualism of the age to submit to any effective system of control.[33] Twice in 1849 the seventy-two Schuylkill operators, deploring the glut produced by the "reckless traffic in coal," pledged to suspend mining for three weeks.[34] From time to time during the 1850's arrangements of this sort were tried both in Schuylkill County and in the northern anthracite field, the Wyoming and Lackawanna valleys of Luzerne County.[35] But the temptation to undercut one's competitors usually prevailed, to the disadvantage of all. "The stock of the carrying [railroad] companies were the foot-balls of the stock board," as one critic

31. Clifton K. Yearley, Jr., *Enterprise and Anthracite: Economics and Democracy in Schuylkill County, 1820-1875* (Baltimore, "Johns Hopkins University Studies in Historical and Political Science," LXXIX, No. 1, 1961), pp. 57-93.
32. *Wilkes-Barre Advocate*, Nov. 6, 1850.
33. Yearley, *Enterprise and Anthracite*, p. 59.
34. *Miners Journal* (Pottsville), March 24, July 14, 1849.
35. *Ibid.*, March 21, 1857; *Wilkes-Barre Advocate*, Feb. 9, 1853; *Pittston Gazette*, Jan. 30, Feb. 27, 1857; *Record of the Times* (Wilkes-Barre), Jan. 18, 1860.

said; "Coal lands the foot-ball of daring speculators, . . . and the miners became the foot-balls of both."[36]

When in 1842 the Schuylkill miners struck to obtain cash payment of their wages, the operators, who were hard pressed for cash themselves, showed no intention of abandoning their expedient of paying in store orders, or credit for provisions. One mine owner proclaimed that "when he wanted guardians to take care of his business he would get the Court to appoint them."[37] This, and the advice, to any individual miner dissatisfied with his wages, to "seek employment elsewhere . . . drop all coalition —allow no one to dictate to you—consult with your employer—go to him, if you want to work, and after making your contract, go peaceably to your duties as good and well meaning citizens should," represented the opinion of both the businessmen and the public of the time.[38]

Here and there in the region a new note was occasionally heard. "We query much," a Mauch Chunk editor mused in 1843,

if the 'strikes,' 'riots,' and the like daring combinations and conspiracies, are not the legitimate offspring of the universal spirit of association—the steam engine of present civilization. We deprecate every union in which the dignity and responsibility of the individual are lost in the masses; and yet we cannot conceive how any great effort can be successfully completed, without association of some kind. Society abridges no real, true and honest right. . . .[39]

At that time such a prophet enjoyed little honor in the anthracite country. But during the 1850's the feeling grew that, as an editor in the Lackawanna valley said, "There ought to be a Co-operative Union among the miners, which should fix authoritatively a just scale of wages, and so with Coal operators, there should be such an understanding as will effectually do away with these strikes which operate only to the damage of all parties."[40]

The northern operators, however, guided by the Delaware, Lackawanna & Western and the Delaware & Hudson railroads, which had already combined coal mining with their coal carry-

36. *Miners Journal* (Pottsville), Dec. 1, 1855.
37. *Ibid.*, July 16, 1842.
38. *Ibid.*, July 23, 1842.
39. *Carbon County Transit* (Mauch Chunk), Aug. 29, 1843.
40. *Lackawanna Herald* (Scranton), June 8, 1854.

ing, were strong enough to resist such advice. One of them wrote during the miners' strike of 1862-1863,

It will never do to yield a single *iota*. Once thoroughly taught a good lesson, it will not soon be forgotten and will save in coming time more than the present cost. It is a most difficult time to conduct at all satisfactorily any operation, the controlling element of which is *Labor*.[41]

The operators publicly resolved that they were "determined to manage their own business in accordance with the principle of justice to themselves as well as to the men; and when they are prevented from doing this they will cease to operate."[42] Public opinion likewise disapproved of the miners' union except for its mutual-benefit system, which relieved the taxpayers from having to support disabled miners, and for its quieting of the usual "riots and rows" among mineworkers of different nationalities. But where wages were concerned, it was generally agreed that the men ought to content themselves, like everyone else, with the law of supply and demand.[43]

During 1867 and 1868 the independent operators of the southern field began to co-operate in order to ensure their control there. Early in 1869 the Mahanoy Valley and Locust Mountain Coal Association, the Mount Carmel Coal Association, and the Coal Association of the Southern Coal Field of Schuylkill County, in proposing to reduce wages to the level of the northern field, resolved on "Firmness, therefore, upon the part of the operators, and a persistent determination to manage their own business, . . . as the only alternative against certain ruin."[44] As a Hazleton operator made clear, a little more bluntly, to a union committee, "he'd do as he pleased; he had done so for thirty years, and would still do so, and was ready to fight the men any time they wished."[45]

Within a few months, however, the organizations of Schuylkill operators helped usher in a new regime that quieted such truculence. Following the initiative of the mineworkers' new Work-

41. Joseph H. Scranton to Moses Taylor, Jan. 8, 1863 (Scranton papers).
42. *Luzerne Union* (Wilkes-Barre), Jan. 21, 1863.
43. *Record of the Times* (Wilkes-Barre), Aug. 16, 1865.
44. *Miners Journal* (Pottsville), Jan. 23, 1869.
45. *Ibid.*, May 1, 1869.

ingmen's Benevolent Association, the operators submitted during
the spring and summer of 1869 to the first in a series of annual
suspensions of mining intended to reduce the coal surplus in the
market, raise coal prices, and permit agreement on a sliding
scale or "basis" for wages. Mining wages in the Schuylkill field
were now pegged to the price of coal rather than to the supply
of or demand for labor or to the arbitrary will of the employer.[46]

The Wyoming-Lackawanna operators, however, continued
obdurate. "I agree with you," W. R. Storrs, the general coal
agent of the D. L. & W. Railroad, assured his president, "that
no concessions can now be made to the men. We must be as
independent as they are."[47] When the men struck to secure the
same "basis" as in Schuylkill County, Storrs advised them, he
reported, to "take the Co. at its word, resume work, make no
demands, nor send no Committees & see what the Co. will do.
Act the manly part of true men, and see whether or no such
action is appreciated."[48] The strike failed. The managers of the
D. L. & W. did, indeed, admire, in all sincerity, any show of
"manliness" or independence by their workers. When later in
1869 a few of the miners threatened to strike against being
docked for "sending out too much slate & dirt with the coal,"
Storrs privately applauded them: "Our men are independent. . . .
don't think they will do it [strike] for this, but it shows their
spirit."[49]

The Schuylkill operators' associations amalgamated late in
1869 into the Anthracite Board of Trade. Negotiations between
this board and the Workingmen's Benevolent Association, however, fell through; the "suspension" of mining in 1870 was in fact
a lockout. Before the operators agreed to compromise, the Philadelphia & Reading Railroad, the principal carrier in the southern
field, had to bring pressure to bear on them. Much the same
sequence of events occurred again in 1871. The operators agreed
not to reopen their suspended mines "until a radical change is
effected in the system of labor," since, they said, the union's

46. G. O. Virtue, "The Anthracite Mine Laborers," *Bulletin of the U. S. Department of Labor,* No. 13 (Nov., 1897), pp. 732-36.
47. W. R. Storrs to Samuel Sloan, June 7, 1869 (D.L. & W. papers).
48. Storrs to Sloan, Aug. 13, 1869.
49. Storrs to Sloan, Dec. 10, 1869.

scheme for raising both coal prices and wages only evinced its greed for "nothing less than a copartnership interest" in the business.[50] Ultimately both sides accepted arbitration, by which, although the employer's right of management and the individual mineworker's right "to make his own contract" were formally affirmed, a new "basis" wage scale was put into effect.[51]

This partnership of capital and labor was always a shaky affair, in spite of the combined efforts of both the workers' and employers' associations to hold their members to the scale. When in 1871 one operator offered higher wages, union members and operators alike abandoned their agreement. In spite of imperfect discipline on both sides, however, they continued the pattern of annual wage agreements through 1872 and 1873. The Reading even issued a railroad pass to John Welsh, the head of the union. "It is in our interest," General Henry Pleasants, the company's mining chief, urged, "to have him visit all parts of the coal region as often as possible because his presence often allays trouble and is calculated to prevent strikes."[52]

The independent operators of the Schuylkill field had always objected to the Reading Railroad as a monopoly, "ruled by foreign interests entirely," whose "whole course . . . has been one of injustice and oppression to the community of this county, . . . a desperate, lawless, and haughty corporation."[53] The free competition of small firms and partnerships of local individuals, even though many of them failed, they believed to be both more efficient and morally better than domination by a corporation with chartered privileges "secured," they said, "by secret legislation unknown to the people."[54] But the balance of power in Schuylkill tipped finally to the side of the Philadelphia & Reading Coal and Iron Company, the railroad's mining subsidiary, when in the early 1870's under the direction of Franklin B. Gowen, it rapidly acquired most of the coal land and control, through leases

50. *New York Herald*, Feb. 16, 1871.
51. *Miners Journal* (Pottsville), April 22, May 20, 1871.
52. Henry Pleasants to George deB. Keim, June 15, 1874 (Philadelphia & Reading Coal and Iron Company papers).
53. *Miners Journal* (Pottsville), Feb. 1, 1851; *Record of the Times* (Wilkes-Barre), Jan. 16, 1875.
54. *Miners Journal* (Pottsville), Feb. 20, 1836; Jan. 14, 1854; Feb. 22, 1862; July 29, 1865; Feb. 13, 1869.

and carrying contracts, of the remaining seventy-odd independent operators.[55] Thereafter the Reading dominated the southern field as the Lackawanna and the Delaware & Hudson, joined at this time by the Erie Railroad, already did the northern field.

The half-dozen anthracite railroads (including the Lehigh Valley and the Central of New Jersey) now operated or leased most of the mines and provided the remaining independents with their only routes to market. With all the minor competitors whipped into line, it was possible for the railroads in 1873 to organize a general system of controlled production and prices in all the anthracite fields. Their Board of Control limited each producer to an annual tonnage calculated not to oversupply the market. This "secret" though often exposed anthracite coal combination, based as it was only on "a friendly understanding," broke down from time to time during the next twenty-five years. In 1898, however, J. P. Morgan, through consolidation of some of the railroads and elimination of a threat of free competition by certain independent operators, made the combination fully effective.[56]

Having to this degree insured prices and production against the free play of the market after 1873, the operators of all the anthracite fields could dispense with the assistance of labor organizations. It had proved dangerous, though useful when better expedients were lacking, to admit the Workingmen's Benevolent Association into their counsels. So the general coal agent of the Lackawanna pointed out in 1871, the year when the men of the northern field struck:

It was when the Union or W.B.A. conceived the idea of controlling the business, putting up wages by limiting the production, and managing the mines, that the men became dissatisfied &c. I need not enlarge. There is no value or security in these coal properties subject to such unwarrantable dictation & interference by irresponsible men.[57]

The general depression made a satisfactory wage agreement impossible in 1874, and in 1875 the operators forced the issue. "The Companies have all agreed to the [wage] reduction & will

55. *Ibid.*, May 7, 1875.
56. Eliot Jones, *The Anthracite Coal Combination in the United States* (Cambridge, Mass., 1914), pp. 40-97.
57. Storrs to Sloan, April 29, 1871.

stand by each other in the contest," the president of the Lackawanna noted with satisfaction.[58] After a scattering of local
strikes, the miners of the northern field submitted. In the Schuylkill field, where the public "perfectly understood that Mr. Gowen
intends in this struggle to convince the men that their organization is utterly powerless when contending against the corporation," the union struck for five bitter and violent months.[59] Welsh
advised compromise, only to have his followers cry treachery
and the companies decline to "recognize the assumed right of
the Miners' Union to dictate" to them.[60] Gowen flatly refused to
negotiate on any question of railroad freight rates or the price
of coal. The contest was unequal; defeat destroyed the union,
and Welsh himself was blacklisted.[61]

For the operators the regulation of wages now became an
incidental matter rather than, as in the days before the combination, the only means of control open to them. In command at
most other points, their right to rule labor was seldom challenged
after 1875, nor did they often need to invoke the right-to-work
doctrine or even the law of supply and demand. Coal mining
was still troubled by an overcapacity to produce, usually blamed
on the railroad companies' prior interest in a steady flow of coal
to market, and the Reading, having imprudently extended its
mining operations, was intermittently in receivership. But toward the mineworkers the operators could assume a wary benev-
olence befitting their power.

Although hostile to any revival of the Workingmen's Benevolent Association, the Philadelphia & Reading Coal and Iron
Company and the three large independent operators in the
Lehigh field voluntarily continued the old union's "basis" or
sliding scale relationship between prices and wages. In fact the
Reading's managers prided themselves on voluntarily paying
more than the minimum prescribed by the basis during depressed
years in the 1880's.[62] It is true that for a time in the late 1870's

58. Sloan to Storrs, Feb. 12, 1875.
59. *Morning Republican* (Scranton), March 29, 1875.
60. *Shenandoah Weekly Herald*, April 24, 1875; *Record of the Times* (Wilkes-
Barre), June 26, 1875.
61. Marvin W. Schlegel, *Ruler of the Reading: The Life of Franklin B.
Gowen, 1836-1889* (Harrisburg, 1947), pp. 62-76.
62. S. B. Whiting to Receivers, July 7, 1880 (Philadelphia & Reading Coal
and Iron Company papers).

Gowen maintained an espionage system in the Schuylkill field in order to counter the spread of the Knights of Labor among his miners.[63] But after Gowen's retirement the company's general manager made a practice of receiving committees of the men with due courtesy, sometimes passed along their grievances as "very properly made and . . . worthy of the most careful consideration," and occasionally even deigned to sign formal wage agreements with them.[64]

In the Wyoming-Lackawanna field, where wages were never calculated on a standard sliding scale, the three coal railroads fixed rates more arbitrarily. Their presidents or mining superintendents conferred at intervals to determine a common wage policy, and, though they avoided more general meetings with independent operators for fear of "unfavorable comment," the latter were fairly content to "do whatever the large companies do."[65] Yet while keeping control in their own hands, the Lackawanna, Erie, and Delaware & Hudson customarily cultivated the good will of the miners. The Lackawanna's general coal agent recognized that "when a Committee of our own men . . . make requests or demands, it may be best to confer with them."[66] He reported many a "pleasant chat" in which, "as a co-worker," he persuaded committees of the miners that "there was two sides to the question, and that the Co. was doing the best it could with them."[67] Officers of other companies shared this attitude. "I have always felt a friendly interest in our men," one of them confided, "and have been the first to advance [wages] when prices would warrant it, and the last to reduce when compelled to do so by reason of lower prices for Coal."[68]

But such soft words were intended to prevent the spread of the Knights of Labor and other organizations among the miners.

63. Weekly Miners Journal (Pottsville), Feb. 21, 1879; Franklin B. Gowen to S. B. Whiting, March 7, 1879 (Philadelphia & Reading Coal and Iron Company papers).
64. Whiting to Receivers, Feb. 11, 1886; agreement of Sept. 14, 1887 (Philadelphia & Reading Coal and Iron Company papers).
65. Storrs to Sloan, July 29, Nov. 25, 1876; April 27, 1880; June 20, 1882; Jan. 28, Feb. 2, 1885; Feb. 19, 1889.
66. Storrs to Sloan, May 4, 1886.
67. Storrs to Sloan, March 20, 1877; Feb. 18, 1888.
68. W. H. Tillinghast to Thomas H. Phillips, Dec. 30, 1885 (Lehigh & Wilkes-Barre Coal Company papers).

"Given the power," one official warned, "they will exercise it—Say who shall be employed—hours of service—[what] wages and when paid—Registration to enforce their demands—practically full control—Bad precedents in the hands of irresponsible leaders."[69] The only serious challenge to the operators, the strike in the Lehigh field in 1887-1888, they squarely met, firm in their belief in the employer's "right to control his own business."[70]

At the end of the century, however, just when the combination of the major operator-carriers became fully effective, the United Mine Workers of America arrived in northeastern Pennsylvania, fresh from their victories of 1897 in the bituminous fields and seeking still a new balance between the rights of management and labor. In 1900 and, after an inconclusive settlement, again in 1902 the U.M.W. struck to obtain through collective bargaining a share in the control of wages and working conditions. The strikers proclaimed as their goal "the freedom accorded them in the early days" of coal mining. "The miner," they announced hopefully, "has the right to set the price for his labor. The lawyer, doctor and merchant each set their own price."[71]

Unconvinced by this excursion into history and ethics, the operators condemned the organizers from the bituminous regions as strangers presuming to tell "the head of a family what conduct he should follow toward his children."[72] In declining the union's invitation to a joint conference, President George F. Baer of the Reading admonished them:

There can not be two masters in the management of business. . . . Discipline is essential in the conduct of all business. . . . Your organizations have no power to enforce their decrees, and thereby insure discipline, and we have no power to maintain discipline except the power to discharge. The moment we exercise this power we would be subjected to an inquisitorial and ineffective supervision, without any certainty as to how or when it will be possible to reach a righteous decision or to enforce that decision when reached.[73]

69. Storrs to Sloan, Feb. 8, 1888.
70. *Scranton Republican*, Oct. 24, 1887.
71. *Ibid.*, May 2, 1900.
72. *Ibid.*, Aug. 10, 1900.
73. U. S. Anthracite Coal Strike Commission, *Report to the President on the Anthracite Coal Strike of May-October, 1902* (Washington, 1903), p. 218.

The sole issue of importance underlying all the specific demands of the union, President W. H. Truesdale of the Lackawanna insisted, was "that these great properties shall be controlled and operated by their owners and not by outsiders."[74] And President E. B. Thomas of the Erie Railroad added the usual companion principle of the "inalienable right of a man to labor, and this without regard to nationality, creed, or association."[75]

This invocation of individualism, however, held a poignant irony for the operators as members of the anthracite combination. Their united strength, acquired as recently as 1898, had in fact been imposed from without by the financial influence of J. P. Morgan. This overlordship Morgan now exerted on the side of collective bargaining, at the urging of Mark Hanna and the National Civic Federation, which had recently begun its campaign to harmonize capital and labor. Morgan also had personal confidence in the probity of John Mitchell, the president of the U.M.W., who was also an official of the Civic Federation.[76]

The anthracite operators perforce accepted arbitration by a commission sanctioned by Morgan and appointed by President Theodore Roosevelt, who was determined to demonstrate at least the moral sovereignty of government in economic matters.[77] Although Baer and his colleagues continued to expostulate that they would "not agree to turn over the management of our business to a labor organization" and rested their case before the commission mainly on the familiar principles of company "discipline" and the right of non-union miners to work, they accepted the commission's report, not only as to specific wages, hours, and other working conditions but also in its establishment of a conciliation board on which the operators and the union would be equally represented. Some of the operators remained a bit touchy at having had to knuckle under. Disputing the union's interpretation of the nine-hour day awarded by the Commission,

74. *Scranton Republican*, Aug. 16, 1902.
75. Anthracite Coal Strike Commission, *Report*, p. 221.
76. E. G. Campbell, *The Reorganization of the American Railroad System, 1893-1900* (New York, 1938), pp. 160-89; Marguerite Green, *The National Civic Federation and the American Labor Movement, 1900-1925* (Washington, 1956), pp. 43-56.
77. Henry F. Pringle, *Theodore Roosevelt: A Biography* (New York, 1931), pp. 264-78.

the Reading locked its men out. When, after a compromise, the miners reported back to work a day earlier than the company desired, the superintendent lectured them, "This company will control its own property and will insist that all its employees obey the regulations and orders," and told them not to come back until the duly appointed time.[78]

Operators might protest that they had already "had to yield so much that they regard each additional concession as a humiliation" or that the agreement had made the men "feel that they are in charge of the mines."[79] But almost the only shred left of their once-fixed principle of exclusive control was their empty refusal, until 1920, to recognize that the mineworkers' committees with whom they met represented that meddling stranger the U.M.W. The practical success of the new regime all but realized Mitchell's vision in which "the representatives of the anthracite miners sit side by side with Mr. Baer, Mr. Olyphant, Mr. Truesdale and Mr. Thomas . . . as plain, good friends and business men and adjust their differences and compose their quarrels without recourse to strikes and lockouts."[80] Between 1903 and 1912 the conciliation board heard two hundred grievance cases, some brought by the mineworkers and others by the operators, all of which (with the aid of an impartial umpire) were settled formally or informally or withdrawn to the relative satisfaction of both sides. The agreement, originally for three years, was regularly renewed thereafter without undue altercation.[81]

An editor in the region observed, only a year after the agreement of 1903, "The arbitrary feeling is no longer manifested. . . . The watchword seems to be fairness."[82] Now that labor costs as well as production and prices were under control, the absolute rights of management were as outmoded as the individual miner's "right to work" independently of the union or, for that matter,

78. *Scranton Republican*, April 24, 1903.
79. *Ibid.*, July 7, 1904; testimony of R. M. Olyphant, in Interstate Commerce Commission, W. R. Hearst *against the Philadelphia & Reading Railway Company et al.* (n.p., 1904), p. 253.
80. *Scranton Republican*, Oct. 30, 1903. R. M. Olyphant was president of the Delaware & Hudson Railroad.
81. Arthur E. Suffern, *Conciliation and Arbitration in the Coal Industry of America* (Boston, 1915), pp. 225-68.
82. *Scranton Republican*, May 2, 1904.

as the individual coal operator's onetime independence of the anthracite combination.

Combination and control were supplanting free competition throughout American industry in the late nineteenth and early twentieth centuries. Usually, however, the trust movement followed the example of the anthracite business only as far as the stage the latter reached in 1898 and stopped short of that of 1903. The National Civic Federation might advocate collective bargaining, but trust control of production and prices by no means led businessmen generally to admit their employees to a share in controlling the cost of labor. Even the anthracite operators, for that matter, accepted collective bargaining and conciliation in 1903 only under duress from higher authority, including the moral suasion that President Roosevelt brought to bear in their case, as a salutary example, but in no other. Sacrificed as they were *pour encourager les autres,* they remained unique among employers of large masses of unskilled and semi-skilled labor.

The United Mine Workers of America likewise was not a typical union of that period. Most of the other unions in the American Federation of Labor consisted of skilled craftsmen, and collective bargaining reigned mainly in trades with a high proportion of such men. In the steel industry after 1900, for example, consolidation and co-operation under the leadership of the United States Steel Corporation resulted in the suppression of the old ironworkers' union, already weakened as it was by the decline of old-fashioned craftsmanship.[83]

It was in 1903, for that matter, that there sprang up the first of a series of twentieth-century movements for the open shop in industry. There had been employers' associations with this purpose since the 1830's, even then complaining, "Heretofore we have not been masters of our business, but have been compelled to comply with the most arbitrary measures of the men in our employ, aided on and encouraged by the Trades' Union."[84] In various trades during and after the Civil War employers' asso-

83. David Brody, *Steelworkers in America: The Nonunion Era* (Cambridge, Mass., 1960), pp. 50-79.
84. John R. Commons and others, *A Documentary History of American Industrial Society* (Cleveland, 1910), VI, 33.

ciations endeavored to restore the blessings of pristine individualism to their workmen and themselves. About 1900 a rash of anti-union crusades spread across the country in cities where unions had been strong.[85] Then in 1903, only a few weeks after the Anthracite Strike Commission issued its report, the National Association of Manufacturers took up the crusade, fulminating against the imminent usurpation by an un-American labor movement of capital's "rights of sovereignty."[86] If private claims to sovereignty suggested anarchy to some, the open-shop advocates retorted that it was unionism that presaged anarchism, and "socialism and despotism" as well.[87]

The doctrine of the right of management to control every aspect of business, however, was falling out of favor. With the public excited over the trust movement, and particularly over what was feared to be its excessive control, a more strictly libertarian argument like the right-to-work formula—or "the maintenance of individualism"—was more prudent. If the employer's authority was mentioned at all, it was usually behind some such mask as "the principle of personal ownership." The latter phrase, indeed, did duty as merely another synonym for the employee's "right to work" as often as for the rights of capital.[88] The open-shop movement appealed to the nostalgia of those who fancied that the competitive past had been a more pleasant economic world than the regulated present. New circumstances had transmuted the old doctrines.

These rags and tatters of nineteenth-century principles nevertheless served a practical new purpose. Labor had once been the only major factor on a company's balance sheet that, in a highly competitive era, was perhaps susceptible to company control. The employer of the 1870's had sought to fix a wage scale in order to remove at least this one element of uncertainty from his calculations. After 1900, when business consolidation was stabilizing prices and production, labor might be the only intract-

85. John R. Commons and others, *History of Labour in the United States* (New York, 1918), I, 401ff.; II, 26ff., 195, 414ff.

86. Green, *National Civic Federation*, p. 98; chap. iii, *passim*.

87. *Ibid.*, p. 105.

88. Albion Guilford Taylor, *Labor Policies of the National Association of Manufacturers* (Urbana, "University of Illinois Studies in the Social Sciences," XV, No. 1, March, 1927), pp. 48, 52; chap. ii, *passim*.

able factor. A strike for higher wages, even if it failed, could without warning derange the cost estimates on which a company's contracts were based. To control labor in the twentieth century, however, would be only to rivet the last major link in a general structure of control.

Today the economic structure rests partly on the continuing consolidation of business, partly on a revival of governmental regulation, and partly on collective bargaining. To all but that minority of rugged individualists who cling to the "right to work" formula, the anarchically competitive economy of the mid-nineteenth century seems remote indeed. When at that time the need for industrial control was first felt, few could express it except in such libertarian terms as the *freedom* of the owner to control his business. Since business, however, consisted of people as well as contracts and balance sheets, the employer's freedom often seemed to workingmen to be no better than the autocratic authority of a tyrant. Today it is difficult not to sympathize with them when one reads the ukases that their employers promulgated in the name of the rights of property. "Our money built these mills," one manufacturer bluntly asserted in 1882, "and we propose to secure whatever benefits may be derived from the business."[89]

But the businessman of the last century merits our sympathy too. He did perceive as early as anyone, from his precarious seat in the vortex of the competitive storm, the urgent need for some principle of control. His claim to an exclusive right to control was not mere selfishness or casuistry. Rather it was one of the first steps in the development of industrial regulation, and with it eventually a greater economic and social harmony and stability, a development that has continued to our own day.

89. Massachusetts Bureau of Statistics of Labor, *Thirteenth Annual Report* (1882), p. 366.

Who Burned the Reichstag? The Present State of an Old Controversy

ROBERT E. NEIL

[1]

On the night of February 27, 1933, the German Reichstag Building went up in flames.[1] The Hitler government, not yet a month old and engaged in a desperate election campaign to win an absolute majority in the national legislature, at once branded this arson, a Communist outrage, a signal for a general insurrection. The next day it promulgated emergency decrees that suspended the civil rights clauses of the Weimar Constitution and placed the whole country under an arbitrary "state of exception" equivalent to martial law.[2] Then the Nazis were able "legally" to arrest not only Communists but anyone else who had made himself unloved by Germany's new rulers and to herd them into hastily improvised concentration camps.[3] Already on the night of February 27-28, even before these so-called "Fire Decrees" had been issued, thousands of persons were dragged from their beds and hauled off to points unknown.[4]

In the days after the fire the government released a series of official statements containing lurid details of the Communist revolution that its quick action had supposedly thwarted.[5] These

1. The Plenary Session Chamber (*Plenarsaal*) was completely gutted, but only minor damage was done in other parts of the building.
2. The principal "Fire Decree" was the *Verordnung des Reichspräsidenten zum Schutze von Volk und Staat* of February 28, 1933 (*Reichsgesetzblatt*, 1933, part I, No. 17, p. 83).
3. Cuno Horkenbach (ed.), *Das Deutsche Reich von 1918 bis heute, Berichtsheft* 1933 (Berlin, n.d.), p. 106.
4. Hermann Göring, *Aufbau einer Nation* (Berlin, 1934), p. 92; Rudolf Diels, *Lucifer Ante Portas* (Zurich, n.d.[1950]), p. 150. Göring at this time was Minister of the Interior for the state of Prussia and Minister without Portfolio in the Reich cabinet; Diels was head of the political section of the Prussian police and was shortly to become the first chief of the Gestapo.
5. Horkenbach, *Das Deutsche Reich*, pp. 72, 75-77. See also the issues of the *Völkischer Beobachter*, the principal Nazi daily, for early March, 1933.

reports were allegedly based on documentary evidence that
Göring's police had found in a raid on the deserted Communist
party headquarters in the Karl Liebknecht-Haus some days before the fire. The government promised prompt publication of
the incriminating documents. The promise was never kept, but
for the moment the Nazi charges had the desired effect: the
old-line conservatives in the Hitler cabinet made no move to
stop the Nazi reign of terror, and the German voters gave the
Nazi-Nationalist government a slim majority in the election of
March 5.

In terms of power politics the Nazis had scored a decisive
victory: they possessed a set of presidential emergency decrees
that amounted to a blank check for the creation of a dictatorship,
and Hitler's coalition government was no longer in the minority.
The Nazi Revolution could proceed under a cloak of "legality."

The Reichstag fire did not, however, remain only a matter
of power politics. It immediately developed into a propaganda
duel between Berlin and Moscow. This duel has been well described by Arthur Koestler, himself a participant:

It ended with a complete defeat for the Nazis—the only defeat which
we [the Communists] inflicted on them during the seven years before
the war. The object of the two contestants was to prove that it
was the other who had set fire to the German Parliament. The world
watched the spectacle with fascination, and with as little understanding of its true meaning as small children have when they watch a
complicated thriller on the screen. For the world was not yet accustomed to the stage-effects, the fantastic swindles and cloak-and-
dagger methods of totalitarian propaganda. . . . The world thought
that it was witnessing a classic struggle between truth and falsehood,
guilt and innocence. In reality both parties were guilty, though not
of the crimes of which they accused each other. Both were lying,
and both were afraid that the other knew more of the actual facts
than he really did. Thus the battle was really a blind-man's-bluff
between two giants.[6]

The Nazi and Communist versions of the fire agreed in two
respects: first, the fire was a political crime, and second, the one
arsonist who had been apprehended could not have burned the
building by himself—he must have had accomplices. They dis-

6. Arthur Koestler, *The Invisible Writing* (New York, 1954), p. 194.

agreed on the political camp to which these accomplices belonged. The single arsonist in the hands of the police was a Dutch vagabond, Marinus van der Lubbe. Lubbe had been caught *flagrante delicto* in the burning building, and he readily confessed that he had fired the Reichstag as an act of "protest, protest." Lubbe also insisted that he had done the job alone. Few believed him. All the experts declared that one man could not have set so large a fire in the short time (about twenty minutes) that Lubbe was in the building before being caught and certainly not with the materials (charcoal lighters, burning towels, and the like) that he had used. The experts agreed that the fire in the *Plenarsaal* must have been prepared with incendiary chemicals and that the task would have required six to a dozen men. Lubbe might have *started* the fire, but he could not have prepared it. That had been done by accomplices, known or unknown to him. The Nazi government claimed that Lubbe himself was a Communist and that his accomplices, yet to be apprehended, were also. The Communists countercharged that Lubbe was not one of theirs, that he was the dupe of the Nazis, and that the real Nazi arsonists had "planted" him in the Reichstag to be caught by the police.

Few accepted the Nazi version of the fire. It was the one true prewar debacle, as Koestler rightly observes, of Dr. Goebbels' propaganda machine. The Reichstag was not yet cold before the British and French ambassadors were reporting home that it seemed likely that the Nazis themselves were responsible for the fire, and informed Germans agreed.[7] Only three days after the fire the Reich cabinet discussed what could be done about the insinuations in the foreign press;[8] and the next day Hitler gave an interview to Sefton Delmer of the *Daily Express*

7. E. L. Woodward and Rohan Butler (eds.), *Documents on British Foreign Policy, 1919-1939*, 2d series, IV (London, 1950), 430-31, 437 (dispatches from Sir Horace Rumbold); André François-Poncet, *Souvenirs d'une ambassade à Berlin, Septembre 1931—Octobre 1938* (Paris, 1946), pp. 162-63. The view of German sceptics was summed up by General von Hammerstein, Commander-in-Chief of the German army, in the remark: "Ich wees nich, wenn se den man nich selber angesteckt haben" (Kunrath Freiherr von Hammerstein, "Schleicher, Hammerstein und die Machtübernahme 1933," *Frankfurter Hefte*, IX [1956], 175).

8. *Documents on German Foreign Policy, 1918-1945*, series C, I (Washington, 1957), 94 (minutes of the cabinet meeting of March 2, 1933). For an example of the foreign press reaction to the fire, see Alfred Grosser, *Hitler, la presse et la naissance d'une dictature* (Paris, 1959), pp. 162-63.

in which he declared: "It is nothing but a damned lie and a malicious libel. As base as it is ridiculous."[9]

The Nazis faced a number of grave difficulties in trying to sell their version of the fire. First, they could produce no scrap of real evidence to show that the Communists had actually been planning a revolution. Second, it was impossible to explain what motive could have led the Communists to burn the building. If they were really planning an uprising, why should they advertise it? And if they were not planning to revolt, why should they burn an isolated public building and thereby call down the wrath of the Nazi government upon them? As the British ambassador, Sir Horace Rumbold, put it: "Although the Communist leadership is poor, the Communist leaders are not entirely devoid of intelligence, and it is difficult to see what advantage they could gain by attempting to burn down the Reichstag a few days before the elections."[10] Third, if, as the government insisted, a whole team of Communist arsonists equipped with incendiary chemicals had set the fire, it was difficult to show how they had entered the locked Reichstag, done their work, and then escaped unobserved. The one way that they could have managed it was through an underground tunnel between the heating plant and the Reichstag building, but this tunnel implicated the Nazis much more strongly than the Communists. Finally, the Nazis could not find Lubbe's alleged accomplices. To be sure, when Lubbe stood trial before the Supreme Court at Leipzig in September, four co-defendants were in the dock with him—Torgler (the leader of the Communist deputies in the Reichstag), and three Bulgarian Communists who had been found living in Berlin. The government was unable, however, to build any real case against these four. It paraded a series of Nazi witnesses to testify that Lubbe, Torgler, and the Bulgarians had been seen with each other in various combinations and under various suspicious circumstances; but by the end of the trial in December the frame-up had become so transparent that even the Public Prosecutor had to ask for the acquittal of the Bulgarians and was reduced to saying that Torgler should be executed because he

9. Quoted in Norman H. Baynes (ed.), *The Speeches of Adolf Hitler, April 1922–August 1939* (Oxford, 1942), I, 234.
10. *Doc. Brit. For. Pol.*, 2d series, IV, 431 (dispatch of March 1, 1933).

"had taken part in the Reichstag fire in some manner or other."[11] The German Supreme Court had not yet been sufficiently "co-ordinated," however, to accept such a nebulous argument; and it acquitted Torgler as well as the three Bulgarians. Only Lubbe, who had admitted his guilt all along, could be sentenced. In 1933 the Nazis were still inexperienced in "show trials," and this one had backfired disastrously.

The Communist version of the fire, on the contrary, achieved general acceptance in the outside world and even in the Third Reich itself, where many faithful Nazis chuckled over the cynical trick that they believed their leaders had played on the Communists. The Communist version, moreover, has long out-lived the political situation in which it was coined. Until very recently it has been accepted as a proven fact that the Nazis burned the Reichstag. This has been the verdict of all reputable non-German and German emigré historians since 1933, and since 1945 the German historical fraternity, free to express a view that it had doubtless long held in silence, has agreed with them.

Two years ago, however, a German weekly news magazine, *Der Spiegel,* published a sixty-thousand-word feature article in eleven installments contending that the Nazis had not burned the Reichstag after all, but that Marinus van der Lubbe had really done it by himself, as he claimed.[12] Though the *Spiegel* series was designed for popular consumption and is, therefore, cast in a rather sensational style, it is based on painstaking investigation and has demolished a number of myths about the fire that had long been accepted as fact. The claim of the *Spiegel's* publisher to have established once and for all the innocence of the Nazis in setting the fire cannot be accepted, but specialists in recent German history have had to admit that at the very least the case has been reopened.[13]

11. Quoted in Douglas Reed, *The Burning of the Reichstag* (London, 1934), p. 317. Reed was the special correspondent of the London *Times* at the Leipzig trial, and his book is still the best work in English on both the fire and the trial. In German there are Ferdinand Kugler, *Das Geheimnis des Reichstagsbrandes* (Amsterdam, n.d.); Alfons Sack, *Der Reichstagsbrand-Prozess* (Berlin, 1934), by Torgler's defense counsel; and a collection of documents by the star Bulgarian defendant, G. Dimitroff, *Reichstagsbrandprozess: Dokumente, Briefe und Aufzeichnungen* (Berlin, 1946).

12. Fritz Tobias, "Stehen Sie auf, van der Lubbe!" *Der Spiegel,* XIII (1959), Nos. 43-52, and XIV (1960), No. 1/2.

13. See, for instance, the statements quoted in *ibid.,* XIII (1959), No. 52, p.

At the moment the status of the Reichstag fire question is this: the case *for* Nazi complicity and the case *against* Lubbe's sole guilt have both been weakened. Formerly the Nazis were considered without question to have been the real culprits and Lubbe merely their dupe, but now the possibility has been opened up that the Nazis were not implicated in the setting (as opposed to the exploiting) of the fire and that Lubbe may have been acting purely on his own. The problem is to clear away the debris of demolished legends to see what incriminating evidence against the Nazis still remains and what proofs of Lubbe's sole guilt can now be advanced.

[2]

The case against the Nazis can be argued on three levels. At the bottom is a layer of very general circumstantial evidence that is the real foundation of the whole case. On top of that is a layer of more specific circumstantial evidence giving added plausibility to the general argument. Finally, at the apex, is a body of corroborating, probative evidence that seems to clinch the whole matter.[14]

What might be called the "basic case" against the Nazis is entirely circumstantial: the Nazis had, in the language of the criminal court, means, motive, and opportunity—the very elements lacking in the Nazi case against the Communists. The means were squads of terrorists within the ranks of the S.A.—the Storm Troopers, practiced in all crimes including murder. These squads were skilled in the use of delayed-action, self-igniting liquids, which they employed to burn the campaign posters of rival parties.[15] The motives of the Nazis are clear. They needed

54; and XIV (1960), No. 11, p. 82; A. J. P. Taylor, "Who Burnt the Reichstag? The Story of a Legend," *History Today*, X (1960), 515-22; and Martin Broszat, "Zum Streit um den Reichstagsbrand," *Vierteljahrshefte für Zeitgeschichte*, VIII (1960), 275-79.

14. It is impossible in an article of this scope to discuss all the evidence that has piled up since 1933 about the fire. Much of it is trival in any case. I have, therefore, confined myself to (*a*) evidence that is sufficiently reliable to be really damning, and (b) evidence that, though unreliable, is so often cited that it must be discussed.

15. Hans Otto Meissner and Harry Wilde, *Die Machtergreifung: ein Bericht über die Technik des nationalsozialistischen Staatsstreichs* (Stuttgart, 1958), p. 299 n. 35; Eugen Kogon, "Die neue Argumentation in Sachen Reichstagsbrand," *Frankfurter Hefte*, XV (1960), 409.

a wave of popular hysteria to frighten the people into voting for them in the impending election, and since they were conducting a revolution with, instead of against, the machinery of state, the Nazis needed an artificial crisis as a pretext for mobilizing the state's machinery against their opponents. The Nazis also had ample opportunity. They had detailed knowledge of the physical layout, they knew the routine of the guardians of the Reichstag building, and they had an unobserved route of access to the building through the tunnel connecting the heating plant with the Reichstag. This tunnel had a spur leading to the residence of the speaker of the Reichstag, who was also the official in charge of the building and its staff. The speaker of the Reichstag since August 30, 1932, had been Hermann Göring!

In view of these facts suspicion was bound to fall on the Nazis. A secondary layer of more specific circumstantial evidence reinforced the suspicion.

Everything that the Nazi leaders did both before and after the fire was perfectly consistent with the theory that they had had it set for their own purposes. For several days before the fire rumors had been circulating in Berlin that the Nazis were going to stage some incident as a pretext for drastic action against their opponents. (The favorite rumor was that there was to be a fake attempt on Hitler's life.)[16] The burning of the Reichstag fit into this context very nicely. It seemed highly suspicious, moreover, that at the climax of the election campaign the three most important Nazis—Hitler, Göring, and Goebbels— should all have chosen Monday, February 27, as a day of rest to spend in Berlin instead of out speech-making, as they were doing just before and just after the fire.[17] Most damning of all, the speed with which they began exploiting the fire strongly suggested that the Nazi leaders had been prepared for it in advance. Thus Göring declared shortly after his arrival at the Reichstag that he knew "intuitively" that the fire was the work of the Communists, and Hitler announced in the burning build-

16. *Doc. Brit. For. Pol.*, 2d series, IV, 430 (Rumbold's dispatch of March 1); Reed, *Burning of the Reichstag*, pp. 282, 295; *The Reichstag Fire Trial: The Second Brown Book of the Hitler Terror* (London, 1934), p. 113.

17. Richard Wolff, "Der Reichstagsbrand 1933. Ein Forschungsbericht," in *Aus Politik und Zeitgeschichte*, a supplement to the weekly *Das Parlament*, Jan. 18, 1956, p. 39.

ing that this was a "God-given sign" to root them out. These opinions were voiced, of course, before there had been time for any investigation of the fire whatsoever. Nevertheless, on the strength of intuition and divine revelation the Nazi leaders ordered the arrest of all Communist deputies and party functionaries and also large numbers of non-Communist opponents of Hitler. Göring later boasted that he had immediately issued the order to arrest between four and five thousand persons.[18] This action could, perhaps, be explained as hysteria; what was truly suspicious was that the arrest orders, once given, were carried out with a speed and efficiency that betrayed long planning—it would have been impossible to improvise such a large-scale police action at a moment's notice.[19] Finally, the various official statements released after the fire were so full of provable inaccuracies, contradictions, and inconsistencies that they could quickly be classed as fabrications and propaganda.[20] To cite but one example, the government claimed that it had known about the Communists' revolutionary plans since the raid on the Liebknecht-Haus on February 24; yet no special steps had been taken to guard against an uprising, and Goebbels and Göring said that the fire had taken them by surprise.[21] Strange behavior for men who professed to have known in advance about the alleged plot! But if what they had really known about in advance was a Nazi plan to burn the Reichstag, then their behavior during and after the fire becomes all too intelligible.

The public behavior of the Nazi chieftains raised suspicions about their real motives. Even more damaging was that apparently only they had had the means and the opportunity to burn the building in the particular way in which it was done. Everything that was learned about the fire suggested that Nazi arsonists had in fact used the heating tunnel and that Lubbe was their dupe.

Lubbe entered the Reichstag at 9:05 P.M. by breaking in a

18. Reed, *Burning of the Reichstag*, p. 230 (Göring's testimony at Leipzig); Göring, *Aufbau einer Nation*, p. 92.

19. *Doc. Brit. For. Pol.*, 2d series, IV, 431 (Rumbold's dispatch of March 1).

20. For an amusing account of Nazi blunders in this regard see Meissner and Wilde, *Die Machtergreifung*, pp. 227-30.

21. Reed, *Burning of the Reichstag*, pp. 246-47; Joseph Goebbels, *Vom Kaiserhof zur Reichskanzlei* (Munich, 1934), pp. 269-70.

window. Two reliable witnesses saw him do this, and they immediately alerted the police. Inside the building Lubbe blundered around in the dark for the next twenty-two minutes setting fire to anything that looked combustible with charcoal lighters, burning towels, and even pieces of his own clothing. During the process he kicked in and passed through numerous windows and glass doors. He spent most of his time in the Reichstag restaurant and kitchen; only at the very end did he stumble into the *Plenarsaal.* Meanwhile, the police and fire department had gone into action. Lubbe was arrested at 9:27, by which time the fires that he had set in the restaurant, kitchen, and halls were fully under control; but at just this moment there was an explosion in the *Plenarsaal* that turned the whole chamber into such a sea of flames that it could not be saved. Lubbe was taken to the police station at the Brandenburg Gate for an initial interrogation that lasted for several hours. There he insisted that he had done the job, without the help or prompting of others, as an individual act of protest (against what it was not clear). Lubbe also stated that in setting the blaze he had used only the materials already described.[22]

Such, in abbreviated form, were (and still are) the undisputed facts about the fire. Did they tell the whole story? Nearly everyone agreed that they did not. The technical experts insisted that the fire in the *Plenarsaal* was different in character from the rather pathetic little ones that Lubbe had set elsewhere in the building; the main fire could have been started only with the use of special chemicals. At the Leipzig trial the experts testified that traces of such chemicals had been found in seven different places in the *Plenarsaal* (and *only* there), and Chief Fire Director Gempp stated that he had found a burning torch and trails of gasoline on the carpet in the hall just outside the chamber.[23] None of these technical findings squared with the story that Lubbe told. It seemed out of the question that he could have been the real author of the fire in the *Plenarsaal.*

22. A timetable of the fire is contained in Reed, *Burning of the Reichstag,* pp. 157-59. Good narrative accounts of the undisputed events of the night are to be found in *Der Spiegel,* XIII (1959), No. 43, pp. 45-51; and Meissner and Wilde, *Die Machtergreifung,* pp. 222-26.

23. Reed, *Burning of the Reichstag,* pp. 139, 181-88, 215; Horkenbach, *Das Deutsche Reich,* p. 71.

He must, therefore, have had accomplices, but how did they get into the building and escape unnoticed? They could not have done it above ground. All entrances to the Reichstag except one were securely locked, and the porter of this remaining entry could account for all persons who had used it to enter or leave the building before the fire.[24] Aside from the window smashed by Lubbe, there was no evidence that anybody else had forced a way into the Reichstag. The tunnel alone remained as a possible entrance. The inference that the arsonists had used it was supported by real evidence: the night porter in the speaker's residence testified that on several occasions in the days before the fire he had heard mysterious footsteps in the tunnel.[25]

If Lubbe's accomplices had come and gone through the heating tunnel—and Göring insisted on this just as firmly as did his opponents, was it likely that they had been Communists? This seemed grossly improbable. Where would they have got keys to the tunnel doors and a knowledge of its layout (the "tunnel" was in reality a whole labyrinth of tunnels)? Even more to the point, would the Communists have dared to undertake such a project—a project for which they had no motive—literally under the noses of Göring's S.A. bodyguard in the speaker's residence? This is what the government contended, but to sceptical Germans and foreign observers it seemed much more credible that if anybody had used the tunnel—and this *was* generally accepted, then it must have been Nazi rather than Communist arsonists.[26]

24. Reed, *Burning of the Reichstag*, pp. 131-32 (testimony of the porter Wendt).

25. *Ibid.*, pp. 153-54. The porter, Paul Adermann, had even fastened pieces of paper and thread to the doors at the ends of the tunnel to make sure that his ears were not playing tricks on him. They were not: the paper and thread were broken by the nocturnal "prowlers." At the time this evidence was held to be very significant. Now, however, it has been deflated: it was an open secret that technical personnel, contrary to regulations, often used this tunnel as a convenient way of getting to the Reichstag itself from the heating plant (*Der Spiegel*, XIII [1959], No. 45, pp. 67-68). This was the reason that Adermann, after describing the noises in the tunnel, had to admit to the court that there was nothing unusual about them (Reed, *Burning of the Reichstag*, p. 153). As to the threads and strips of paper, Adermann seems merely to have been an officious individual checking up on a violation of regulations.

26. Göring himself drew immediate suspicion on the Nazis in this connection by ordering soon after his arrival at the fire that the tunnel be searched, an order that was carried out by the commander of Göring's personal bodyguard (Reed, *Burning of the Reichstag*, pp. 156-57; *Second Brown Book*, p. 308, Meissner and Wilde, *Die Machtergreifung*, p. 227).

The Nazi propaganda campaign had thus backfired. Göring and Goebbels had convinced everyone that Lubbe had had accomplices and that they must have used the tunnel, but nobody would then draw the desired conclusion that these accomplices had been Communists. By selling the first but not the second half of their story, the Nazis had succeeded only in implicating themselves; they had tied an albatross firmly around their own necks.[27]

If the real arsonists had been Nazis, then Lubbe must have been their dupe, and there was strong circumstantial evidence to support this conclusion. The timing of Lubbe's entry into the Reichstag was significant. Just before 9:00 each night the mail-man made his rounds of the boxes inside the Reichstag; at 10:00 a night watchman checked the entire building; but between 9:00 and 10:00 the Reichstag was not patrolled. The Nazis, through Göring, were doubtless well aware of this routine. Could it be coincidence alone that led Lubbe to break in at 9:05? Furthermore, Lubbe could not by himself have accomplished even the miscellaneous burning and breakage in the restaurant, kitchen, and halls. According to the police reconstruction of Lubbe's movements, he must have performed 167 separate actions in a mere twenty-two minutes.[28] The police claimed to have checked all of this with a stopwatch and found it to be accurate, but when the Supreme Court held an official re-enactment of the fire in the Reichstag building, all observers agreed that Lubbe could not possibly have done so much in so little time.[29] It also seemed incredible that Lubbe, working in the dark, could have kicked in quarter-inch windows, passed through broken glass doors, and set numerous fires without suffering a single cut, bruise, or burn despite the fact that his flimsy shoes were going through at the toes and that at the last he was stripped to the waist, having used his jacket and shirt to set fires.[30]

27. By the time that the Nazis realized their blunder, it was too late. At Leipzig Goebbels was reduced to suggesting that the Communists had burned the building, not as a signal for revolution, but because they knew that it would be blamed on the Nazis! (Reed, *Burning of the Reichstag*, p. 244).

28. *Second Brown Book*, pp. 63-68, gives an itemized list of these various actions.

29. Reed, *Burning of the Reichstag*, pp. 126-27, 169-70.

30. *Ibid.*, p. 120.

All of this was suspicious enough, but Lubbe's behavior at the Leipzig trial seemed to clinch the argument that he was being used as a tool. According to the police Lubbe had answered their questions volubly and in fluent German during his interrogations in the days after the fire; an interpreter had not been needed. Psychiatrists testified that at that time Lubbe had been perfectly normal—indeed, above average in intelligence. Yet at Leipzig Lubbe sat with his head between his knees and dripped saliva and mucus all over the floor. All who saw him believed that he was either mentally deficient or drugged. On only two occasions did Lubbe "awaken" and show any interest at all in his trial, and then he spoke a mixture of broken German and Dutch unintelligible to the court without the services of the translator. The rest of the time he would only answer, under constant prodding, "yes" or "no" or sometimes both to the same question. It seemed exceedingly unlikely that Lubbe could have made to the police the detailed statements that they claimed; or, if he really had made full and coherent statements without the aid of an interpreter, then he must have revealed something so damaging to the Nazis that they had had him "processed" into harmlessness for the trial. Rumors were soon circulating that the Nazis had destroyed the records of the initial police interrogations of Lubbe and that the drug being used on him was scopolamine.[31]

The case against the Nazis at the first level—circumstantial evidence that they and not the Communists had the motive, the means, and the opportunity to set fire to the Reichstag—was thus supported by a second layer of more specific circumstantial evidence. But this was not all. In the months following the fire concrete information piled up, which, if true, actually proved Nazi guilt, and over the years, especially since 1945, additional probative evidence has accumulated. Much of this evidence is

31. Wolff, "Der Reichstagsbrand 1933," pp. 26, 28. Wolff, whose research was commissioned by an agency of the Bonn government and who might therefore be expected to have had full official co-operation in tracking down sources, claims that all copies of the transcripts of Lubbe's interrogations have indeed vanished without trace. In fact, all seven copies are still in the files where they have always been since 1933 (*Der Spiegel*, XIII [1959], No. 44, pp. 42-52, where extracts from the "vanished" protocols are published). In addition to other errors of this kind, Wolff's whole "research report" displays a marked inability to distinguish between real evidence and mere hearsay and also a willingness to cite dubious sources if they support his own opinions.

worthless, but seven items carry enough weight to merit discussion.

About a month after the burning of the Reichstag copies of an anonymous document that purported to give the real story of the fire began circulating from hand to hand in Germany. According to this document the Nazis had from the beginning wanted to suppress the Communist party, but this action had been blocked by their Nationalist partners in the government coalition. In order to overcome the resistance of the Nationalists, the Nazis decided to stage a particularly outrageous incident and pin it on the Communists. The incident was the Reichstag fire. All the principal Nazi leaders were aware of the plot and were, therefore, in Berlin on the day of the fire; the squad of arsonists was led through the heating tunnel by Edmund Heines, S.A. leader for Silesia; and Lubbe was left behind to incriminate the Communists.

By the end of April this document had become known abroad, and extracts from it were printed in the *Manchester Guardian* on April 26 and 27. The paper attributed authorship of the report to "a prominent German conservative leader" with inside sources of information about the sessions of the Reich cabinet. A few days after the *Manchester Guardian's* publication of parts of the report, Dr. Ernst Oberfohren, until recently the leader of the Nationalist deputies in the Reichstag, was found in his apartment dead of a gunshot wound. Anti-Hitler circles drew the natural conclusion: Oberfohren was the author of the anonymous report (henceforth known as the "Oberfohren Document"), and he had been silenced by the Nazis.[32]

A second item of evidence involved one Georg Bell, who on April 3, 1933, was murdered in a Tirolean village by Nazi agents. Bell had been a well-known political contact man and information peddler in the last years of the Weimar Republic. In particular, he had been a friend of Ernst Röhm, the commander of the S.A. After Bell's death it was alleged that he had been murdered to prevent his telling what he knew about the Reichstag fire.

32. The circumstances surrounding the Oberfohren Document are discussed in Wolff, "Der Reichstagsbrand 1933," pp. 35-36, and its text is printed on pp. 46-48. An extract of the text may also be found in Walther Hofer, *Der Nationalsozialismus: Dokumente 1933-1945* (Frankfurt/M., 1957), pp. 51-52.

According to this story Bell had had a list of Röhm's homosexual "friends," and one of the names on the list had been that of Marinus van der Lubbe. Bell had allegedly known all about the fire, had told an English reporter about it in advance—a fact which was supposed to have been reported *before* the fire in the *Neue Zürcher Zeitung*—and had been trying to sell what he knew to another Swiss paper before his murder.[33]

At the time the Reichstag was burned the Chief Fire Director of Berlin was Walter Gempp. He had held the post for years and had achieved an international reputation. Gempp personally directed the fighting of the Reichstag fire. Soon after the event he allegedly made the following charges: that Göring had deliberately hindered the work of the fire department, that suspiciously large numbers of S.A. men were already on the scene when the fire brigades arrived, and that the firemen had found quantities of unused incendiary materials in unburned parts of the Reichstag. In March, 1933, Gempp's superiors suddenly dismissed him from his post for "permitting Communist activities in the force"—a preposterous charge, and in 1937 he was arrested and brought to trial for taking bribes. The court convicted Gempp and sentenced him to prison, but before the sentence could go into effect, he was found hanging in his cell.[34]

The typesetter "Beni" Thaler is the source of the fourth piece of evidence. He was one of the two eyewitnesses to Lubbe's entry into the Reichstag, and it was said that he had seen more: through a ground floor window he had observed a group of uniformed S.A. men with burning torches moving around inside the Reichstag. When word of this story reached the S.A., Thaler was brought to Berlin-Brandenburg S.A. headquarters for questioning. There he was "accidentally" allowed to witness the beating of prisoners in the courtyard. Thaler took the hint. When he testified at the Leipzig trial some months later, he said

33. Wolff, "Der Reichstagsbrand 1933," pp. 33-34.

34. Annedore Leber, *Das Gewissen steht auf: 64 Lebensbilder aus dem deutschen Widerstand 1933-1945*, herausgegeben in Zusammenarbeit mit Willy Brandt und Karl Dietrich Bracher (Berlin, 1954), pp. 106-107. In 1955 several Berlin fire department officers who had been on duty at the Reichstag fire twenty-two years earlier prepared a lengthy memorandum documenting Gempp's alleged charges that there had been irregularities in the fighting of the fire (Wolff, "Der Reichstagsbrand 1933," pp. 32-33; *Der Spiegel*, XIII [1959], No. 47, pp. 55-61).

nothing about the S.A. squad that he had allegedly seen in the Reichstag. Thaler was killed in 1943, but earlier in the war years he is supposed on several occasions when he was drunk to have told his story to comrades who have survived.[35]

In the four previous items of evidence, fact and allegation were intertwined; the present story, in contrast, is built entirely on allegation—even the existence of an "agent" Waschinski may be disputed. Like Georg Bell, Paul Waschinski was an under-cover political agent and information monger. His principal employer in February, 1933, was Count Helldorf, commander of the Berlin S.A. Helldorf got word that a Dutch tramp had been making inflammatory speeches to crowds of unemployed in one of the Communist, working-class suburbs of Berlin; the agitator had said that public buildings like the Reichstag ought to be burned in protest against economic and political conditions. Helldorf assigned Waschinski to "shadow" and establish contact with the Dutchman. Agent Waschinski succeeded in his mission and even spent the night of February 26-27 with Lubbe in the Shelter for Destitutes in Hennigsdorf, a west-side suburb. On Helldorf's orders Waschinski persuaded Lubbe to break into the Reichstag shortly after 9:00 on the night of the twenty-seventh (at the very time that Helldorf, Waschinski claimed, had ar-ranged for the real Nazi arsonists to be coming through the tunnel). What sort of story Waschinski had concocted to accom-plish this is uncertain; but, whatever it was, Lubbe was properly duped. As soon as Lubbe had been worked into the trap, Waschinski rushed off to alert the police. Waschinski was im-prudent enough to talk about his exploit, with the result that he was murdered in the Blood Purge of June 30, 1934. One of his S.A. friends, however, is said to have escaped to Paris, where he revealed the whole story.[36]

The Waschinski story, if true, explains how the Nazis "planted" Lubbe in the Reichstag. Another story purports to tell

35. Meissner and Wilde, *Die Machtergreifung,* p. 304 note 81a; *Der Spiegel,* XIII (1959), No. 50, p. 34.
36. Attention was called to Waschinski as early as 1933-34 (see, for instance, *Second Brown Book,* pp. 218-21); but the fullest version of this story is that of Meissner and Wilde, *Die Machtergreifung,* pp. 204-22, with copious notes. Harry Wilde insists that he got the story direct from the S.A. refugee in Paris (Meissner and Wilde, *Die Machtergreifung,* pp. 297-98, note 21).

how the fire was actually started. According to it one of the
S.A. men who fired the Reichstag was a professional criminal
named Rall. Some months later Rall, who in the meantime had
been expelled from the S.A., was arrested for burglary. Since
this was during the Leipzig trial, Rall saw a chance to revenge
himself on the S.A. and perhaps also to get his release by telling
what he supposedly knew about the fire. Instead, he got himself
murdered. Certain Gestapo officials who were hostile to the S.A.
heard about the matter and were able to piece together for themselves the full details of Rall's story after his death. They are
said to have learned that the idea of burning the Reichstag had
originated with Goebbels, that Göring had co-operated in the
plan, that SA-Gruppenführer Karl Ernst had made the technical
arrangements, and that the squad of ten arsonists had been led
through the tunnel by one "Heini" Gewehr.[37]

Whether or not he had led an arson squad including Rall into
the Reichstag, a thug named "Heini" Gewehr had in fact been
in the S.A., and he outlived the Third Reich. During the Nuremberg trial a prosecution witness told the Rall story as evidence
against Göring. One of Göring's assistant defense counsels, seeking to discredit this testimony, found out where Gewehr was
interned and suggested that he be brought to Nuremberg to deny
the whole story and thus partially clear Göring of complicity in
the fire. To the surprise of his attorney, Göring was far from
pleased with this suggestion. Instead, he replied: "You have to
be very careful with witnesses like that! Even if the S.A. really
did set fire to the Reichstag, that doesn't mean that *I* knew anything about it."[38] In the upshot Gewehr was not called to testify,
an omission that is held to implicate Göring still further and to
lend credibility to the Rall story.

Whatever his personal guilt may have been, Göring at least
conceded to his counsel that perhaps the S.A. "really did set fire

37. *The Trial of the Major War Criminals before the International Military
Tribunal, Nuremberg, 14 November 1945–1 October 1946* (42 vols.; Nuremberg, 1947-1949), XII, 252-53 (testimony of Hans Bernd Gisevius, a former
Gestapo official and later member of the resistance movement). Gisevius has
published a full account of this story in Hans Bernd Gisevius, *Bis zum bitteren
Ende: vom Reichstagsbrand bis zum 20. Juli 1944* (rev. ed.; Hamburg, 1960),
pp. 50-70.
38. Werner Bross, *Gespräche mit Hermann Göring während des Nürnberger
Prozesses* (*Flensburg and Hamburg*, 1950), p. 196. My translation.

to the Reichstag." Göring admitted as much on two other occasions after the war, first to State Secretary Meissner when they were interned together at Bad Mondorf and later to an Allied interrogator at Nuremberg during pre-trial questioning.[39] Göring denied to the end personal complicity in the fire, but even he had to admit that Nazis might have set it—probably, he said, one of Karl Ernst's "unruly S.A. units."

Two prominent witnesses have testified, however, that they heard Göring himself boast of having burned the Reichstag. The first occasion was a conversation in the Reich Chancellery shortly after the fire. Hermann Rauschning, then Nazi President of the Senate in Danzig, heard Göring tell how "his boys" had set the fire but had had too little time to "burn down the whole shack."[40] The other occasion was Hitler's birthday in 1942. General Halder, then Chief of Staff of the German army, was among the officers sitting around the *Führer's* lunch table at military headquarters on the eastern front. When someone brought up the artistic merit of the Reichstag building, Halder heard Göring say: "The only one who really knows the Reichstag is I, for I set fire to it."[41]

[3]

There is, thus, an imposing body of evidence that it was the Nazis who burned the Reichstag. It is now possible, however, to question this verdict because some of the evidence that supports it has been discredited.[42]

The third category of evidence—concrete, probative information—has been hardest hit by the findings of Fritz Tobias published in the *Spiegel*. First, it has definitely been established that the Oberfohren Document is not by Oberfohren, that his

39. Otto Meissner, *Staatssekretär unter Ebert-Hindenburg-Hitler: der Schicksalsweg des deutschen Volkes von 1918-1945, wie ich ihn erlebte* (Berlin, 1950), p. 283; Wolff, "Der Reichstagsbrand 1933," pp. 43, 45-46 (transcript of Göring's interrogation, which is Nuremberg Document 3593-PS).

40. Hermann Rauschning, *Gespräche mit Hitler* (Zurich-Vienna-New York, 1940), p. 76.

41. *Trial of Major War Criminals*, IX, 434 (Halder's affidavit read into evidence by Justice Robert Jackson during his cross-examination of Göring).

42. Space forbids explanation in detail of how various pieces of evidence have been discredited. I shall limit myself mainly to summarizing conclusions; for the arguments see the *Spiegel* series.

death was suicide rather than murder, and that his suicide had
nothing to do with the document attributed to him. The Oberfohren Document has, therefore, no weight as evidence; it is
merely a collection of rumors in pamphlet form to which Oberfohren's name was attached posthumously for purposes of anti-
Nazi propaganda.[43] Second, Lubbe's homosexuality was a deliberate fabrication of the Communists to link him to the
leadership of the S.A. Whatever it was that Georg Bell had on
the Nazis to warrant his murder, it was not Lubbe's name on one
of Röhm's "love lists."[44]

Third, the Gempp legend has also been discredited. There is
no real evidence the Gempp ever made the charges attributed
to him; indeed, he disputed them most energetically in his testimony at the Leipzig trial.[45] Further, Gempp's dismissal, trial,
and death were not related to the fire. Along with sixteen other
high officials, he had repeatedly accepted large bribes from the
Minimax Corporation, a manufacturer of fire-fighting equipment.
Authorities in the Ministry of Justice had already been investigating the case before the Nazis came to power. Far from pushing the case against Gempp and the others, the Hitler government kept it as quiet as possible because certain right-wing
politicians seem to have been involved in the scandal. Finally,
however, the accused were brought to trial, found guilty, and
given prison sentences. Thereupon several of the convicted men
committed suicide before their sentences could go into effect
because, through a legal technicality, this saved their families
from losing their survivors' pensions. Gempp was among those
who took this way out. Gempp's death, like Oberfohren's, was

43. *Der Spiegel*, XIII (1959), No. 48, pp. 49-56; and XIV (1960), No. 7,
p. 14.
44. *Ibid.*, XIII (1959), No. 50, pp. 30-33. There is no evidence that Bell
knew anything at all about the fire. The assertion, repeated by Wolff ("Der
Reichstagsbrand 1933," p. 34), that Bell had told an English correspondent about
the fire in advance and that this information was printed in the *Neue Zürcher
Zeitung* before the fire is false: there is no such item in the *Neue Zürcher Zeitung*.
45. Leber (*Das Gewissen steht auf,* pp. 106-107) misleads her readers on
this point by saying only that Gempp "told what he knew" at Leipzig. Bracher
goes even further and states that Gempp repeated his alleged charges in testifying before the Supreme Court (Karl Dietrich Bracher, "Stufen totalitärer Gleich-
schaltung: die Befestigung der nationalsozialistischen Herrschaft 1933/34,"
Vierteljahrshefte für Zeitgeschichte, IV [1956], 36-37). This is the opposite of
the truth: Gempp categorically denied that he had ever made such charges.

suicide rather than murder.[46] There is no truth either in the charges attributed to Gempp or in similar charges by others that the fire department was called too late, that the work of the fire-men was obstructed, or that they stumbled onto evidence incriminating the Nazis. The fighting of the Reichstag fire was a perfectly normal, efficient operation without suspicious irregularities.[47]

Fourth, "Beni" Thaler could not have seen uniformed S.A. men with flaming torches moving around in the ground floor of the Reichstag: the windows were made of frosted glass. Besides, is it likely that an S.A. incendiary squad would have gone about its business in uniform? Thaler may have seen lights in the ground floor, but he could not have seen who carried them.[48]

The *Spiegel's* attack on a fifth legend, the Waschinski legend, is surprisingly weak—surprisingly, because a strong case can be made against it. All that the *Spiegel* has done is to show that the man who spent the night of February 26-27 with Lubbe signed his name in the police register as Franz Watschinski (instead of Paul Waschinski) and that he was not the "mysterious" unidentified young man who brought the news of the fire to the police station at the Brandenburg Gate.[49] These two discoveries hardly represent an imposing accomplishment, nor do they discredit the Waschinski legend. The story should indeed be re-

46. *Der Spiegel*, XIII (1959), No. 46, pp. 41-48. Bracher attempts to save the Gempp legend by pointing out that the Nazis frequently attacked former Republican officials with false corruption charges (K. D. Bracher, W. Sauer, and G. Schulz, *Die nationalsozialistische Machtergreifung: Studien zur Errichtung des totalitären Herrschaftssystems in Deutschland 1933/34* [Cologne and Opladen, 1960], p. 81, note 25). True enough, but this particular case seems too well documented to be a Nazi conspiracy, and it seems unlikely that sixteen other officials would have been falsely indicted just to get at Gempp. Had the Nazis wanted to silence Gempp, they could have clapped him into a concentration camp at any time instead of waiting till 1937 to bring him to trial.

47. *Der Spiegel*, XIII (1959), No. 47, pp. 50-61, contains a very detailed analysis of the activities of the fire department at the Reichstag and refutes point-by-point the postwar allegations of certain Berlin fire officials (cf. note 34, above).

48. *Ibid.*, XIII (1959), No. 50, p. 34. It is true that the S.A. did question and intimidate Thaler. Nevertheless, the Thaler incident must, at the very least, be reduced from probative to circumstantial evidence.

49. *Ibid.*, XIII (1959), No. 45, pp. 55-63. A great deal has been made of this "mysterious young man in knee boots" whose name the police neglected to take. The partisans of the Waschinski legend claim that he was the man (Meissner and Wilde, *Die Machtergreifung*, p. 304 n. 81). In actuality it was only an innocent passer-by named Neumann.

jected as evidence, but for other reasons. All that can be documented about it is that Lubbe spent the night before the fire in the company of a man named Franz Watschinski. The rest of the story is nothing more than a set of unsupported assertions based on one concrete fact—a man's name in an overnight register—and on the failure of the police to find and produce him at the trial. The full Waschinski story was allegedly told to Harry Wilde, then in exile in Paris, now a well-known West German journalist-historian, by one of Waschinski's former S.A. friends who had fled Germany after the Blood Purge of 1934; but we have only Wilde's word for this. Wilde claims that he made detailed notes on his conversations with the S.A. man, yet he cannot even remember the man's name.[50] Since Wilde is known in Germany as the author, under a pseudonym, of a popular history of the Third Reich based mainly on invention and fabrication,[51] it is natural to be suspicious of his story. But even if Wilde did get his information as he says from a refugee S.A. man, it has little value as historical evidence. The S.A. man, Wilde reports, claimed to have heard the story from Waschinski himself, but who is to say that he did or even that there ever was an "agent" Waschinski? Any reader, including, of course, Wilde himself, of the *Brown Books* and other anti-Nazi propaganda could have constructed such a story out of whole cloth. The Waschinski legend, whoever its real author, belongs in the same category as all the other "authentic" rumors about the fire that circulated freely at the time in German emigré and other anti-Nazi circles.[52]

Finally, the *Spiegel* has cast grave doubt on the Rall legend propagated since the war by the former Gestapo agent turned resistance member, Hans Bernd Gisevius. The *Spiegel* insists

50. Meissner and Wilde, *Die Machtergreifung*, pp. 297-98, note 21.
51. H. S. Hegner (Harry Schulze-Wilde), *Die Reichskanzlei von 1933-1945: Anfang und Ende des Dritten Reiches* (rev. ed.; Frankfurt/M., 1960).
52. Most of this alleged evidence against the Nazis was simply fabricated by the Communist propaganda headquarters headed by Willy Muenzenberg in Paris. It was this organization that prepared the two *Brown Books*. On the workings of the Communist fabrication mill see Koestler, *Invisible Writing*, chap. xvii, especially pp. 198-99 (Koestler was himself one of Muenzenberg's underlings). Though the *Brown Books* must be used with extreme caution, it should be emphasized that they do contain some accurate information and devastating critiques of official German documents regarding the fire and the Leipzig trial.

that Rall, far from being one of the ten S.A. men who allegedly burned the Reichstag, had in fact been expelled from the S.A. in 1932 (instead of after the fire in 1933), and that at the time of the fire he was already sitting behind prison bars on a burglary charge, not wandering through the heating tunnels of the Reichstag.[53] The *Spiegel's* attempted refutation of the Rall story is not as convincing as its attack on the other legends about the fire because the source of the *Spiegel's* information on Rall is Rudolf Diels, the first chief of the Gestapo, who—if Gisevius is right—was himself involved in the murder of Rall. Yet, if the Rall legend has not been discredited beyond question, the burden of proof falls on its advocates; and Gisevius' tale can no longer be classed as evidence of Nazi guilt unless it can be more fully substantiated.[54]

Thus, the *Spiegel* has managed to discredit a considerable amount of the concrete evidence that had supposedly corroborated the circumstantial case against the Nazis. This does not, of course, prove that they did not set the fire. The only way to do that, short of establishing an alibi for every Nazi for the night of the fire, is to prove that somebody else did set it; and so the *Spiegel* undertakes to show that Lubbe alone burned the Reichstag, as he claimed. The main objection to this theory is the testimony of the experts that a whole squad of men with special incendiary materials would have been required to prepare the fire in the *Plenarsaal*. Indeed, it was on this expert opinion that all the Nazi and Communist charges and countercharges of conspiracy were ultimately based. The *Spiegel* has made mincemeat of the testimony of the experts at the Leipzig trial.[55] Of the three experts who testified, no two had the same theory about the fire aside from the opinion that Lubbe had not set it by himself. One, for instance, thought that the blaze had been caused

53. *Der Spiegel*, XIV (1960), No. 18, pp. 14-18.
54. At Nuremberg and in the 1946 edition of his book *Bis zum bitteren Ende* Gisevius stated that "Heini" Gewehr, the supposed leader of the S.A. squad including Rall, had been killed on the eastern front. Gisevius was wrong: Gewehr is still alive. In 1960 a criminal investigation was opened to determine whether he had any part in the fire. Despite Gisevius' appearance as a witness, the public prosecutor of Düsseldorf dismissed the proceedings against Gewehr on January 4, 1962 (*Der Spiegel*, XVI [1962], No. 4, p. 37). The whole Rall legend is thus called even more strongly into question.
55. *Ibid.*, XIII (1959), No. 49, pp. 47-55.

by too little air in the chamber while another attributed it to excessive drafts. The "expert" who advanced the theory about self-igniting chemicals turns out to have been a man whom his colleagues considered a "daydreamer and public menace." Although this man claimed to have found traces of his pet chemical in the *Plenarsaal,* the official indictment against Lubbe and the others (which was based on the written opinion of the experts), conceded that:

The very careful salvage operations in the *Plenarsaal* have provided no clues as to the manner in which the *Plenarsaal* was prepared for ignition or what chemicals were used for that purpose. Likewise, no clues have been found to indicate that any highly inflammable liquids, e.g., petroleum, benzine, benzol, or ether, were employed in setting the fire.[56]

The experts simply started from the opinion—for which they had no tangible evidence—that Lubbe could not have set the fire alone, and then constructed conflicting theories—for which again they had no evidence—of how the job might have been accomplished. One expert, Dr. Schatz, actually changed his theory in the course of his testimony to make it conform more closely to what had been observed by the other witnesses. But, even if there were no tangible evidence to support it, was the opinion of the experts sound that one man could not have set the fire? It was not. The history of famous fires shows that more often than not they have resulted from causes which the Leipzig experts, to be consistent, would have had to pronounce inadequate. In 1956, for instance, the Vienna Stock Exchange, a building similar to the Reichstag in its furnishings, was burned down in a fire started by a cigarette butt entirely without help from self-igniting chemicals or arson squads. And, concerning the Reichstag itself, Gempp, whose other alleged statements were so readily cited by the anti-Nazis, told reporters shortly after the fire that the wood paneling of the *Plenarsaal* was so fully dried out, that it had burned like tinder.[57] Contrary to the long-accepted view, therefore, it seems entirely possible that Lubbe could have set the fire in the *Plenarsaal* all by himself.[58]

56. Quoted in *ibid.,* XIII (1959), No. 43, p. 60.
57. Horkenbach, *Das Deutsche Reich,* p. 71.
58. As a matter of fact, this was the view taken by the two Criminal Com-

[4]

Such, in very condensed form, are the *Spiegel*'s findings. They have discredited most of the concrete, corroborative "evidence" on the third level of the case against the Nazis and cast doubt on an important piece of specific circumstantial evidence on the second level—that the fire in the *Plenarsaal* could not have been caused by Lubbe alone. What remains? Tobias and the *Spiegel* have not touched the bulk of the circumstantial evidence. The basic case—means, motive, and opportunity—remains intact. So also does the fact that the Nazis at once took the very steps to exploit the fire that one would have expected of them if they themselves were the arsonists. Göring freely admitted on later occasions that he had had his arrest lists drawn up in advance and was only waiting for a pretext to use them;[59] and it can be proved that in exploiting the fire for their own purposes the Nazis deliberately lied to the German people and even to their conservative colleagues in the Hitler government.[60]

Merely showing that the Nazis could have set the fire, that they had a strong motive to do so, and that they cynically exploited the deed does not, of course, prove that they did in fact burn the Reichstag. But the only other conceivable explanation —that Lubbe alone set the building ablaze—cannot be reconciled with some of the evidence still outstanding. For instance, the *Spiegel* has not been able to discredit two highly damaging pieces of concrete evidence—the statements of Rauschning and Halder that they heard Göring boast of setting the fire. Both men have reconfirmed their statements, which carry real weight.[61] Furthermore, it is very significant that after the collapse of the Third

missioners who carried out the police investigation of Lubbe and the fire. Though the Nazis suppressed the findings of the police, the two detectives stuck to their opinion and expressed it again after the war (*Der Spiegel*, XIII [1959], No. 44, p. 52; Franz von Papen, *Der Wahrheit eine Gasse* [Munich, 1952], p. 303).

59. Reed, *Burning of the Reichstag*, p. 228; Göring, *Aufbau einer Nation*, p. 94; *Trial of Major War Criminals*, IX, 433; Diels, *Lucifer*, pp. 150-51.

60. Diels, *Lucifer*, pp. 144-45; Martin Sommerfeldt, *Ich war dabei . . . 1933 bis 1939* (Darmstadt, 1949), pp. 26-31 (by Göring's press chief); cabinet minutes of February 28 and March 2, 1933 (*Doc. Ger. For. Pol.*, C, I, 88-90, 94); and Göring's pre-trial interrogation at Nuremberg (Nuremberg Document 3593-PS, printed in full in Wolff, "Der Reichstagsbrand," pp. 42-46).

61. Halder reconfirmed his Nuremberg affidavit in a letter to Wolff (p. 39); and Rauschning reconfirmed his story in a letter to *Der Spiegel* (XIII [1959], No. 52, p. 47).

Reich Göring himself was willing to admit that it seemed possible to him that S.A. men had burned the Reichstag on their own initiative—indeed, Göring even conceded that he and other top Nazis had speculated at the time on who in the lower echelons might have been responsible. It was hard to imagine how such persons could have duped Lubbe, but, as Göring said, "everything is possible."[62]

The controversial figure of Lubbe remains the hardest of all the outstanding factors to reconcile with the theory of Nazi innocence. To do that, it is necessary to make Lubbe alone responsible not just for the major blaze in the *Plenarsaal* but also for all the minor damage elsewhere in the building. This is what the police, who believed in his sole guilt, tried to do. The investigating officers produced detailed accounts of Lubbe's actions, allegedly dictated by him in fluent German decorated with "flowers of speech," yet no one except the police and a few other officials ever heard Lubbe speak a single sentence of coherent German.[63] True, these "vanished" accounts have now been found, and they do not, as had formerly been claimed, contain anything to implicate the Nazis; but neither do they prove that Lubbe alone was guilty. What these accounts really suggest is that the police made their own reconstruction of the fire, carefully seeing that every item of damage was accounted for, and then got Lubbe to agree to it point by point. In any case, whether Lubbe actually dictated his statement or the police overzealously suggested it to him, it is incompatible with the time involved: nobody but the police believed that Lubbe alone could have carried out so many actions in so little time. Even if the firing

---

62. Wolff, "Der Reichstagsbrand," p. 45 (quoted from Nuremberg Document 3593-PS). Göring believed that if any Nazi had been responsible, it had probably been Karl Ernst, and that the S.A. had set the fire because they thought that Hitler was moving too slowly and because they themselves wanted a pretext to engage in more open violence against the Communists and other opponents (*Ibid.*, pp. 43, 45).

63. The *Spiegel* lamely tries to explain this away by saying that by the time of the trial Lubbe had grown so apathetic when he found that nobody would believe him that he simply did not take the trouble to speak good German! (*Der Spiegel*, XIII [1959], No. 52, p. 41). Yet even some of the witnesses for the prosecution who had heard Lubbe haranguing the unemployed in the days before the fire had to admit that he had spoken such a mixture of broken German and Dutch that they could not really understand him (Reed, *The Burning of the Reichstag*, p. 177).

of the *Plenarsaal* did not require more than one man, the total amount of damage must have. This tallies, moreover, with a claim that Gempp *did* make: he found a torch lying in the hall outside the *Plenarsaal,* and there was a trail of gasoline on the carpet of the Bismarck Hall.[64] Lubbe had neither torch nor gasoline.

Those who believe that the Nazis were innocent must also account for the extraordinary and suspicious condition of Lubbe at the Leipzig trial. Not only could Lubbe no longer speak fluent and flowery German, he had been reduced almost to an animal. The Nazis insisted that Lubbe was faking, that his behavior was a Communist tactic to paralyze and discredit the trial. The anti-Nazis contended that he must have been drugged or otherwise "processed." The *Spiegel* now argues that Lubbe had simply undergone a complete physical and mental breakdown as a result of being chained day and night for seven months while awaiting trial, of realizing that he was not going to get the sole credit for his Herostratic deed, and of learning that, thanks to a Nazi *ex post facto* law, the so-called "Lex Lubbe," he could now be executed for a crime that had carried only a prison penalty when he had committed it.[65] All of these theories presuppose that Lubbe was perfectly normal at the time of the fire and of his first interrogations. If that were true, what sort of intuition prompted the government press service to release the following statement on February 28, less than a full day after the fire: "The Communists will probably contend that we are dealing here with a mental deficient, yet it can already be stated definitely that the criminal is fully normal mentally"?[66] And why did the Examining Magistrate, Dr. Vogt, who took over the investigation where the police officials left off, testify in flat contradiction of their elaborate reports that it would "never be possible from van der Lubbe's statements to reconstruct his movements in the Reichstag"?[67]

In a criminal court the Nazis might get off with a Scotch

64. *Ibid.,* p. 139.
65. *Der Spiegel,* XIII (1959), No. 51, pp. 39-48, and No. 52, pp. 41-51, advances this theory and discusses Lubbe's condition at the trial in great detail.
66. *Völkischer Beobachter* (South German edition), March 1, 1933 (quoting a government communiqué of February 28). My translation.
67. Reed, *The Burning of the Reichstag,* p. 72.

verdict: not proved. The historian's problem, however, is that of a grand rather than a trial jury: Who should be indicted? In a puzzle like the Reichstag fire this question is best answered by accepting the solution that puts the least strain on the imagination, the alternative that presupposes the fewest coincidental factors. If one argues that the Nazis were innocent, then one has to assume that by some remarkable coincidence a Dutch vagabond with dubious mental equipment but with exactly the right sort of suspicious background (Lubbe had belonged to a splinter-group of anarchists who had broken away from the main Dutch Communist party), provided the Nazis with just the sort of pretext they needed at just the time it would be most useful in just the city where all their leaders were assembled and in just the building to which they and only they had easy access. Further, one must assume that by sheer coincidence he broke into the Reichstag at the only time (between 9:00 and 10:00 P.M.) that his enterprise had the slightest chance of success, that he then blundered about in the dark performing an inhuman number of tasks without injuring himself in any way, and that on capture he gave an eloquent account of his actions to the police only to sink in the next seven months to the level of an animal. If, on the other hand, one argues that the Nazis were guilty, then one has only to assume that somehow they managed to dredge up, dupe, and perhaps drug Lubbe—acts that even Göring admitted were possible. Nothing else would have posed a problem, and no other coincidences are involved.[68]

68. While this article was in the hands of the editor, Tobias published his findings in book form: Fritz Tobias, *Der Reichstagsbrand. Legende und Wirklichkeit* (Rastatt/Baden, 1962). Though it contains a wealth of additional detail and documentation, Tobias' book raises no basic points not already made in the *Spiegel* series.

International Control of the Atom:
Roots of a Policy

OSCAR E. ANDERSON, JR.

On Tuesday evening, December 27, 1945, the American Historical Association met at the Willard Hotel in Washington. Carlton J. H. Hayes, recently ambassador to Spain, delivered the presidential address: "The American Frontier—Frontier of What?" He pleaded for Americans to renounce narrow nationalism and take their rightful place in the Atlantic community. Secure in such a citadel, "we could co-operate the more loyally and effectively, because the less suspiciously, with all the United Nations and do our full part in developing the new world order from wishful thinking to functioning reality."[1]

When the historians left the Willard that night, they could read in the morning papers of important headway along the course Professor Hayes had charted. Secretary of State James F. Byrnes had persuaded the Soviet Union to join the United States and the United Kingdom in recommending that the United Nations General Assembly establish a commission to consider problems arising from the discovery of atomic energy. The news seemed a good omen. Working with the nation's closest wartime ally, the Truman Administration had advanced a promising proposal which Russia had received favorably. This turn of events must have struck many of the departing historians as only the fortunate result of an impromptu attempt to deal with the great challenge of the age. They could not have known the years of thinking that lay behind it.

The plan to seek international control of the atom originated in the minds of Vannevar Bush and James B. Conant. It was Bush, the director of the Office of Scientific Research and De-

1. *American Historical Review*, LI (1946), 213.

velopment, who, in the fall of 1941, won President Roosevelt's
support for a try at the bomb. In 1942 he became chairman of
the Military Policy Committee, which provided top-level guidance for the Manhattan District. At his side throughout the war
was President Conant of Harvard. Chairman of the National
Defense Research Committee and scientific adviser to General
Leslie R. Groves, the Manhattan District commander, Conant
like Bush thought in terms of both science and high policy.

Bush and Conant knew that the atomic bomb would have a
revolutionary impact on the society of nations. So did other
scientific men, but these two were in a position to do something
about it. From the first, they opposed sending the British information beyond what the United Kingdom could use in the
current war. They took this stand partly in hopes of hastening
the end of the fight against the Axis, partly to reduce the chances
of a break in security that would tip off the enemy. But their
main reason was a conviction that the President should not prejudice an attempt to settle the long-range international issue on its
own merits. The British, they believed, were interested in postwar commercial applications that could only complicate matters.[2]

Bush and Conant prevailed, despite Prime Minister Churchill's formidable pressure for a completely joint effort. At Quebec
in August, 1943, Roosevelt and Churchill agreed to co-operate in
order to bring the bomb project to fruition at the earliest possible
moment. While they specified full and effective sharing of information on common research and development efforts, they restricted interchange on design, construction, and operation of
large-scale plants to such *ad hoc* arrangements as seemed necessary to expedite the work. Any postwar advantages of an industrial or commercial character, the British government conceded,
would be dealt with on terms specified by the President. The
Prime Minister went even further and expressly disclaimed any
interest in these aspects beyond what the President considered
"fair and just and in harmony with the economic welfare of the
world."[3]

2. Bush explained his view of British motivation in Bush to Hopkins, March
31, 1943, Papers of Harry L. Hopkins, Franklin D. Roosevelt Library, Hyde
Park, N. Y. See also Conant to Bush, March 25, 1943, which Bush sent along
as an enclosure.

3. The original of the Quebec Agreement is filed in the Records of the Man-

Neither Bush nor Conant had been in a hurry to force a decision on postwar issues, but in the late summer of 1944, they recognized the time had come for careful thought. A vast production complex had risen in the long valleys of eastern Tennessee and on the desert banks of the Columbia. The atomic bomb was far from a ready weapon in the arsenal, but hopes were bright that at least one would be available in a year. In France the eastward dash of the Third Army brought the end of the European war in sight. In Chicago scientists of the Metallurgical Laboratory raised searching questions about the future.

From Chicago came the most immediate stimulus to action. Scientists there, nearing the end of their assignment, were eager to press beyond current objectives and investigate the long-term potential of nuclear energy for both peaceful and military ends. Groves and his advisers considered this both unnecessary and unwise in view of the hour's grave uncertainties. In July the Chicago group learned that Groves contemplated placing the Metallurgical Laboratory on a curtailed, stand-by status. Resentment ran high on the Midway. Arthur H. Compton, the director at Chicago, asked a committee headed by General Electric executive Zay Jeffries to prepare a prospectus on future goals.[4] Then Compton saw Bush in Washington and stressed the importance of a minimal research effort to develop information needed at the peace table and to lay the foundation for rapid progress under postwar conditions. Both men pledged that they would give careful thought to the future but prevent general discussions that might detract interest and attention from the war effort. To make sure he had relieved the fears of the Chicago scientists, Bush had the Military Policy Committee ask Dean Richard C. Tolman, a physicist who was assisting Conant, to lead a study of postwar needs.[5]

hattan Engineer District, World War II Records Division, National Archives and Records Service, Alexandria, Virginia. The *New York Times* published the complete text on April 6, 1954.

4. Project Council Policy Meeting, July 5, 1944, Metallurgical Laboratory Report CS-1913; Jeffries to Compton, July 14, 1944, Records of the Office of Scientific Research and Development, Headquarters, U. S. Atomic Energy Commission, Washington, D. C.; Compton, *Atomic Quest: A Personal Narrative* (New York, 1956), p. 232.

5. Bush to Compton, Aug. 10, 1944, Bush to J. Franck, Aug. 28, 1944, OSRD Records. The Military Policy Committee had acted on August 5, two days before Compton's talk with Bush.

During the fall of 1944 the Jeffries and Tolman committees scouted the frontiers of nuclear energy. In reports submitted in November and December, both called for continuing federal support of research and development. Going beyond the technical sphere, the Jeffries group argued that a world-wide organization was necessary to prevent the atom from becoming the destroyer of nations.[6] Neither document had any immediate impact. This did not mean that the Army pigeonholed and forgot them. It meant only that both reports were ready before anyone could use them. Bush and Conant were alert to the need for planning. They knew the value of research. They did not require reports to tell them the importance of devising effective arrangements for national and international control. But until they could interest the officials who had to make these essentially political decisions, the detailed analyses of the working scientists had little utility.

The Chicago scientists reassured, Bush and Conant turned to the stimulation of postwar planning at the policy-making level. On September 19 they addressed a letter to Henry L. Stimson urging the Secretary of War to talk with the President about plans for national legislation to control atomic power and a treaty to regularize the relationships with Great Britain and Canada. Actually, their ideas went far beyond what they were ready to put in writing. Bush and Conant were thinking of an international control agency, one that would include Russia. While they favored co-operating in the raw-materials field and putting interchange on a permanent basis, they did not want the United States to commit itself so completely to Britain as to prejudice relations with Russia. They hoped to avoid precipitating a nuclear arms race before the United States had made a fair try at multilateral control.[7]

Meanwhile, President Roosevelt had been thinking of the day the war would end. Late in August, 1944, Justice Felix Frankfurter had arranged for Niels Bohr to see the President. The

6. Prospectus on Nucleonics, Nov. 18, 1944, Report of Committee on Postwar Policy, Dec. 28, 1944, Manhattan District Records.
7. Bush and Conant to Stimson, Sept. 19, 1944, Comments by Conant, handwritten on Bush to Conant, April 17, 1944, Conant, Some Thoughts on International Control of Atomic Energy, May 4, 1944, OSRD Records.

great Danish physicist had a suggestion: Britain and the United States should announce the bomb to the world in an effort to build confidence and prepare the way for international control. Roosevelt listened politely but made no promises.[8]

The next person to turn the President's attention to the future of atomic energy was Winston Churchill. On Sunday, September 17, the Prime Minister left Quebec to visit the Roosevelts at Hyde Park. As the train rolled south, he could reflect with satisfaction on the week just past. The second great conference at the frowning citadel above the St. Lawrence had ranged far beyond coming military campaigns. President Roosevelt and Secretary of the Treasury Henry Morgenthau had shown their growing understanding of the economic problems Britain would face once Germany had surrendered. Although the heads of government had made no commitments on Tube Alloys (the British code word for the fission program), Churchill would have his opportunity in the quiet, informal atmosphere of Dutchess County. The time must have seemed unusually propitious. His interest in atomic energy never had been narrowly commercial, but he could not close his eyes to the advantages the new technology might offer Britain with her sick coal industry and her desperate need for exports. With Roosevelt taking a large view of Britain's crisis, Churchill must have felt confident his 1943 disclaimer on industrial and commercial advantages would prove no obstacle.

On September 18 President and Prime Minister talked atomic energy. They considered Bohr's suggestion, but neither thought it time to tell other nations. When the discussion turned to industrial applications, Churchill found Roosevelt liberally inclined. Both men agreed on what amounted to an Anglo-American approach to the postwar world. They initialed an *aide-mémoire* recording their view that "full collaboration between the United States and the British Government in developing Tube Alloys for military and commercial purposes should continue after the defeat of Japan and unless and until terminated by joint agreement."[9]

8. Bohr used a memorandum of July 3, 1944, as the basis of his remarks. A copy is filed in Manhattan District Records.

9. Churchill, *Closing the Ring* (Boston, 1951), pp. 146-61; notes made by John J. McCloy after meeting in Secretary Hull's office, Sept. 20, 1944, attach-

On Friday, September 22, Roosevelt was back in Washington. He telephoned Bush to come to the White House. Bush found the President in the company of Admiral Leahy and Lord Cherwell, the physicist who was Churchill's most trusted economic adviser. Roosevelt talked at some length of the situation after the war, affirming his belief in the necessity of keeping Britain strong. Economic aid was one way. Atomic energy was another. There should be complete interchange after the defeat of Japan. Bush spent an uncomfortable hour. With Cherwell present, he could not say what was uppermost in his mind—that collaborating too closely with Britain might alienate Russia. When the President mentioned commercial use and the need for domestic control, Bush told him of the letter he and Conant had just sent Stimson on this very issue. Searching for a hearing under more auspicious circumstances, Bush offered to tell Stimson that the President would like to talk with him. Roosevelt agreed that this would be desirable.[10]

After lunch the following Monday, Bush saw Stimson. The more he thought about it, he told the Secretary, the more it seemed that the President contemplated an Anglo-American agreement to hold atomic energy closely and use it to control the peace of the world. This might lead to extraordinary efforts by Russia to develop the bomb secretly and to a catastrophic conflict. Might not another policy prevent such a disaster? Complete scientific interchange among all countries would minimize the danger of a secret race on military applications. One might even hope for an international organization that would permit all nations to share control. Stimson conceded that someone ought to analyze this possibility carefully, but he was pessimistic about holding the President's attention long enough to get to the bottom of the subject. When Bush suggested that he and Conant draft a statement of what they considered a reasonable approach, Stimson seized the offer. He thought a short report to the President might at least bring a pause for further study.[11]

ment to Henry L. Stimson Diary, Yale University Library, Sept. 20, 1944. The American copy of the Hyde Park *aide-mémoire* is filed in Papers of Franklin D. Roosevelt, Roosevelt Library, Hyde Park, N. Y.

10. Bush, Memorandum of Conference, Sept. 22, 1944, and Bush to Conant, Sept. 23, 1944, OSRD Records.

11. Bush to Conant, Sept. 25, 1944, OSRD Records.

Bush and Conant had their paper ready five days later. There was every reason to believe, they asserted, that atomic bombs would be demonstrated before August 1, 1945. The advantage then resting with the United States would be temporary. Any nation with good technical and scientific resources could catch up in three or four years. It was foolhardy to seek security in secrecy. It was fully as unwise to depend on the control of raw materials. The only chance of heading off an arms race was to propose free interchange of all scientific information under an international office. As soon as practical, the technical staff of this agency should have access to laboratories, industrial plants, and military establishments throughout the world. Such a system offered the great advantage of laying before people everywhere the true state of the armament situation. If that were done, there was reason to hope that the weapons never would be employed. One could even dream that their existence might decrease the chance of another major war.[12]

The autumn of 1944 passed without action. Toward the end of October Stimson spoke to Bush about the memorandum. He did not say what he was going to do, and Bush concluded he had not yet decided. Privately, Bush thought Stimson should add his own comments and place the document in the hands of the President. Ultimately, Roosevelt should have a solid group of men to study the implications of atomic energy and counsel him on possible moves. In November Bush had to go to Europe to confer on using the proximity fuze against the Germans. Not until December 13 did he have an opportunity to advise Stimson face to face that the time had come to tell the Department of State about the bomb and to name a committee on domestic policy. Stimson did not commit himself on the committee, but he gave Bush to understand he would discuss bringing in State with the President. Stimson was still mulling over the question of international exchange. So great was its moment, he said, that arriving at a policy demanded enormous care.[13]

12. Bush and Conant to Stimson, with enclosure, Sept. 30, 1944, OSRD Records.

13. Bush to Conant, Oct. 24, 1944, Bush and Conant to Stimson, Oct. 27, 1944, Bush, Memorandum of Conference, Dec. 8, 1944, Bush to Conant, Dec. 13, 1944, OSRD Records.

Just at this juncture Stimson learned of an ominous development. The British had permitted French scientists working in Canada to visit their liberated homeland. Since the limited interchange authorized at Quebec had acquainted the Frenchmen with some aspects of the Manhattan project, their return raised the possibility of a security leak. As Stimson saw the affair, it was more than military secrecy. It put France in a position to play power politics—to bring or threaten to bring Russia into the picture.[14]

When Stimson, accompanied by General Groves, saw the President on Saturday, December 30, his complaint against British policy on the French scientists dominated the conversation. Roosevelt saw no reason for admitting France to the atomic partnership. He accepted Stimson's suggestion that the French involvement as well as impending raw-materials negotiations made it advisable to admit Secretary of State Stettinius to the little group of top officials who knew the great secret. The next day Stimson called at the White House again, this time alone. The talk turned to the approaching conference with Churchill and Stalin and Russia's increasing intransigeance. Stimson reported General John R. Deane's warning from Moscow that further easy concessions would gain nothing, that the United States should be more vigorous in insisting on a *quid pro quo.* Stimson observed this had a bearing on S-1 (he always used the code name). He was troubled about withholding information from the Russians, but he was convinced that it was essential to delay until the United States was sure of getting something for its frankness. Roosevelt said he thought he agreed.[15]

Bush was disappointed when he learned that Stimson had failed to discuss either the planning committee or postwar international safeguards. But the frustrations of Washington did not discourage him easily. On the committee, he would prod Stimson's assistant, Harvey H. Bundy. As for international control, that subject might well come up in discussing the French im-

14. Stimson Diary, Dec. 15, 29, 1944; Groves to Stimson, Dec. 14, 26, 1944, Manhattan District Records.
15. Stimson Diary, Dec. 29, 30, 1944; Groves, Memorandum, Dec. 30, 1944, [Stimson], Memorandum of Conference with the President, Dec. 30, 1944, Manhattan District Records.

broglio with Stettinius. So it happened. Stimson's overtures to Stettinius paved the way for a Bush conference with Assistant Secretary of State James C. Dunn on January 20. Bush used the opportunity to outline the international approach he and Conant had suggested to Stimson. Dunn thought Bush and Conant ought to present their views directly to Stettinius.[16]

Early in February, 1945, Bush saw two excellent opportunities to press Stimson to deeds. The first was a resurgence of the previous summer's concern for the future of the Metallurgical Laboratory. On February 1 Bush reminded Bundy that Stimson needed a high-level committee on postwar plans. On the thirteenth Bundy reported that Stimson had approved establishing the committee.[17]

Bush's second opportunity came when the Yalta communiqué announced the San Francisco conference on world organization. Thursday morning, February 15, Bush showed Stimson a draft letter to Roosevelt that proposed writing his plan for an international control agency into the United Nations Charter. Stimson believed that Bush was thinking along the right lines, but he was inclined to tread more cautiously. He thought it inadvisable to put the plan into full force until the United States had obtained all it could from Russia in the way of liberalization in exchange for atomic energy. As the two men talked, Stimson observed that it might be a good idea to start by opening exchange on some single form of scientific research.

Later that day Bush sent Conant a revised letter to the President urging that the United Nations Charter provide for an International Scientific Section. That no peace-loving nation have reason to fear the clandestine research activities of another, this agency should establish full interchange of information on all scientific subjects that had evident military applications. To curb aggressor nations, it should propose ways of policing research activities. If the attempt to secure peace by international organization went well, it should recommend ways to extend interchange to the actual military applications of science. This could

16. Bush to Conant, Jan. 2, 1945, Bush to Bundy, Jan. 30, 1945, OSRD Records; Stimson Diary, Jan. 3, 1945.
17. Bush to Bundy, Jan. 30, Feb. 1, 1945, Bush to Conant, Feb. 13, 1945, OSRD Records.

be done subject by subject. Ultimately, the United Nations might assume control of all excessively powerful weapons. Sometime in the next few weeks Bush sent his letter to the White House.[18]

Though Stimson had accepted the idea of an advisory committee, he had done nothing to bring it into being. Growing impatient, Bush and Conant cornered Bundy on March 3. Several matters demanded attention, they said: public announcements, draft legislation, international control, the technical program. Unless something were done, confusion would fill the vacuum when the bomb became public knowledge. On Monday, March 5, Bundy spent two hours laying the impending issues before Stimson. From domestic regulation to international control, the story captured the Secretary's imagination.[19]

On Thursday, March 15, Stimson lunched with the President. After explaining the timetable on the bomb and how important it was to prepare, Stimson said there were two schools of thought on future control. One favored a secret attempt by the United States and Britain. The other proposed an international effort based on free interchange of scientific information and unlimited access to the laboratories of the world. Stimson told the President a decision was necessary before the first bomb was used. The White House must be ready with a public statement at that time. Roosevelt agreed. Stimson considered the talk successful. Yet it accomplished nothing. Perhaps the Secretary did not present his thoughts specifically enough. Probably the President was too exhausted to act. Whatever the case, Stimson never saw his chief again. Postwar planning had advanced no further when on April 12 the news flashed from Warm Springs that Roosevelt was dead.[20]

Meanwhile, the Yalta communiqué had stirred the hopes and fears of the Chicago scientists. Those sensitive to political issues viewed the San Francisco conference as the occasion to capitalize on the nation's atomic advantage and win what they considered the best guarantee of peace—a strong international research

18. Bush to Conant, Feb. 15, 1945, OSRD Records; Stimson Diary, Feb. 13, 15, 1945. Bush said in a letter to Bundy, April 25, 1945, OSRD Records, that he had sent his letter to the President.
19. Bundy to Stimson, March 3, 1945, Bundy, undated notes on talk with Stimson, Manhattan District Records; Stimson Diary, March 5, 1945.
20. Stimson Diary, March 15, 1945.

center with full access to the scientific activities of all nations. Their spirits sank at the death of Roosevelt, and a sense of desperation gripped the laboratory.[21]

Unknown to the troubled scientists at Chicago, Stimson saw President Truman on April 25. Forcefully, he stated the Bush-Conant thesis that the United States could not retain its present nuclear advantage indefinitely. The very existence of modern civilization was at stake. As American leaders approached the new world organization, they must appreciate the bomb's awful power. Effective safeguards meant unprecedented inspection and controls. A primary question was whether the United States should share this weapon with other nations and, if so, on what terms. American leaders had a moral obligation they could not shirk without incurring responsibility for any disaster that might follow. On the other hand, could they but use the weapon properly, they had opportunity to establish a pattern that might save the peace of the world and civilization itself. Stimson said that he would appoint a committee to recommend early steps in anticipation of postwar problems and to furnish advice on policies that would be appropriate once the bonds of secrecy had been loosened. Stimson returned to the Pentagon convinced that he had accomplished much.[22]

The same day Stimson briefed the President, Bush raised a new question: When was the best time to tell Soviet leaders about the bomb and the hopes for its control? Niels Bohr had turned up at OSRD headquarters and warned that Russia might soon fall heir to whatever work the Germans had accomplished. He thought the United States should raise the question of international control early so its overtures would not seem an attempt at coercion. Indeed, it was important to start consultations before the new weapon made its debut in warfare. This would permit negotiation before public discussion aroused passions and introduced complications. Bush sent Bundy a memorandum from

21. Compton to Groves, March 5, 1945, OSRD Records; Alice K. Smith, "Behind the Decision to Use the Atomic Bomb," *Bulletin of the Atomic Scientists,* XIV (1958), 293-95.

22. Stimson Diary, April 23-25, 1945; Stimson, Memorandum Discussed with the President, Manhattan District Records. Stimson's memorandum as published in *Harper's Magazine,* CXCIV (1947), 99-100, omitted a specific reference to Russia.

Bohr with a strong endorsement. Time was growing short. Some of the best minds in the country should be put to work on international policy. The Secretary should appoint the advisory committee and set this matter before it promptly.[23]

On May 2 Stimson called on the President and suggested names for the committee. During the next few days Stimson invited seven distinguished men to serve—Bush, Conant, Under Secretary of the Navy Ralph A. Bard, Assistant Secretary of State William L. Clayton, Massachusetts Institute of Technology president Karl T. Compton, his old friend and War Department aide George L. Harrison, and James F. Byrnes, who would be the President's personal representative. Stimson said he was calling the advisory group an "Interim Committee" because Congress probably would wish to appoint a permanent commission to supervise, regulate, and control.[24]

When Conant received his notice, he was troubled. He doubted, he told Stimson, that Bush and he should represent the scientists who had been actively at work in the laboratory. Many of this group feared that soon the United States and the Soviet Union would be locked in a secret armament race, particularly if the United States should use the bomb in battle before notifying the Russians of its existence. Conant would serve if Stimson insisted, but he hoped the Interim Committee would ask a few of the leading scientists to present their views on international relations either to the committee or directly to the President. Stimson did insist, and Conant, after a check with Bush, recommended asking Arthur Compton, Ernest O. Lawrence, Robert Oppenheimer, and Enrico Fermi to serve the committee as a Scientific Panel.[25]

The Interim Committee met formally on May 31 and June 1

23. Bush to Bundy, April 25, 1945, Manhattan District Records. The Bohr memorandum was the one Bohr had used in talking with Roosevelt the preceding August supplemented by an addendum dated March 24, 1945. Both documents are filed in Manhattan District Records.

24. Stimson Diary, May 2, 3, 1945; Stimson to Bush, May 4, 1945, OSRD Records.

25. Conant to Stimson, May 5, 1945, OSRD Records. There were two factors that may have contributed to Conant's heavy stress on notifying the Russians before using the bomb. First, he no doubt knew of Bohr's conversation with Bush. Second, he may well have seen a letter from Smyth to Tolman (April 26, 1945, Manhattan District Records), which argued that telling the Russians about the bomb in general terms might strengthen their motives for co-operating.

and listened to the experts, not only the Scientific Panel but a quartet of industrialists as well. The committee canvassed the proposal for an international control agency and the related but more immediate question: Should the United States tell the Russians?[26] On Wednesday, June 6, Stimson reported to the President that the Interim Committee opposed revealing the S-1 work to Russia or anyone else until the first bomb had been used successfully against Japan. Should the Russians raise the subject at the coming Big Three conference, Stimson suggested that Truman turn the query aside. Then Stimson took up international control. The Interim Committee's only suggestion was that each country promise to make public all work being done on atomic energy. To assure fulfilment of this pledge, it favored constituting an international control committee with complete power to inspect. Stimson recognized that this proposal was far from perfect and that Russia might not assent to it. Emphatically, he advocated a policy of no disclosures until control was established. Before the meeting ended, both Stimson and the President were considering the possibility of demanding settlement of the troubled situations in Poland, Rumania, Yugoslavia, and Manchuria as considerations for taking the Russians into partnership on S-1.[27]

In two weeks the Interim Committee had second thoughts. The chain of events that stimulated them began June 2 when Arthur Compton invited the Chicago scientists to make suggestions on the future of nuclear energy for the guidance of the Scientific Panel. The Metallurgical Laboratory responded with a will. One of the first reports finished was from a Committee on Political and Social Problems headed by chemist James Franck. It inveighed against using nuclear bombs against the Japanese without warning. This would cost the United States support throughout the world, precipitate a deadly competition, and prejudice the possibility of reaching an international agreement on control. A demonstration of the power of the bomb in some uninhabited area would create more favorable conditions for agreement. Compton saw that the Franck paper reached Harri-

26. Notes of the Interim Committee Meeting, May 31, June 1, 1945, Manhattan District Records.
27. Stimson Diary, June 6, 1945.

son, Stimson's alternate as Interim Committee chairman. Harrison insisted that the Scientific Panel consider it. On June 16 Compton, Lawrence, Oppenheimer, and Fermi reported that they could propose no technical demonstration likely to end the war. They believed, however, that the circumstances of military use made a difference. They advocated that the United States approach its principal allies before employing its new arms—not only Britain but also Russia, France, and China. It should advise them that considerable progress had been made on atomic weapons and welcome suggestions on how the powers might cooperate in making this development contribute to better international relations.[28]

At the Interim Committee meeting on June 21 (all but Stimson were present), the Scientific Panel's call for the United States to notify its allies made a sharp impression. There was no question about informing Britain; a clause in the Quebec Agreement required that. France and China seemed irrelevant. The real issue was international control, and Russia, the great imponderable. From the first Bush and Conant had opposed any policy that unnecessarily risked prejudicing relations with Russia. Now they had the best possible opportunity to make their point that the United States ought to bid for Soviet co-operation before dropping the bomb. They persuaded their colleagues to suggest that Stimson bring to the President's attention the possibility of telling Stalin at Potsdam that the United States was working on the bomb and expected to use it against Japan. While refusing to give further information the President might express his hope

28. Compton to Bush, June 2, 1945, Compton to Stimson, June 12, 1945, with enclosure, Political and Social Problems, Interim Committee Log, June 15, 16, 1945, Oppenheimer to Stimson (attention Harrison), June 16, 1945, with enclosure, Manhattan District Records; N. Hilberry to Bartkey *et al.*, June 4, 1945, Records of the Argonne National Laboratory, U. S. Atomic Energy Commission, Lemont, Ill.; Compton, *Atomic Quest*, p. 236. Alice K. Smith has expressed doubts that the Scientific Panel saw the Franck report. "Behind the Decision to Use the Atomic Bomb," *Bulletin of the Atomic Scientists*, XIV (1958), 306. Her position depends on the assumption that the Scientific Panel met June 9 and 10, while the report was not finished until June 11, and on Oppenheimer's recollection that he did not see the report until it was printed after the war. Mrs. Smith has been led astray by Compton's inexact reference to the date of the meeting in *Atomic Quest*, p. 239. She may still be correct that the panel did not see the report, though this seems most unlikely. There can be no doubt, however, that the four scientists knew the report existed and were familiar with its argument.

that the weapon become an aid to peace and that this be the subject of later discussions.[29]

Stimson considered this suggestion thoroughly and presented it at the White House on July 3. The Chief Executive listened attentively and indicated his approval.[30] Yet at Potsdam things worked out differently. Stimson was disturbed to see the repressive Russian system in action. Had the Interim Committee been thinking in a vacuum? On July 19 he dictated a memorandum setting forth his view that no world organization for controlling the atom could function effectively if it had to depend on a nation that did not permit its citizens free speech and whose governmental action was controlled by the autocratic machinery of secret political police. The United States should ask itself if it dared share atomic energy with Russia under any system of control until the Kremlin put into actual effect the liberal Constitution of 1936. Should American leaders decide that a free society was indeed necessary for successful control, they ought to proceed slowly in making any disclosure on atomic energy or agreeing to Russian participation. At the same time—herein lay the hope—they should explore constantly how the United States could use its headstart to remove the basic difficulty—the character of the Soviet state.[31]

The next day Stimson had the American ambassador to Russia, Averell Harriman, read his memorandum. Stimson was depressed at Harriman's pessimism on the chances of persuading the Kremlin to change its system. Nevertheless, on the afternoon of July 21, when he gave the President General Groves's full report on the Alamogordo test, Stimson left a copy of his paper. The next morning Truman said that he had read it and concurred in its analysis.[32]

The decision on telling the Russians rested with the President. He and Secretary of State Byrnes had considered the matter

29. Notes of the Interim Committee Meeting, June 21, 1945, Manhattan District Records.

30. Stimson Diary, July 2, 3, 1945.

31. Stimson Diary, July 19, 1945; Reflections on the Basic Problems which Confront Us, July 19, 1945, *Foreign Relations of the United States: Diplomatic Papers. The Conference of Berlin (The Potsdam Conference), 1945* (Washington, 1961), II, No. 1157, pp. 1155-57.

32. Stimson Diary, July 20-22, 1945.

carefully. They had checked with Churchill; they had listened to Stimson. Finally, they decided to inform Stalin as casually and briefly as possible. When the plenary meeting adjourned early the evening of the twenty-fourth, Truman strolled casually around the conference table and told Stalin simply that the United States had a new weapon of unusual destructive force. Stalin showed no special interest, saying only that he was glad to hear it and hoped the Americans would make "good use of it against the Japanese." Truman had taken the minimum step necessary to warn Russia of the advent of the bomb. Technically, he forestalled a Russian charge that the United States and Britain had not dealt frankly. Actually, he did not go far enough to have much chance of winning Russian confidence as a prelude to an effort at international control. The President said nothing about the bomb as a power for peace, nothing about later talks on how to make this dream reality.[33]

Stimson returned from Potsdam in deep discouragement. Only reluctantly did he consent to recommend release of the Smyth report on American development of the bomb. No country infected with the OGPU, he told his advisers, could become part of an effective system of international control. The Russian people, living in an atmosphere of repression, could not be as alert as a free people. If the Russians did not have the spark of initiative, he did not want to give them scientific information that would kindle it.[34]

With the end of the war against Japan, Stimson withdrew to St. Huberts in the Adirondacks. Resting in his mountain retreat, he came to view things in a more constructive light. Back in Washington on September 12, he saw the President. While retaining his Potsdam misgivings about the Soviet Union, Stimson had concluded that the United States could not use the bomb as

33. Truman, *Memoirs*, I, *Year of Decisions* (Garden City, N. Y., 1955), p. 416, is the only first-hand account of the conversation. Byrnes, *Speaking Frankly* (New York, 1947), p. 263, Churchill, *Triumph and Tragedy* (Boston, 1953), pp. 669-70, and Leahy, *I Was There* (New York, 1950), p. 429, tell how they watched the conversation and what Truman told them afterwards. According to Byrnes, who talked with the President on the ride back to their quarters at Babelsberg, Truman told Stalin that the United States planned to use its new bomb very soon unless the Japanese surrendered.

34. Stimson Diary, Aug 1-3, 1945; W. H. Kyle, Notes of a Meeting on the Smyth Report in the Office of the Secretary of War, Aug. 2, 1945, Manhattan District Records.

a lever to accelerate the granting of individual liberties in Russia. Such changes would come slowly. The United States could not delay its approach until the process was complete. Unless the "Anglo-Saxon bloc" offered the Russians full partnership in the development of atomic energy, Stimson feared that the Soviet Union would begin "a secret armament race of a rather desperate character." Stimson told the President he favored a direct offer by the United States and Britain to control the bomb and encourage the development of atomic power for peaceful purposes. The United States might propose to stop weapons work if the British and the Russians would do likewise. It might impound its current stockpile if all three nations would forego the bomb as an instrument of war. Further, the United States might consider a covenant for exchanging information that would advance commercial and humanitarian applications. Stimson opposed acting through an international organization. This tactic would take too long, and the Russians would never consider it seriously.[35]

On Friday, September 21, 1945, Stimson attended his last cabinet meeting and outlined the proposal he had made to the President. Secretary of Commerce Henry A. Wallace, Under Secretary of State Dean G. Acheson, and the next Secretary of War, Robert P. Patterson, gave Stimson influential support. Among those who questioned his plan, Secretary of the Navy James V. Forrestal saw the bomb and the knowledge that produced it as "property of the American people" that the Administration could not give away until sure the people approved. Until the United States had tested thoroughly the validity of Russian commitments, it should not try to buy Soviet understanding and sympathy.[36]

Bush, who attended the session at Stimson's request, sought to clarify the issue. Stimson's proposal did not involve relinquishing the secret of the bomb. That secret rested not in basic scientific data but in the details of bomb design and in manufacturing

35. Proposed Action on Control of Atomic Bombs, enclosure, Stimson to Truman, Sept. 11, 1945, Interim Committee Log, Sept. 12, 1945, Manhattan District Records; Henry L. Stimson and McGeorge Bundy, *On Active Service in Peace and War* (New York, 1947), pp. 642-48.

36. Stimson Diary, Sept. 21, 1945; Walter Millis (ed.), *The Forrestal Diaries* (New York, 1951), pp. 94-96; Truman, *Year of Decisions*, pp. 525-28.

processes. The question was whether the United States could trust Russia. Was it not reasonable to suggest that, as a test case, the United States offer a *quid pro quo* exchange of the basic scientific information that it could not keep secret anyway? Until the Russians passed such a test, Bush believed that the United States should hold tightly the technology of the bomb.[37]

Truman's October 3 message to Congress on a national atomic energy policy reflected his support of the Stimson-Bush approach. While he did not mention Russia, he announced that he would initiate discussions, first with Britain and Canada, and then with other nations, in an effort to agree on conditions "under which cooperation might replace rivalry in the field of atomic power." These talks would not involve disclosure of the manufacturing processes leading to the bomb. They would attempt to arrive at safe conditions for promoting the exchange of scientific information for peaceful and humanitarian ends.[38]

Truman was slow to carry out his promise of a quest for international control. Byrnes, who had been at the London meeting of the Council of Foreign Ministers since early September, returned thoroughly exasperated by weeks of wrangling. He saw the President's message creating new difficulties. No international control plan was safe without inspection. How did anyone expect to see Russian bomb factories when Americans could not even enter Poland and Hungary? Byrnes was convinced the United States should hold off until sure of a decent peace. On October 10 he told Forrestal and Patterson he was going to advise the President to procrastinate.[39]

Meanwhile, a potent influence from abroad urged the President to act. On October 16 Prime Minister Attlee reported to Truman that he was under heavy Parliamentary pressure for a statement of policy on international control. He was going to make a short statement the next day, but he wanted a conference with the President before attempting a further exposition. Unless the wartime partners had a clear position, he said, the atom

37. Bush summarized his views in a memorandum to the President, Sept. 25, 1945, OSRD Records.

38. *Congressional Record*, 79 Cong., 1 sess., pp. 9322-23.

39. Meeting of Secretaries of State, War, and Navy, Oct. 10, 16, 1945, Manhattan District Records; *The Forrestal Diaries*, p. 102.

might jeopardize the prospective meeting of the United Nations General Assembly. Mackenzie King of Canada shared this concern; he should be party to the discussions. Warning that he could not put Parliament off for long, Attlee volunteered to come to Washington at once. This was a plea Truman could not ignore. The invitations went forward. On October 30 the announcements were made in both Washington and London.[40]

Though Attlee would arrive in only ten days, neither the White House nor the Department of State had made any preparations. Bush saw this as an opportunity to advance his long-maturing plan for a sound first step on the thorny road to international control. On November 5 Bush gave Byrnes a paper that argued that Russia was the chief obstacle to moving down the road of international understanding, to averting a secret arms race and the catastrophe of nuclear war. If there were any way to remove this barrier, it lay in making agreements the Kremlin would find it advantageous to keep. This meant proceeding step by step, so that Russian leaders would face clear alternatives. They should have to choose between conforming to the plan and facing hostile public opinion throughout the world. Bush presented the mechanics in greater detail than ever before. At the outset the United States should announce that it proposed going "the whole distance" but that the steps must come in sequence, the success of one essential to the next. The first, Bush thought, was to invite Russia to join Britain and the United States in proposing that the United Nations General Assembly create a scientific agency and charge it with the full dissemination of fundamental information in all fields of science, including atomic energy.[41]

The President and Byrnes made Bush's proposals the basis of the American presentation to Attlee and King. The Bush plan received official sanction on November 15 when the President and the two Prime Ministers announced they would urge the United Nations to set up a commission to make proposals for exchanging basic scientific information, confining atomic energy to

40. Attlee to Truman, Oct. 16, 1945, Records of the U. S. Department of State, Washington, D. C.; *New York Times*, Oct. 31, Nov. 1, 1945.
41. Bush to Byrnes, Nov. 5, 1945, OSRD Records.

peaceful uses, eliminating all weapons of mass destruction, and safeguarding states that complied.[42]

This "Agreed Declaration of Washington" made no provision for a direct bid to Russia. During the next week or so Byrnes, whose primary concern remained the whole sweep of East-West relations, decided that the time had come for another meeting of the foreign ministers of the Big Three—this time in the Soviet capital. After obtaining Truman's agreement he dispatched a cable to Molotov on November 23. The Russians extended invitations to a meeting in December. Byrnes may have had atomic energy in mind when he asked for a Moscow meeting, but not until November 29 did he suggest to Britain's Foreign Minister, Ernest Bevin, that the agenda include the proposal for a United Nations commission on controlling the atom. Later the same day Lord Halifax called at the Department of State to report that although His Majesty's Government doubted Russia's willingness to join in sponsoring the proposal of November 15, they would welcome Soviet co-operation. Would Byrnes consider asking Russia to act with the Anglo-American powers? Now the way was open. On December 1 Byrnes formally notified the United Kingdom he planned to discuss both the method of proposing the commission and the nature of its authority.[43]

To Byrnes's amazement atomic energy occasioned less debate than any other item on the agenda at Moscow. The Russians agreed to sponsor a proposal for a United Nations Atomic Energy Commission with the same functions that Truman, Attlee, and King had spelled out in Washington a month earlier.[44]

The United States had made its overture to the Kremlin. What about its British ally? Was the tie too close? The first four months of 1946 saw the answer. The flow of technical data had slowed to a trickle with the end of the war. Now the Administra-

42. Atomic Energy Agreed Declaration by the President of the United States, the Prime Minister of the United Kingdom, and the Prime Minister of Canada, Nov. 15, 1945, Papers of Harry S. Truman, Truman Library, Independence, Mo.; *New York Times,* Nov. 16, 1945.

43. Byrnes, *All in One Lifetime* (New York, 1958), pp. 319, 326-27; Byrnes to A. Harriman, Nov. 23, 1945, Byrnes to J. G. Winant, Nov. 29, 1945, Memorandum of Conversation, Lord Halifax and Secretary Byrnes, Nov. 29, 1945, Aide Mémoire, Dec. 1, 1945, Department of State Records.

44. Byrnes, *Speaking Frankly,* pp. 266-68, and *All in One Lifetime,* pp. 332-33, 336-37.

tion refused to replace the Quebec Agreement with an expanded arrangement that would supply Britain with whatever information she needed for her atomic energy program. The zeal of Congress for protecting the nation's atomic secrets and the espionage revelations coming out of Ottawa made it impossible for American officials to give fresh authorization for interchange. Still, it was more than this. President Truman was unwilling to do anything that would jeopardize the chances for successful action in the United Nations Atomic Energy Commission.[45]

Bush and Conant had won their point. Perhaps it was all a vain hope. Did any plan, however well conceived and executed, have a chance? One thing seems certain. The passage of time made success less likely. Why did it take so long to start building on the Bush-Conant concept of an international effort at control?

Explanations come easily. The choices were difficult, especially for the leaders of a democracy. They would have been difficult under the most favorable of circumstances. As it was, the stress of war colored every judgment. At the most critical juncture, a President died. His successor had to take over at a time when tremors on distant shores sent demands for decisions sweeping in like tidal waves.

All this does not fully explain the delay. The United States did not lack high-minded, far-sighted men. The deficiency lay somewhere between thought and executive action. The machinery of decision-making groaned and sputtered. The gears of coordination never really engaged. Americans had learned to build a bomb that released an appalling amount of destructive energy in a few millionths of a second. They had required more than a year to take the first step toward controlling it.

The news the night of December 27, 1945, was indeed encouraging. Its roots lay in careful thought, not hurried improvisation. Yet behind the headlines, there loomed a disturbing question. Would the United States be as effective in peace as enterprising in war?

45. Minutes, Combined Policy Committee, Dec. 4, 1945, Feb. 15, 1946, April 15, 1946, Department of State Records; Truman, *Memoirs,* Vol. II, *Years of Trial and Hope* (Garden City, N. Y., 1956), pp. 12-14; Truman to Attlee, April 20, 1946, Annex 37, Diplomatic History of the Manhattan Project, Manhattan District Records.

Bibliography of the Scholarly Writings
of Frederick B. Artz

BOOKS

France under the Bourbon Restoration, 1814-1830. Harvard University Press, Cambridge, Mass., 1931.

Reaction and Revolution, 1814-1832. Harper and Brothers, New York, [c. 1934].

The Intellectual History of Europe from Saint Augustine to Marx. Ginn and Company, Boston, [c. 1941].

1917 and 1941. (*America in a World at War*, No. 14). Farrar and Rinehart, New York, [c. 1941].

The Mind of the Middle Ages: 200-1500 A.D.: An Historical Survey. Alfred A. Knopf, New York, 1953; 2nd edition, 1954; 3rd edition, 1958.

From the Renaissance to Romanticism: Trends in Style in Art, Literature, and Music, A.D. 1300-1830. University of Chicago Press, Chicago, 1962.

ARTICLES

"La Crise des incendies en 1830 et les compagnies d'assurances," *Revue d'histoire moderne*, IV (1929), 96-105.

"The Electoral System in France during the Bourbon Restoration, 1815-1830," *Journal of Modern History*, I (1929), 205-18.

"Les Débuts des partis modernes en France (1815-1830)," *Revue d'histoire moderne*, VI (1931), 275-89.

"Ercole Consalvi," *Encyclopaedia of the Social Sciences* (New York, 1930-35), IV, 210.

"European Civilization, 1815-1850: Some Unfinished Business," *Journal of Modern History,* IX, (1937), 304-13.

"Les Débuts de l'education technique en France, 1500-1700," *Revue d'histoire moderne,* XII (1937), 467-519.

"L'Education technique en France au dix-huitième siècle, 1700-1789," *Revue d'histoire moderne,* XIII (1938), 361-407.

"Bonapartism and Dictatorship," *South Atlantic Quarterly,* XXXIX (1940), 37-49.

"L'Enseignement technique en France pendant l'époque révolutionnaire, 1789-1815," *Revue historique,* CXCVI (1946), 257-86, 385-407.

BIBLIOGRAPHY

"Restoration and July Monarchy," *The American Historical Association's Guide to Historical Literature* (New York, 1961), pp. 476, 494.

REVIEWS OF BOOKS

(The reviews are listed under the names of the journals in which they were published. In each case the name of the author and the title of the book reviewed follows the citation of volume and page numbers.)

[*American Historical Review*]

XXXIV (1928), 157-58. Jehan d'Ivray, *L'Aventure Saint-Simonienne et les femmes.*

XXXV (1930), 599-601. E. de Beau de Loménie, *La Carrière politique de Chateaubriand de 1814 à 1830.*

XXXV (1930), 913-14. M. E. Elkington, *Les Rélations de société entre Angleterre et la France sous la Restauration (1814-1830).*

XXXVI (1931), 812-13. Georges Weill, *L'Eveil des nationalités et le mouvement libéral (1815-1848).*

XXXVII (1931), 161. Henry Bérenger, *Chateaubriand.*

XXXVII (1932), 376-77. Charlton J. H. Hayes, *The Historical Evolution of Modern Nationalism.*

XXXVII (1932), 795-96. Robert R. Ergang, *Herder and the Foundations of German Nationalism.*

XXXVIII (1933), 370. F. J. C. Hearnshaw, editor, *Social and Political Ideas of Some Representative Thinkers of the Age of Reaction and Reconstruction, 1815-1865.*

XXXVIII (1933), 594. *"1830." Etudes sur les mouvements libéraux et nationaux de 1830.*

XXXVIII (1933), 833. Chateaubriand, *Les Natchez,* edited by Gilbert Chinard.

XL (1934), 168-69. Charlotte T. Muret, *French Royalist Doctrines since the Revolution.*

XLI (1936), 843. K. M. Hoffman, *Preussen und die Julimonarchie, 1830-1834.*

XLIV (1939), 982. André Maurois, *Chateaubriand.*

XLV (1940), 713-14. Ernest J. Knapton, *The Lady of the Holy Alliance: The Life of Julie de Krüdener.*

XLVII (1942), 851-52. Paul R. Sweet, *Friedrich von Gentz, Defender of the Old Order.*

XLVIII (1943), 331-32. Vernon J. Puryear, *France and the Levant from the Bourbon Restoration to the Peace of Kutiah.*

LI (1946), 705-706. Shelby T. McCloy, *Government Assistance in Eighteenth Century France.*

LIII (1948), 812-13. H. G. Schenk, *The Aftermath of the Napoleonic Wars: The Concert of Europe—an Experiment.*

LV (1950), 595-97. G. de Bertier de Sauvigny, *Le Comte Ferdinand de Bertier (1782-1864) et l'énigme de la Congrégation.*

LVIII (1953), 433. David O. Evans, *Social Romanticism in France, 1830-1848.*

LIX (1954), 411-12. G. D. H. Cole, *Socialist Thought: The Forerunners, 1789-1850.*

LX (1955), 579-80. *Socialist Thought: Marxism and Anarchism, 1850-1890.*

LXI (1956), 392-93. G. de Bertier de Sauvigny, *La Restauration.*

LXII (1957), 388. Frank E. Manuel, *The New World of Henri Saint-Simon.*

LXV (1960), 677-78. G. de Bertier de Sauvigny, *Metternich et son temps.*

LXVI (1960), 207. J. Lucas-Dubreton, *Le Culte de Napoléon, 1815-1848.*

LXVI (1961), 432. J. P. T. Bury, editor, *The Zenith of European Power, 1830-1870 (The New Cambridge Modern History,* Vol. X).

[*Annals* of the American Academy of Political and Social Science]

CLXXXVII (1936), 248. Edward H. Tatum, *The United States and Europe, 1815-1823.*

[*Journal of Central European Affairs*]

I (1941), 351. R. Auernheimer, *Prince Metternich.*

II (1943), 432-33. E. V. Tarlé, *Napoleon's Invasion of Russia, 1812.*

III (1943), 339-40. Albert Guérard, *Napoleon III.*

III (1944), 497. Jacques Lorraine, *Behind the Battle of France.*

VI (1947), 203. Golo Mann, *Secretary of Europe, Life of Friedrich Gentz.*

X (1950), 62-63. Arnold Whitridge, *Men in Crisis: The Revolution of 1848.*

[*Journal of Economic History*]

VII (1947), 87-88. Alexander Gray, *The Socialist Tradition.*

[*Journal of Modern History*]

IX (1937), 262. *Bibliographie critique des principaux travaux parus sur l'histoire de 1600 à 1918. Année 1934.*

X (1938), 295. Sherman Kent, *Electoral Procedure under Louis Philippe.*

XI (1939), 395-96. Duc de Broglie, *Mémoires du Duc de Broglie (Jacques-Victor-Albert, 1821-1901),* Vol. I.

XIII (1941), 556-57. F. H. Brabant, *The Beginning of the Third Republic in France*; John B. Wolf, *France: 1815 to the Present*; D. W. Brogan, *France under the Republic*; Richard W. Hale, *Democratic France.*

XIX (1947), 80-81. Harold Nicolson, *The Congress of Vienna.*

XX (1948), 178. Robert Burnand, *La Vie quotidienne en France de 1870 à 1900.*

XXIII (1951), 169-70. Felix Ponteil, *La Monarchie parlementaire, 1815-1848.*

XXIII (1951), 288. Crane Brinton, *Ideas and men.*

XXXI (1959), 393-94. Georg Iggers, *The Cult of Authority, the Political Philosophy of the Saint-Simonians.*

XXXII (1960), 293. Paul Leuilliot, *L'Alsace au début du XIXe siècle,* Vol. I.

XXXIII (1961), 448. Paul Leuilliot, *L'Alsace au début du XIXe siècle,* Vol. II

[*Politica*]

II (1936), 104-105. C. K. Webster, *The Congress of Vienna, 1814-1815.*

[*Saturday Review*]

July 28, 1951, p. 9. Arthur Bryant, *The Age of Elegance, 1812-1822.*

November 27, 1954, p. 20. Richard Winston, *Charlemagne.*

January 1, 1955, p. 58. Richard R. Bolgar, *The Classical Heritage and Its Beneficiaries.*

Contributors

OSCAR E. ANDERSON, JR., *summa cum laude, '*40; A.M., Harvard, '41; Ph.D., Harvard, '48. Capt., U.S.A.A.F., 1941-46. Assistant Professor of History, University of Cincinnati, 1948-53, Associate Professor, 1953-58; Assistant Historian, U.S. Atomic Energy Commission. 1958-62; International Programs Specialist, National Aeronautics and Space Administration, 1962-   Research Training Fellow, Social Science Research Council, 1947-48. Author of *Refrigeration in America: A History of a New Technology and Its Impact* (Princeton University Press, 1953); "The Pure-Food Issue: a Republican Dilemma, 1906-1912," *American Historical Review*, LXI (1956), 550-73; *The Health of a Nation: Harvey W. Wiley and the Fight for Pure Food* (University of Chicago Press, 1958); with Richard G. Hewlett, *The New World, 1939/1946 (A History of the United States Atomic Energy Commission,* Vol. I) (Pennsylvania State University Press, 1962).

ROWLAND BERTHOFF, *cum laude, '*42; Ph.D., Harvard, '52. 1st. Lt., A.U.S., 1942-46. Instructor in History, Princeton University, 1953-57, Assistant Professor, 1957-62; Associate Professor, Washington University, 1962-.   Fulbright Scholar, University College of Wales, Aberystwyth, 1952-53; Fellow of the American Council of Learned Societies, 1960-61. Author of *British Immigrants in Industrial America, 1790-1950* (Harvard University Press, 1953); "The American Social Order: a Conservative Hypothesis," *American Historical Review*, LXV (1960), 495-514; "The Working Class" in *The Reconstruction of American History*, John Higham, ed. (Hutchinson, London, 1962); and other articles on social and political history. Present research and writing —social history of the Pennsylvania anthracite region, 1825-1915.

ELLSWORTH C. CARLSON, '39; A.M., Harvard, '49; Ph.D., Harvard, '52. Assistant Professor of History, Oberlin College, 1950-54; Associate Professor, 1954-62; Professor, 1962-   ; Chairman of department, 1961-   . Fellow of the Social Science Research Council, 1949-50; Fulbright Lecturer, Philippines, 1956-57; Fulbright Lecturer, Institute of Chinese Civilization, Taiwan, summer 1962. Chairman, Board of Trustees, Oberlin Shansi Memorial Association, 1958- . Author of *The Kaiping Mines, 1877-1912* (Harvard University Press, 1957). Present research and writing—relationships between missionaries and the communities in which they worked in nineteenth-century China, with special attention to Foochow, 1847-1881.

RICHARD N. CURRENT, '34; M.A., Fletcher School of Law and Diplomacy, '35; Ph.D., Wisconsin, '40. Taught at Lawrence College, 1945-47; Mills College, 1947-50; University of Illinois, 1950-55; Woman's College, University of North Carolina, 1955-60; Professor of History, University of Wisconsin, 1960- . Lecturer, Doshisha and Kyoto universities, Japan, summer 1958; State Department Lecturer, India, 1959; Fulbright Lecturer, University of Munich, summer 1959; Harmsworth Professor of American History, Oxford University, 1962-63. Bancroft Prize, 1956. O. Max Gardner Award, University of North Carolina, 1960. Author of *The Lincoln Nobody Knows* (McGraw-Hill, 1958) and five other books and numerous articles; with J. G. Randall, *Lincoln the President: Last Full Measure* (Dodd, Mead, 1955), and with T. H. Williams and Frank Freidel, *A History of the United States* (Knopf, 1959). Present research and writing—a study of the carpetbaggers.

A. HUNTER DUPREE, *summa cum laude* '42; A.M., Harvard, '47; Ph.D., Harvard, '52. Ensign, Lt. (j.g.), and Lt., U.S.N.R., 1942-46. Assistant Professor of History, Texas Technological College, 1950-52. Research Fellow, Grey Herbarium, Harvard University, 1952-54, 1955-56. Visiting Assistant Professor of History, University of California (Berkeley), 1956-58; Associate Professor, 1958-61; Professor, 1961- ; Assistant to the Chancellor, Berkeley Campus, 1960-62. Member of the Council, History of Science Society, 1955-58, 1960- . Author of *Science in the Federal Government: A History of Policies and Activities* (Harvard University Press, 1957); *Asa Gray: 1810-1888* (Harvard Press, 1959); and numerous articles. Present research and writing— principal investigator under a National Science Foundation Grant to the University of California for "Studies in the History of Science in the Federal Government, 1940-1960."

SYDNEY NETTLETON FISHER, '28, A.M., '32; Ph.D., Illinois, '35. Instructor in Mathematics, Robert College, 1928-31; Instructor in History, Denison University, 1935-36; Instructor in English, Robert College, 1936-37; Instructor in History, Ohio State University, 1937-42; Assistant Professor, 1942-47; Associate Professor, 1947-54; Professor, 1954- ; Co-ordinator, Graduate Institute for World Affairs, Ohio

State University, 1961- . Assistant Chief, Economic Analysis Section, Middle East Division, Foreign Economic Administration, 1943-44; Country Specialist, Commercial Policy Division, Department of State, 1944-46. Editor, *Middle East Journal,* 1952-53; Director of Publications, Middle East Institute, 1952-53; member of the Executive Committee, American Association of Middle East Studies, 1961- . Author of *The Foreign Relations of Turkey, 1481-1512* (University of Illinois Press, 1948); *The Middle East: a History* (Knopf, 1959; Routledge and Kegan Paul, 1960); and numerous articles. Editor of *Evolution in the Middle East: Revolt, Reform, and Change* (Middle East Institute, 1953); *Social Forces in the Middle East* (Cornell University Press, 1955); and *The Military in the Middle East* (Ohio State University Press, 1962). Present research and writing—history of Turkey in contemporary times.

ROBERT M. KINGDON, *summa cum laude,* '49; A.M., Columbia, '50; Ph.D., Columbia, '55. Instructor in History, University of Massachusetts, 1952-56; Assistant Professor, 1956-57; Visiting Instructor in History, Amherst College, 1953-54; Assistant Professor of History, State University of Iowa, 1957-59; Associate Professor, 1959-61; Professor, 1961- . Rotary Foundation Fellow, University of Geneva, 1951-52. Fellow of the American Council of Learned Societies, 1960-61. Member of the Council, American Society for Reformation Research, 1960-63. Author of *Geneva and the Coming of the Wars of Religion in France, 1555-1563* (Librairie E. Droz, Geneva, 1956); "The First Expression of Theodore Beza's Political Ideas," *Archiv fuer Reformationsgeschichte,* XLVI, Heft 1 (1955), 88-100; "The Political Resistance of the Calvinists in France and the Low Countries," *Church History,* XXVII (1958), 220-33; and numerous other articles on intellectual and church history. Present research and writing—the history of printing and sixteenth-century politics in France and Switzerland.

ROBERT E. NEIL, '53; A.M., Harvard, '54. U.S. Army, 1954-56. Instructor in History, Oberlin College, 1960-62; Assistant Professor, 1962- . Woodrow Wilson Fellow, 1953-54; member of the Society of Fellows, Harvard University, 1957-60. Present research and writing—history of "The Nazi Revolution" in Germany, 1933-1934.

DAVID H. PINKNEY, *magna cum laude,* '36; A.M., Harvard, '37; Ph.D., Harvard, '41. Research analyst, Office of Strategic Services, 1941-43; Ensign and Lt. (j.g.), U.S.N.R., 1943-46; Political Analyst, Department of State, 1946. Assistant Professor of History, University of Missouri, 1946-52; Associate Professor, 1952-57; Professor, 1957- ; Chairman of department, 1956-59. Fellow of the Fund for the Advancement of Education, 1954-55; Guggenheim Fellow, 1960-61. Member, Board of Editors, *Journal of Modern History,* 1955-58; member, Board of Editors, *French Historical Studies,* 1958- ; Secretary-Treasurer, Society for French Historical Studies, 1956-63; Secretary, Executive Committee, Modern European History Section, American Historical Association, 1961- . Author of *Napoleon III and the Rebuilding of Paris* (Princeton University Press, 1958) and numerous articles on French history. Present research and writing—French Revolution of 1830.

THEODORE ROPP, *summa cum laude,* '34; A.M., Harvard, '35; Ph.D., Harvard, '37. Instructor in History, Harvard, 1937-38; Visiting Lecturer, 1947-48; Instructor in History, Duke University, 1938-42; Assistant Professor, 1942-48; Associate Professor, 1948-59; Professor, 1959- ; Ernest J. King Professor of Military History, Naval War College, 1962-63. Fellow, Social Science Research Council, 1958-59. President, North Carolina Conference, American Association of University Professors, 1959-61; member, Committee E, A.A.U.P., 1962- . Trustee, American Military Institute, 1961-63; member, Secretary of the Army's Historical Advisory Committee, 1962- . Author of *War in the Modern World* (Duke University Press, 1959; 3d ed., rev., Collier Books, 1962) and articles on the history of warfare. Present research and writing—military conscription in Canada and the British Commonwealth; the Battle of Cannae.